Nova Scotia

COLOURGUIDE

Eighth Edition

Edited by Colleen Abdullah

Formac Publishing Company Limited

Halifax

Contents

Formac Publishing Company Limited recognizes the support of the Province of Nova Scotia through the Department of Tourism, Culture and Heritage. We acknowledge the financial support of the Government of Canada through the Book Publishing Industry Development Program (BPIDP) for our publishing activities.
For photo credits please see page 216.

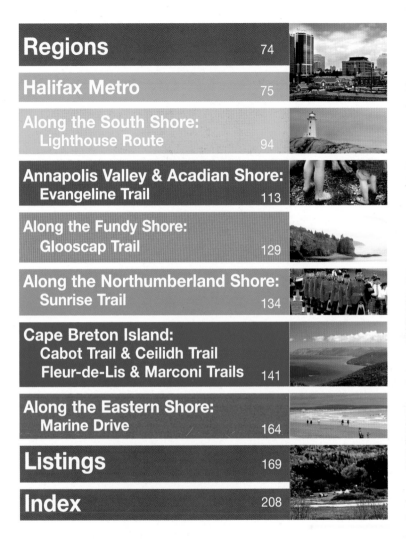

Library and Archives Canada Cataloguing in Publication

The Nova Scotia colourguide / editor, Colleen Abdullah. — 8th ed.

(Formac colourguides)
ISBN 978-0-88780-864-7

1. Nova Scotia — Guidebooks. I. Abdullah, Colleen

FC2307.P66 2009   917.1604'5   C2008-907944-2

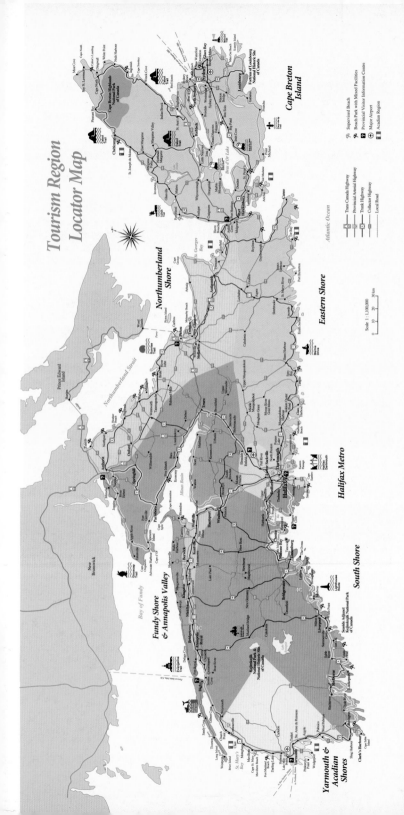

Tourism Region Locator Map

Cape Breton Island

Northumberland Shore

Eastern Shore

Halifax Metro

Fundy Shore & Annapolis Valley

South Shore

Yarmouth & Acadian Shores

New Brunswick

Prince Edward Island

Atlantic Ocean

Bay of Fundy

Northumberland Strait

Scale 1:1,100,000

0   10   20   30 km

Cape Breton Highlands National Park of Canada

Fortress of Louisbourg National Historic Site of Canada

Kejimkujik National Park & National Historic Site of Canada

Kejimkujik National Park & National Historic Site of Canada Seaside Adjunct

Supervised Beach

Beach Park with Mixed Facilities

Provincial Visitor Information Centre

Major Airport

Acadian Region

Trans Canada Highway

Provincial Arterial Highway

Trunk Highway

Collector Highway

Local Road

Getting Around

Though Nova Scotia is Canada's second-smallest province, its land mass is equal to the combined area of the states of Massachusetts, New Hampshire and Vermont. A visitor can easily fill a day or two in one location or spend weeks exploring the countryside and enjoying its many attractions.

Shaped somewhat like the lobster found off its coast, Nova Scotia stretches 730 kilometres from Yarmouth to Sydney. You can drive this distance in less than eight hours along new highways, but plan to take the older, more scenic routes for a relaxing trip with plenty of opportunities for sightseeing and for visiting interesting local museums and shops. For those with limited time, however, the 100-series highway routes, which extend to all areas of the province, are an excellent way to reach particular destinations in a hurry. While they bypass the picturesque villages, many of them offer panoramic vistas not seen on older routes.

Cabot Trail

Amherst Entry Point

Most motoring visitors enter the province at Amherst, at the border point with New Brunswick. A trip through the Wentworth Valley via the Cobequid Pass toll highway is the fastest route to the central point of Truro, or take the slower route, winding around Folly Lake. If scenic Cape Breton Island is your destination, you might want to meander along the Northumberland Shore on the Sunrise Trail (Route 6) to Pictou. Then you can follow the Trans-Canada Highway to Cape Breton. If time is limited, follow the Trans-Canada Highway to Baddeck, where you can make a stop at the Alexander

The MacKay Bridge, leading into Halifax

Whalewatching in Cape Breton

Walking the mud flats at Blomidon

Graham Bell Museum, and then head for the Cabot Trail, taking the counter-clockwise route from Ingonish to Cheticamp. If additional days can be scheduled, be sure to include a visit to the Fortress of Louisbourg and the Glace Bay Miners' Museum.

If you are heading for Halifax and you want a scenic drive, take the Glooscap Trail (Route 2) along the Minas Basin to Truro where you can join Highway 102, which will take you in to the Halifax-Dartmouth metropolitan area.

A few days can be enjoyed taking in the sights of the city and its museums, but be sure to include a drive to spectacular Peggys Cove. Day trips can be planned to the South Shore or Annapolis Valley, but it's better to plan two or three days to make the loop along one route to Yarmouth, following the shoreline one way, and driving through the province's agricultural heartland on the other. Or you can shorten the loop by cutting across on Route 8 between Liverpool and Annapolis Royal, passing Kejimkujik National Park en route.

Yarmouth Entry Point

Arriving at Yarmouth by ferry from Maine, you are faced with the choice of following the Lighthouse Route

Annapolis Valley as viewed from the Look Off on the North Mountain

(see p. 94) along the province's scenic South Shore, or taking the Evangeline Trail (see p. 113) along the Acadian Shore and through the pastoral Annapolis Valley. Both routes lead to Halifax. Enjoy the best of both worlds by taking one route when you arrive and allowing enough time to enjoy the other on the return journey. You might plan one to three days to enjoy charming villages and historic sites each way.

Halifax Entry Point

If you fly into Halifax International Airport, your first stop will probably be Halifax. The Halifax metro area demands at least a day for sightseeing, but two or three days would be better. For information about the area, the Halifax Citadel National Historic Site, evening entertainment and Historic Properties and waterfront see p. 75.

Plan on two to three days exploring the Annapolis Valley, the Fundy Shore (Glooscap Trail, see p. 129) and the South Shore. A day could be enjoyed along Marine Drive, and if more time is available, a visit to Cape Breton should be planned.

Allow a day or two for the drive to Cape Breton, taking in some sights along the way, like historic Sherbrooke Village on Marine Drive (see p. 164).

A couple of days in Cape Breton will leave you wanting to stay longer. From Sydney you can visit the Fortress of Louisbourg (see p. 159), and take in the Miners' Museum in Glace Bay (see p. 163). The Cabot Trail (see p. 141) can be driven in a day, but you will want to make a list of things to do and places to stop on your next trip. An overnight stay at Baddeck, or perhaps Cheticamp or Margaree, will let you enjoy a taste of the Celtic and Acadian cultures of those areas.

Bishops Landing on Halifax Waterfront

Take another day to enjoy part of the pastoral Sunrise Trail along the warm Northumberland Shore (see p. 134) on your way back to Halifax.

Land & Sea

Robert J. McCalla and Al Kingsbury

Atlantic coast

Located on Canada's East Coast, within a day's drive of the United States border and just hours from the major airports in Boston and New York, Nova Scotia prides itself on being "Canada's Ocean Playground," with its 7,450-kilometre coastline of beaches, coves, salt marshes, headlands and cliffs. Its geology, climate, plants and animals — as well as its people — have all been shaped by the sea.

Nova Scotia is part of the Appalachian Region, which extends from the southeastern United States to Newfoundland in the northeast. Along the Atlantic coast, rugged beauty, like the mass of granite rising from the sea at Peggys Cove, draws thousands of visitors each year. By contrast, Cape Breton Island and the northern mainland along the Northumberland Strait boast some fine beaches.

Five Islands

The world's highest tides have carved spectacular sea cliffs along the shores of the Bay of Fundy. The effects of the Fundy tides are most dramatic at Advocate Bay along Cape Chignecto (see p. 131) and in the area of Cape Split, which divides the Minas Channel from the Minas Basin.

Millions of years ago, this area was swampland; deposits of organic matter later became coal, which has been mined at Joggins, Springhill and in communities in Pictou, Inverness and Cape Breton counties. You can tour underground coal seams at the Springhill Miners' Museum (see p. 130) and the Miners' Museum at Glace Bay (see p. 163). Embedded within the sedimentary rocks is an excellent record of past plant and animal life. The areas around Joggins and near Parrsboro are famous for fossils (see p. 131).

The province's land surface has been scarred by glaciers at least four times during the last 100,000 years, leaving behind deposits of drumlins (egg-shaped hills) and erratics (large boulders).

The melting of the glaciers caused a rise in sea level that flooded the shoreline, creating deep bays and sheltered harbours along the Atlantic coast. Halifax Harbour, one of the world's finest, owes its existence to both glacial erosion and a rise in sea level.

Bay of Fundy at low tide

Tides

Coastal Nova Scotia is influenced by the twice-daily ebb and flow of the tides. These effects are most spectacular in the upper reaches of the Bay of Fundy, where the tidal range has exceeded 16 metres, and at low tide huge mud flats are exposed. Several companies take advantage of the upriver surge, known as the tidal bore, by providing white-water rafting excursions on the Shubenacadie River. The tidal phenomenon can be seen along many of the rivers that flow into Cobequid Bay and the Cumberland Basin.

Climate

Nova Scotia has a modified continental climate. The sea makes winters warmer and summers cooler than in the Canadian interior. The same effect takes place within the province — temperatures become more continental as you move away from the coast. And while you can blame the ocean for Nova Scotia's cold, damp springs (the sea is slow to warm), it is also responsible for our fine autumns (it takes just as long to cool).

Precipitation is plentiful and evenly distributed throughout the year. On average, Halifax records precipitation on 171 days of the year. The Cape Breton Highlands and southwestern mainland receive more moisture than the northern

A farm in the Gaspereau valley

9

Fall colours along Cape Breton's Cabot Trail

mainland and the Annapolis Valley, mainly because of onshore winds.

Flora

The forests of Nova Scotia are mixed, typical of the Acadian Forest found throughout the Maritime Provinces. Softwood — mostly balsam fir, red, white and black spruce and white pine — are generally found in poorly drained areas, while hardwood — mainly red maple, yellow birch, sugar maple and white birch — prefer drier ground. During autumn, many Nova Scotian hillsides blaze with colour as hardwood leaves turn from soft greens to vivid yellows, oranges and reds. The most dramatic display of fall colour is seen along Cape Breton's Cabot Trail.

The natural open spaces in Nova Scotia — the salt marshes, bogs, coastal dunes, shallow lakes and ponds, stream banks and barrens — have their own distinctive plant communities. In the salt marshes, for example, angiosperms, algae and grasses trap sediment and help in the transition of the marsh from a saltwater environment to a freshwater one. You'll find many of these marshes in the Minas Basin and Chignecto Bay, although large areas like Grand-Pré have been converted to dykeland.

Birds and Mammals

With its diverse landscape and strategic position along the Atlantic flyway, Nova Scotia hosts a wide variety of birds. Some, like jays, grouse and sparrows, are typical of boreal forest regions. Others create more of a stir. Bald eagles and ospreys can be found close to marine and freshwater feeding areas, particularly in the more remote areas of the northern mainland and on Cape Breton Island. Eagle tours are provided in Cape Breton's Bras d'Or Lakes region (see p. 153-154).

In August, huge flocks of shorebirds (sandpipers, plovers and phalaropes) gather in the upper reaches of the Bay of Fundy to feed on the nutrient-rich mud flats before resuming their southward migration (Evangeline Beach, near Grand-Pré, is a crowded stopover). They can also be found at Brier Island and along the Atlantic coast in sheltered harbours with exposed mud flats and salt marshes.

The best place to observe seabirds — razorbills, guillemots, kittiwakes, cormorants, and puffins — is at Hertford and Ciboux, tiny islands off the coast of Cape Dauphin in Cape Breton. The "Bird Islands" are protected sanctuaries and can only be reached by boat tours that leave from Big Bras d'Or and Englishtown.

Nova Scotia's land mammals range in size from the mole to the moose. Moose and deer are found throughout the province. The coyote, a relatively recent arrival, is the most vilified of Nova Scotia's mammals, given its

penchant for killing sheep.

Marine mammals, including seals, whales, porpoises and dolphins, are among the province's most popular attractions. Numerous species of whales visit Nova Scotia's coastal waters. The Bay of Fundy near Brier Island is a good place to see fin and humpback whales; pilot and minke whales are often sighted in the Gulf of St. Lawrence, especially along the west coast of Cape Breton Island.

Settlement

The prehistoric evidence of native settlement is sparse. At the time of European contact, an estimated 3,000 – 3,500 Mi'kmaq were living in the area that is now Nova Scotia, New Brunswick and Prince Edward Island. In Nova Scotia the largest concentration was probably on Cape Breton Island.

A recent theory places the Chinese in Cape Breton long before John Cabot. European exploration of Nova Scotia may have included the Norse, but there is no hard evidence to show this. Prince Henry Sinclair of Orkney is believed by some to have sailed to Nova Scotia in 1398. Certainly the English and Portuguese had explored the coast by the beginning of the 16th century.

The story of European settlement starts with the French at Port Royal in 1604 and includes the Acadian population, which numbered 13,000 at the time of their deportation in 1755.

Today, more than 950,000 people live in Nova Scotia. Although upwards of 370,000 live in Halifax Regional Municipality, Nova Scotia is mainly a rural and small-town area. Even the urban communities are small. Truro has fewer than 12,000 people; Yarmouth, in southwest Nova Scotia, has a population of only 7,200; Amherst, at the border with New Brunswick, has fewer than 10,000; Lunenburg's population is under 2,500; and 102,000 reside in Cape Breton Regional Municipality.

There are more than 70 ethnic groups in the province (identified by mother tongue), but the vast majority of people trace their roots to the British Isles. Nova Scotia's telephone books are full of Scottish surnames, especially on Cape Breton Island and along the Northumberland Shore. Still, other peoples — the Mi'kmaq and Acadians are most visible — have retained strong cultural identities that will certainly enrich your visit to Nova Scotia.

Seal at Shubenacadie and white-tailed deer at Little Harbour

Genealogy

Terry Punch

Old Burying Ground in Halifax

Nova Scotia was home to Canada's first French settlement four centuries ago, and several waves of people — English, Blacks, Scots, Germans, Irish and Dutch — have followed, so it's not surprising that many descendants of those immigrants visit the province each year in search of their family roots. Residents, too, have developed a keen interest in genealogy, and have put extensive efforts into compiling, preserving and cataloguing data. As a result, many sources of research are available that can be used both before and during a visit to the province by people trying to trace their roots.

Details critical to finding family links are name, place and date (within two to three years) of births, deaths and marriages. If a place within Nova Scotia is not known, religion or ethnicity might help to localize a family. My book, *In Which County? Nova Scotia Surnames from Birth Registers: 1864 to 1877*, gives the distribution of 5,000 surnames. And before you do too much work, you should check Allan E. Marble's *A Catalogue of Published Genealogies of Nova Scotia Families*. Perhaps your family has been researched before, and you will need only to connect or update your branch of the family tree.

Nova Scotia kept no government records of births and deaths before 1864. Township books help in some areas, as does an incomplete set of marriage bonds going back to 1763. Otherwise, church registers, newspaper notices or headstone data must be used. Births 1864–77, deaths 1864–77 and 1908–55, marriages 1864–1930 and marriage bonds 1763–1864 are searchable at www.gov.ns.ca/nsarm/databases. More recent records are held by the Deputy Registrar-General. A death register for Halifax, 1890–1908 is available at that website.

The major repository in the province is the Nova Scotia Archives & Records Management (NSARM) on University

St. Paul's Church, Halifax

Avenue in Halifax. Hours of operation are in the listings section of this book.

Church records are an invaluable resource for genealogical research, and many of these are available in Nova Scotia. Typically, registers open in the 1800s, although some start decades earlier. Catholic records of the French era (pre-1755) are best explored through the Centre d'Etudes Acadiennes at New Brunswick's Université de Moncton. Members of the Church of Jesus Christ of Latter Day Saints (Mormons) microfilmed many church records, and these are accessible through their worldwide library system. NSARM has many pre-1908 church registers, especially Anglican, Methodist and Presbyterian ones. Other records are in church repositories or in local custody.

Many headstone inscriptions have been transcribed, and the results are often available at NSARM or with local historical or genealogical societies. Most surviving inscriptions date from 1840, and these are particularly useful for deaths in the 1875–1950 period. Headstones bear interesting names ("Experience Lavender" — White Point), reveal origins ("native of Midleton, County Cork, Ireland" — Holy Cross, Halifax), or indicate military service (Michael Gabriel, "Private, 40th Battn C.E.F." — North River).

Newspaper announcements of marriages and deaths were predominantly those of Anglophones, the prominent and the Protestant until about 1850, after which coverage grew increasingly general. NSARM has microfilm of most of the old newspapers, and vital records from the Halifax press (1769–1856) have been published by the Genealogical Association of Nova Scotia. Other information available at the archives includes census data, poll tax records, land grants and deeds and probate records.

Township books were kept in areas settled by New Englanders in western Nova Scotia. These generally covered births, marriages and deaths from the 1760s to the 1820s. They often recorded only those families having shares in the township — neglecting minorities, transient families and immigrants.

Census indexes for 1901 and 1911 are on line at www.automatedgenealogy.com. The Genealogical Association of Nova Scotia (GANS) publishes *The Nova Scotia Genealogist*, with readers' queries, book reviews, short articles and other useful information. GANS offers a series of publications containing the 1838 census data for many counties and another that lists deaths and burials in the province from 1749 to 1850. Other helpful organizations can be found in the listings section of this book. For further particulars of existing records and where to find them try consulting two standard works I've written about the subject: *Genealogist's Handbook for Atlantic Canada Research* and *Genealogical Research in Nova Scotia*. They are available at NSARM and at many local libraries or may be purchased from GANS.

Museums

Fisheries Museum in Lunenburg

Nova Scotia's modern history is diverse, abundant and — by New World standards — long. The area has also witnessed some cataclysmic events in the evolution of the earth. Fascinating stories of the ages before human settlement are visible in its rocks and land formations. The history of its first people, the Mi'kmaq, stretches back 16,000 years to the end of the last Ice Age. Europeans visited Nova Scotia as early as the 11th century and came to stay in 1604. Thankfully, the riches of the past have been collected, treasured and preserved and are now artfully and creatively presented at more than 100 museums in Nova Scotia.

The Nova Scotia Museum presents the unique social and natural history of the province at 27 museums across the province. A Nova Scotia Museum Pass (available at museum.gov.ns.ca, by calling 800 632-1114 or at any Nova Scotia Museum site) is a great bargain ($42 per adult; $82 per family) and will admit you to all Nova Scotia Museum sites. Parks Canada administers several important National Historic Sites in the province, including the Halifax Citadel and the Fortress of Louisbourg. There are also many excellent community museums. Check before you visit a museum, as many are only open during the summer season.

If you are coming to Nova Scotia by ferry, you can get your first history hit as soon as you disembark in the old seaport of Yarmouth. Kids love fire trucks. Get their vacation off to a roaring start at the Firefighters' Museum of Nova Scotia. Here, you'll find a rare collection of firefighting memorabilia from the 19th and early 20th centuries. While you're in town, the award-winning Yarmouth County Museum is worth a walkabout.

The stories of Nova Scotia's earliest settlers unfold along the Evangeline Trail. Along the Acadian Shore you will witness evidence of the faith, industry and tenacity of Nova Scotia's 17th-century French settlers. Beautiful St. Mary's Church in Church Point is the largest wooden church in North America (56 metres from floor to steeple). The church houses le Musée Ste-Marie, its collection comprising church artifacts such as vestments, furnishings, documents and photographs.

Fort Anne National Historic Site

When you arrive at the graceful old town of Annapolis Royal, you can stretch your legs on the earthworks of Fort Anne National Historic Site, which affords great views of the Annapolis Basin. The gunpowder building is the only surviving structure of the first 1708 French fort. The museum in the officers' quarters (circa 1797) presents a chapter in the struggle between France and Britain for supremacy in the New World. An amazing tapestry represents 400 years of the area's history.

Nearby, Port Royal National Historic Site is a reconstruction, based on a detailed drawing by Samuel de Champlain, of Canada's first European colony — a fur-trading post established here in 1605. Inside the high wooden walls surrounding the habitation, costumed interpreters perform the daily chores that made it possible for the French to maintain a European lifestyle.

Grand-Pré National Historic Site

Grand-Pré National Historic Site commemorates the deportation of the Acadians in 1755. The site paints a vivid picture of the lives of the first French settlers around Minas Basin. As a prelude to your visit, you might read Longfellow's epic poem *Evangeline*, or the novel *The Sea is So Wide* by Evelyn Eaton, both fictional stories based on the tragic events of 1755.

The town of Windsor claims bragging rights to being the birthplace of Canada's great game on ice. At the Hockey Heritage Centre, fans can see wooden pucks, handmade one-piece hockey sticks and early memorabilia of the game. Also in Windsor are two Nova Scotia Museum sites — the mid-Victorian Haliburton House, former home of Thomas Chandler Haliburton, writer of the famous Sam Slick stories, and the late-Victorian Shand House.

Re-enactors at
Louisbourg

Along the Fundy Shore there's history of another, much older sort — the history of ancient rocks and life forms. The Joggins Fossil Centre, recently designated a UNESCO World Heritage Site, has an excellent collection of 300-million-year-old fossils and explains the geological phenomena in this area. There are also guided tours of the nearby fossil cliffs.

The Fundy Geological Museum at Parrsboro is a great place to take young dinosaur enthusiasts. There are some Jurassic tales here to tell the kids back home.

Nova Scotia has an extensive shipbuilding heritage. Huge wooden vessels were built on the beaches of this shore. The Age of Sail Heritage Centre at Port Greville highlights the history of lumbering and shipbuilding with artifacts and hands-on exhibits. On the other side of Minas Basin is the Lawrence House Museum in Maitland where the *William D Lawrence*, the largest wooden ship ever built in Canada, was launched in 1874.

Visitors can go deep into a dark coal mine at the Miners' Museum in Springhill, a coal-mining town that has seen more than its share of tragedy, and learn about the stories of heroism and survival around the chilling disaster of 1891, the subterranean fire of 1916, the explosion of 1956 and the major "bump" of 1958.

At Pictou's Hector Heritage Quay, costumed heritage interpreters and stirring exhibits let you feel the hardships of the 1773 voyage that brought early Scottish settlers to "New Scotland." Step aboard the full-size replica of the ship *Hector* and imagine yourself crossing the Atlantic in the crowded space below decks.

In nearby Stellarton, the Nova Scotia Museum of Industry celebrates 200 years of progress, with more than 18,000 artifacts and many interactive exhibits.

Across the Canso Causeway in Cape Breton, the Alexander Graham Bell National Historic Site at Baddeck deserves a half-day visit. It shows the diverse interests and accomplishments of the man behind the telephone. Most of Bell's later years were spent in Baddeck, and the museum demonstrates the impressive breadth of his inventiveness, including his method for teaching speech to the deaf, his giant kites, airplanes and hydrofoils. At the Fortress of Louisbourg National Historic Site, you will be transported back to 1744. Dozens of costumed actors portraying townsfolk and soldiers carry on as if the 21st century weren't just beyond the site's walls. There's a lively tavern, period homes to explore and women at work in the authentic kitchen gardens. Atop the ramparts at the back of the fortress there's a bird's-eye view of the harbour and town, with the children at play and the soldiers doing their drills. The fortress is best experienced over a full day.

When you return to the mainland, take the ruggedly beautiful Marine Drive for a very different view of Nova

Scotia. Along the way, at the Lighthouse Interpretive Centre at Port Bickerton, the lore of the lighthouse and the lightkeeper is kept alive. The lighthouse gives a great view of the sea and community.

Sherbrooke Village is a living history museum, depicting rural life in Nova Scotia between 1860 and the First World War. A weaver's cottage, a blacksmith's shop, a doctor's office and the home of an affluent master mariner are as they looked 100 years ago.

The Fisherman's Life Museum in Jeddore Oyster Pond is a little gem. An early 1900s inshore fisherman, his wife and family of 13 daughters lived here. Women of the Eastern Shore tell stories of the family and how they lived, while they bake, tend the garden and preserve its wonderful produce, just as it was done several generations ago.

Many visitors are unaware of Halifax's close connection to the *Titanic* disaster. It was from Halifax that search and recovery operations were conducted. The Maritime Museum of the Atlantic has the world's largest collection of wooden artifacts from the *Titanic* (sit in a replica deck chair from the *Titanic* for a great souvenir photo). The powerful exhibit "A Moment in Time" captures the devastation wrought by the Halifax Explosion of 1917. Exhibits on the Age of Sail, shipwrecks and the navy are part of the big picture of a great port city in a maritime province.

Halifax is crowned by the star-shaped Halifax Citadel National Historic Site. The Citadel is surrounded by a dry

Halifax Citadel

Heritage sheep,
Ross Farm

defensive ditch: don't fall in! The earthen ramparts provide great views of the city and harbour. Constructed between 1828 and 1856, the Citadel is a fine example of a bastioned fort of the "smooth bore" era. The site's newest exhibit, Fortress Halifax — Warden of the North, describes Halifax and its defences. In summer, students portray soldiers of the Royal Artillery and the 78th Highlanders of 1869 and fire the noonday gun. Fun to watch — but cover your ears.

At the Museum of Natural History there is something to fascinate all ages and tastes — a house full of live exotic butterflies (in summer), life in a busy beehive (located safely behind glass), a nature centre with live critters, as well as world-class fossils and travelling exhibits.

A gateway to North America for more than one million people, Pier 21 National Historic Site recollects the experiences of many individuals who arrived between 1928 and 1971. The facility houses interactive displays and artifacts, touching first-hand accounts and exhibits celebrating the ethnic diversity and cultural heritage of Canada.

Along the Lighthouse Route there are a couple of museums you really shouldn't miss. It's an easy day trip from Halifax to New Ross and the town of Lunenburg, a UNESCO World Heritage Site.

In 1816, William Ross, an army captain, and his wife Mary arrived in Nova Scotia with 172 disbanded soldiers to take up lands granted to them by the Crown. Today, the Ross Farm Living Museum of Agriculture is alive with costumed heritage interpreters who take you back to the early 1800s at a vintage store, the Ross farmhouse, barns and workshops, a village school, a blacksmith's shop and a cooper's shop. The farm is populated with heritage animals — horses, cows, oxen, sheep, pigs and poultry. The baby farm animals are always popular with children. Kids who have never seen a cow up close can try to milk one. Slightly older children (and their grandparents) might enjoy demonstrations of spinning, flax processing, bread making, yarn dying and woodworking.

In Lunenburg, the Fisheries Museum of the Atlantic is one of the Nova Scotia Museum's largest and most popular sites. *Bluenose* buffs will enjoy the exhibit of memorabilia and photos of the famous schooner built here. Old salts will tell you all you want to know about lobster fishing and demonstrate fishing skills. There's an exhibit on Lunenburg's rum-running days and a wonderful aquarium with peepholes at just the right level for pint-sized observers. You can board the schooner *Theresa E. Connor*, and see what the life of a Grand Banks fisherman was like.

For information on these and the many other museums in Nova Scotia consult the *Nova Scotia Doers' and Dreamers' Guide* or visit novascotia.com/en/home/whattodo/attractions/museums.

Art & Crafts

Susan MacAlpine Foshay

Along with its many kilometres of spectacular scenery, Nova Scotia can boast an abundance of artists and craftspeople. With your *Nova Scotia Colourguide* in hand, supplemented by any number of provincial tour guides — *The Guide to Craft and Art in Nova Scotia* (www.craft-design.ns.ca) and *Studio Rally Map* (www.studiorally.ca), and road maps readily available at tourist information centres along the way — you'll find many wonderful surprises awaiting discovery. Whether you are looking for rug hooking, metal work, jewellery, pottery, quilts, paintings, sculpture or work in wood, or you are just browsing, there is much to see.

John Thompson of Leather Works in Cape Breton

Artist's studios, galleries and shops are, by and large, located on secondary highways and in towns and villages, thus favouring a leisurely approach to your adventure. Leaving Halifax behind (we'll return), let's head off towards the South Shore along the Lighthouse Route in the direction of Chester, Mahone Bay and Lunenburg. If time allows, there is a most rewarding secondary highway drive along Route 333 that will take you past the forge and home of blacksmith and sculptor John Little in East Dover. John is known around the world for his forging and is also acknowledged by respected members of the international music community for his forged metal sculptures for musical performance. This route will also lead you to Peggys Cove and then, rejoining Highway 103, to Chester and

Handmade casserole dish with cedar waxwing. Lucky Rabbit Pottery in Annapolis Royal.

beyond. Amicus Gallery in Chester offers a variety of fine art and craft to suit all tastes, and Trees Gallery in Mahone Bay and The Black Duck in Lunenburg are good stops. They are just a few of the many galleries and shops in this area. This route is also home to many artists, whose studios you'll find by referring to the *Studio Map* and *The Guide*, mentioned above. In Lunenburg you can pick up a map that shows a self-guided walking tour of about 20 galleries, showing diverse media and styles. As you travel along the coast from Bridgewater, you'll arrive in the village of Petite Rivière, where the Maritime Painted Saltbox features the fine folk art of Tom Alway and Peter Blais in charming surroundings.

Whether Liverpool's Roger Savage is painting on Sable Island or on the magnificent beaches along the coast of Queen's County, his watercolours capture the very essence of coastal Nova Scotia. Savage's gallery carries not only his paintings, but also a wide selection of reproductions of his work.

The southernmost end of the province offers Tin Pot Textiles in Yarmouth, a studio devoted to the arts of knitting and rug hooking, but you'll need to plan ahead as it is only open by chance or appointment. En route between Yarmouth and Digby don't miss Sous le Soleil, where Jay LeBlanc's gallery and studio has original works in stained glass as well as other media.

If you are short on time, from Liverpool you can cross the province on Highway 8 and resume exploration in Bear River with Rob Buckland-Nicks and Flight of Fancy. Rob's work, birds of Canada painted on natural stone, will intrigue you. Flight of Fancy offers a wide variety of high quality work in many media by other artists from Nova Scotia. Heading east you'll pass through Upper Clements,

Folk art by William Roach, Sunset Art Studios in Cheticamp

where Emery and Sheila Salsman have their Sun Room Glass gallery offering beautiful stained glass. Just next door is Annapolis Royal, one of Canada's cultural capitals, and home to many artists and craftspeople. Make note here of Lucky Rabbit Pottery studio, shop and garden where Deb Kuzyk and Ray Mackie combine magic and practicality in their

Kathy Brown,
Spinnakers in the Northwest Arm

functional porcelain. At Kentville, cross over the North Mountain to catch a breathtaking view of the Bay of Fundy and visit Bob Hainstock in his printmaking studio located right at the crest of the hill. Continue down to Halls Harbour for a lobster feast and then to David Lacey's studio where he paints impressionistic and magic realism land- and seascapes. On the way back to Kentville from Halls Harbour, head east towards Canning and visit the studio of Steven Kennard, a photographer and a wizard woodworker whose exquisitely turned exotic woods are cherished keepsakes.

As you leave the Bay of Fundy behind, heading towards Halifax/Dartmouth, stop in Mount Uniacke at James Brown's Steady Brook Saddlery. Whether or not you are an equestrian, Brown's working saddlery will be sure to impress — finely tooled leather work and exquisite silver detail, mohair cinchas and quality saddle blankets are readily available. Then at Lower Sackville, head towards Truro. An alternate route back at Windsor is to travel to Truro along the Noel Shore, which skirts the Minas Basin. A number of artists reside along this route.

From Truro, the scenic route to Amherst will reveal such accomplished artists as painter Joy Laking and mixed media artist Krista Wells, to name only two. Once in Amherst, a small town nestled at the edge of the Tantramar Marsh, visit Deanne Fitzpatrick, an entertaining and gracious host, whose hooked rugs are sure to enchant you. Some narrative, some boldly geometric, Deanne's rugs are always skillfully executed. She also offers kits for both the beginner and for the more advanced rug hooker.

Visit some of our magnificent beaches as you travel east along the Northumberland Shore heading towards New Glasgow

Catfish Moon
Studios in
Annapolis Royal

Jumping through Hoops, The Clever Hen Pottery in Chester

and sculptor/weaver Dawn MacNutt. Known the world over for her woven human-like forms, MacNutt creates work in metal and natural materials projecting the serene and evoking the spiritual.

Lyghtesome Gallery in Antigonish will amaze you with its diversity and its quality of work. While the gallery does have an extensive selection of original work by Nova Scotia printmakers and watercolourists, it also carries sculpture and pottery. The work of Linda Johns, a brilliant artist from the area, is featured here.

A visit to Cape Breton will further enhance your Nova Scotia pilgrimage. Wherever you stop you will be immersed in local culture and confronted with a beautiful and varied landscape, in addition to an abundance of artists creating anything and everything you can imagine. Quality and variety are the watchwords! After crossing the causeway and heading counterclockwise around the island, stop at Del Zoppo's Grey Seal Weaving studio at Lower L'Ardoise. Her damask weaving is unparalleled and the location of her studio is nothing short of sublime. Continue on towards Fortress Louisbourg National Historic Site where you will be transported out of the here and now and into a time of great significance in the history of Canada – a unique historical environment that will appeal to all. Many of the artifacts on display and used in reconstructing the Fortress are reproductions made by Nova Scotia craftspeople, and you can admire iron hinges, earthenware, leather- and woodwork at close range. There is much to see, do and absorb here, so be prepared to stay the day.

Beyond Sydney, located on the edge of the Atlantic Ocean is Dominion where you will find the studio of watercolourist Kenny Boone. Boone's landscapes, seascapes, beaches and forests have wide appeal.

Farther on, as you embark on the Cabot Trail (a must-see under any circumstances), stop in Indian Brook and visit John Roberts's studio and shop, where you will find beautiful leather goods that will stand the test of time. And if your interest is in quality knitwear, stop in North East Margaree at Sheep's Clothing. While they feature contemporary knitted clothing and accessories based on traditional designs, they also excel in making reproduction items for re-enactors and living history museums. Any route you happen to take in Cape Breton will yield artists and craftspeople, so press on and keep your eyes open for the signage.

Back on the mainland, head for Guysborough and the Eastern Shore route, which will bring you to Halifax along the rugged coast of the Atlantic Ocean. Skipping Stone Gallery in the town of Guysborough represents a number of Nova Scotia painters and a number of craftspeople. If folk art appeals to you, Barry Colpitts is located in East Ship Harbour and creates a wild variety of whirligigs, yard

Mussel bowl, Stewart Applegath of Cape Breton Clay

art and funky furniture. In sharp contrast, Leslie Hauck's Spinner's Loft in West Jeddore gives insight into the process of hand spinning yarns and knitted garments.

Before you make your final approach into the Halifax Metro area, at Musquodoboit Harbour head down the West Petpeswick Road and stop at the studios of Kath and Rob Rutherford. Rob's work is a macro view of regional landscapes (silkscreen prints and acrylic paintings), whereas Kath's engravings and oil paintings are a micro view featuring still life and reflecting local tradition. Once in Halifax you will find an endless list of galleries, studios and shops where you can immerse yourself in work by local artists and craftspeople. While Halifax does not yet have a gallery neighbourhood, one area that is developing into a cultural destination is the waterfront, particularly the southernmost area where, from April to October, the cruise ships dock. The area is also home to the Nova Scotia Centre for Craft and Design and the Mary E. Black Gallery, as well as the new Port Campus of NSCAD University (whose main campus downtown houses the Anna Leonowens Gallery, a great spot to see student artwork). A little off the beaten track, the area is definitely worth a visit. Located throughout the city there are a number of excellent public galleries, not least of which is the Art Gallery of Nova Scotia, and while finding the university galleries may take a little perseverance, your efforts will be satisfied with dynamic exhibitions, both contemporary and historic. Commercial galleries also proliferate and offer amazing work available for purchase at all price points.

The Art Gallery of Nova Scotia (below) and Maude Lewis's house, installed in the Gallery

Theatre

Linette Chiasson

Neptune Theatre's production of *The Producers*

With more than thirty working venues and a list of companies that grows longer every year, actors, directors and playwrights are flocking to Nova Scotia, producing works that are commanding international attention.

The first theatrical production in Nova Scotia (and arguably in the New World) was a masque devised by Marc Lescarbot, a settler at Port Royal, in 1606. The theatrical tradition of the area is continued to this day at King's Theatre, site of the Annapolis Royal Summer Theatre Festival, held each year in July and August.

The numerous theatre festivals in Nova Scotia constitute a good reason for a trip just in themselves. Festival Antigonish is a popular event, with attendees from around the globe — a treat for any theatre lover and set in a jewel of a town. The Liverpool International Theatre Festival, held at the Astor Theatre every other May, and the Chester Theatre Festival at the Chester Playhouse in July and August are well worth checking out, as is the Halifax Fringe Festival in September. The Internet is a valuable tool when planning a festival expedition, with listings and information about plays and show times.

In the metro area, there are a host of companies and venues to see — most notably Shakespeare by the Sea, set against the natural beauty and fantastic forts and ruins around Point Pleasant Park each summer. Dartmouth-based Eastern Front Theatre, located at Alderney Landing, a fun few minutes by ferry from downtown Halifax, is the area's

Performers at Halifax Feast's Dinner Theatre

only professional company whose mandate places emphasis on producing plays of regional provenance and social relevance. It's a short walk from here to Crichton Avenue, where you will find the Dartmouth Players, an amateur company that attracts some fine local talent and provides solid entertainment. The Theatre Arts Guild is a Halifax institution that has been presenting good entertainment to theatre-goers at its Pond Playhouse for many years.

The well-known Neptune Theatre started life in 1915 as the Strand Theatre vaudeville house, but since 1963 the company has been producing shows almost year-round and has expanded its reputation as a touring venue since it's extensive renovation in 1997. The Fountain Hall main stage is a grand space with beautiful acoustics, while the smaller Studio Theatre provides a more intimate setting. With the addition of the studio series, the Neptune season offers a fine mix of old and new works with an emphasis on Canadian content. Ticket

Shakespeare by the Sea

prices are available on the theatre's website, but if you're not able to book ahead, a limited number of rush tickets are sold a half hour before most performances for about half price. Both of the Neptune venues also serve as host theatres for touring productions and smaller companies, so it's worth calling the box office ahead of time to find out what's happening when you're going to be in town.

Keep your eyes peeled, and peruse *The Coast* (a free Halifax weekly) for complete area entertainment listings, as there are many smaller companies in the metro area that produce shows on a less regular schedule. Names to watch for include the Irondale Ensemble, Zuppa Circus, 2B and Exodus Theatre. Watch also for

Steven McCarthy in
2B theatre
company's
Revisited

performances at some of the smaller venues, like The Space on Agricola Street and Bus Stop Theatre, also in the city's North end. Daltheatre, the Dalhousie University theatre department, runs an interesting season from the Sir James Dunn Theatre in the Dalhousie Arts Centre — also the home of the Rebecca Cohn auditorium. Year-round fun can be found at Halifax's two dinner theatres — Historic Feast Dinner Theatre and Grafton Street Dinner Theatre, both within the downtown core. Don't forget to make reservations. Keep an eye on Theatre Nova Scotia's website at www.theatrens.ca for frequently updated information about productions in Halifax and across the province.

Two Planks and a Passion, a professional theatre company located in the pastoral landscape of Nova Scotia's Annapolis Valley and home of the Ross Creek Centre for the Arts, offers inspired outdoor productions in July and August. The company, dedicated to bringing theatre to the masses, also tours extensively.

Mermaid Theatre, an internationally acclaimed touring puppet theatre based in Windsor, is targeted at children, but is equally magical for adults. It's well worth the trip from anywhere in the province.

If your taste runs to unusual venues, there's the Ship's Company Theatre in Parrsboro. The theatre is housed in a converted car ferry, the MV *Kipawo*, and the performances are just as innovative. For more historic savour, there's the Savoy Theatre in Glace Bay, built in the 1920s in the manner of a Victorian show house. Although extensively renovated in the 1970s, the theatre retains all of its original period charm. In addition to its regular season, it hosts a wide range of touring and cultural activities, including an original Cape Breton show with comedy and music blended in perfect proportion. If you're planning a visit to Peggys Cove, see

Old Red
Schoolhouse
Theatre, Peggys
Cove

what's playing at the Old Red Schoolhouse, a charming venue for theatre and live music.

With so much to choose from, theatre aficionados will have no difficulty finding exciting productions across the province. The key is to keep abreast of the

many new companies, productions and venues popping up all the time. Check websites, ask at your place of accommodation, and pay attention to signs and posters. For more information on how to contact the companies mentioned here (and others), see the listings section of this *Colourguide*.

Ship's Company Theatre, Parrsboro

Shaw's *The Devil's Disciple* at Neptune Theatre

Music

Peggy Walt

Internationally acclaimed fiddler Natalie MacMaster

Nova Scotia is alive with the sound of music. The province for all seasons is also the province for all sounds. From pop to Celtic, down-home bluegrass to hard-core jazz — a tour of Nova Scotia can be a symphony of sounds.

One of the headliners in this musical landscape is Symphony Nova Scotia (www.symphonynovascotia.ca) — the only Canadian professional symphony orchestra east of Quebec City, presenting an exciting repertoire of classical and pop music in its various series. Under Maestro Bernhard Gueller, SNS's season runs from September to May at Halifax's Rebecca Cohn Auditorium, with traditional symphonic repertoire and diverse local artists such as rapper Buck 65, and singer/songwriters Joel Plaskett and Jill Barber. Symphony players comprise many smaller ensembles such as the Rhapsody Quintet (www.rhapsodyquintet.com) and the Blue Engine String Quartet. SuddenlyLISTEN (www.suddenlylisten.com) produces improvisational music concerts, as does the Upstream New Music Ensemble.

Complementing the orchestra's season, in late May and early June the Scotia Festival of Music produces a two-week long world-class chamber music series in Halifax with artists of exceptionally high calibre (www.scotiafestival.ns.ca).

The St. Cecilia Concert Series (www.stcecilia.ca) brings a wide range of performers to Nova Scotia audiences in the Halifax region and on the South Shore. During the summer months visitors will be delighted to find Music at the Three

Churches in Mahone Bay (www.threechurches.com), Musique Saint Bernard (www3.ns.sympatico.ca/musiquestb/), on the Acadian Shore, and Musique Royale (www.musiqueroyale.com) at various historic venues around the province, as well as Lunenburg's Boxwood Festival (www.boxwood.org). There is also a wealth of community and church choirs throughout the province performing seasonal repertoire (www.nscf.ns.ca/links.htm), including groups such as Camerata, the Cape Breton Chorale, Men of the Deeps, The Aeolian Singers, Gilbert and Sullivan Society, and Nova Voce.

Award-winning singer/songwriter Jill Barber

For traditional musical tastes, each area of Nova Scotia offers its own musical pedigree: in Cape Breton, the fiddle shares the stage with Celtic singers; in southwest Nova Scotia, Acadian musicians blend Louisiana Cajun, modern folk and fiddle tunes for a distinctive and lively sound. Each community has its own stellar entertainers: for example, fiddler Buddy MacMaster is king of the Ceilidh Trail, and from the French-speaking communities in the district of Clare come celebrated groups such as Grand Dérangement and Blou, heard at festivals such as the Festival Acadien de Clare (www.festivalacadiendeclare.ca). Acadian kitchen parties are held at various local restaurants on the French Shore throughout the summer as part of Musique de la Baie (www.baiesaintemarie.com).

Community dances are popular all over Nova Scotia, but few can compare with the Mabou Ceilidh Family Square Dance (www.angelfire.com/ca2/wmsquaredancing/). A tradition for more than 20 years, this community ceilidh is a weekly event all year round. The musicians range from stars such as Natalie MacMaster to gifted youngsters who are itching to get into the spotlight. People at all levels of dancing ability are welcome to participate. You can learn the steps from seasoned regulars.

Canadian hip hop artist Buck 65

Communities such as Italy Cross in the Bridgewater area have found their own way to bring Canadian talent to their villages. Seaside Folk, a non-profit organization of music fans, hosts monthly concerts at the Italy Cross fire hall, featuring performers as diverse as Scotland's Battlefield Band to local favourites such as Dan McKinnon. And then there's Pictou's Hector Festival, celebrating Celtic music and heritage each August at the deCoste Centre (www.townofpictou.ca).

All the pomp and circumstance of the province's rich military history comes alive at Halifax Metro Centre the first week in

DRUM! Halifax

July, with the Royal Nova Scotia International Tattoo (www.nstattoo.ca). Nova Scotia's spine-tingling massed pipes and drums share the floor with the best international military bands, as well as dancers, a massed choir and international performers. Pipe and drum bands abound throughout the province and are often found in local competitions such as The Gathering of the Clans each July 1 in Pugwash.

On Cape Breton Island, the tempo picks up in June, especially in Port Hawkesbury. With a weekly Ceilidh at the Creamery (Tuesdays; www.ceilidh.ca) and free Granville Green concerts (Sundays, July and August, www.granvillegreen.com), the port town is making a strong case for itself as the musical capital of the island. There are ceilidh dances each Wednesday all summer long at The Barn in the Margaree Valley (www.normaway.com).

Bluegrass is blooming in Nova Scotia. Communities such as Bridgewater, Avon Valley and Stewiacke (www.downeastgrass.com) have built amazing concerts and camping festivals spotlighting the unique down-home sounds of this provincial treat. You can also camp at Antigonish's Evolve Festival (www.evolvefestival.com). For something different, in August Truro hosts the Dutch Mason Blues Festival, billed as three days of Blues, Bikes and BBQ. In summer, concerts are advertised in the local newspapers, tourist information centres and on community cable channels. You can also check Music Nova Scotia's website at www.musicnovascotia.com to find out who is playing where.

Lunenburg Folk Harbour Festival

One of the best places to enjoy the music scene is in downtown Halifax. *The Coast*, a free weekly newspaper, gives details on the what and where of live music, be it pop, jazz, fusion, hardcore rock or anything in between. Halifax also hosts the best pub scene in Canada. Mainstays such as The Old Triangle, Lower Deck and Stayner's Pub feature live entertainment. In the fall, Halifax is home to the hit show DRUM! (www.drumshow.ca), a musical celebration of four founding cultures of Nova Scotia (Mi'kmaq, Acadian, Scottish and Black), utilizing rhythm, dance and video montages in a powerful celebration of Nova Scotia's culture and history. And pop music enthusiasts will want to check out the Halifax Pop Explosion, held each October (www.halifaxpopexplosion.com).

The Atlantic Jazz Festival (www.jazzeast.com), which takes place in early July, is the place to see solo jazz artists and ensembles from Canada and around the world. In addition to free jazz during the day on Spring Garden Road, the festival hosts evening events in a variety of venues throughout the city.

More great music from around the world abounds at the annual Multifest, held on the Dartmouth waterfront each June (www.multifest.ca). Flamenco, African drumming, Korean dance and great food await you. And there is more flamenco music in the small but growing scene at Fall for Flamenco (www.flamencofestival.ca).

Guerilla Vacation, Atlantic Jazz Festival, Halifax

Another banner event is held in the town of Canso on Marine Drive, a three- to four-hour drive from Halifax. The Stan Rogers Folk Festival, named for one of the country's best-loved folk musicians, can lay claim to being one of Canada's best folk festivals, held each July (www.stanfest.com)

Two music festivals in August exemplify Nova Scotia's rich history of community spirit and entrepreneurism: the Lunenburg Folk Harbour Festival (www.folkharbour.com) and the New Glasgow Riverfront Music Jubilee (www.jubilee.ns.ca). Lunenburg, a fishing town steeped in history, hosts folk musicians such as Susan Crowe, Ron Hynes, Lennie Gallant and many others. The Jubilee, set against the backdrop of the beautiful New Glasgow riverfront, offers the best in East Coast and Canadian talent ranging from pop to Celtic.

Wolfville's Deep Roots Festival in mid-September in the beautiful Annapolis Valley showcases local, national and international folk artists (www.deeprootsmusic.ca).

The festival season draws to a close in October with the internationally acclaimed Celtic Colours International Festival (www.celtic-colours.com) in Cape Breton, drawing enthusiastic crowds to listen to the best of Celtic music from the new and old worlds — Slainte Mhath, Mary Jane Lamond, Bela Fleck and Capercaillie.

Halifax's Rhapsody Quintet

Music has always been an important part of the Nova Scotian way of life and Nova Scotia has made important contributions to the world's music, being the birthplace of opera singer Portia White, country crooners Hank Snow and George Canyon, and Springhill's Anne Murray. Performers always find a warm reception in the province. Indoor (Dalhousie Arts Centre, Halifax Metro Centre, Centre 500) and outdoor venues have recently featured notables from Leonard Cohen to The Rolling Stones. Concerts, outdoor festivals and ceilidhs are enthusiastically attended by people of all ages.

For details about music festivals and events call 800 565-0000, check out www.novascotia.com or ask at a local visitor information centre.

Dining

Rob Crawford

Prosciutto-wrapped Monkfish with Chard and Cape Breton Mustard Pickles from Chives Canadian Bistro, Halifax

Nova Scotia dining establishments have come a long way in recent years. Chefs are travelling around the world and returning to this province with international experience, then sourcing from local suppliers to provide fresh, often organic, ingredients for creative and innovative menus.

In a province almost completely surrounded by ocean, fresh seafood is a given. Lobster of course is king. But we have queen crab and Digby scallops, blue mussels and farm-raised salmon. Haddock and halibut are among favourite fresh offerings. Lamb, beef, pork and poultry are raised locally. Annapolis Valley apples, Cumberland County blueberries, juicy red strawberries and bog cranberries, each in their season, grace restaurant menus. Traditional treats like blueberry grunt and apple crisp vie with creative interpretations in salads and entrées. Fresh vegetables are available in abundance.

It may come as a pleasant surprise to many that the fruit of the vine is grown widely and well in this province. Nova Scotia wineries produce distinctive wines that have garnered awards and international appreciation.

In Nova Scotia dining establishments associated with inns and hotels offer some of the best cuisine in the province. Having lodging nearby after dinner is a bonus, especially after a long day of travel. Here are only a few of many exceptional restaurants within walking range of good accommodations.

Rhubarb Grill in Indian Harbour is on the Oceanstone Inn & Cottages property. The secluded location makes for a great escape for Nova Scotia residents as well as visitors to the province. Frequent changes to the menu and décor keep the restaurant feeling new. Chef Kent Thiebault is constantly trying out new dishes and refining favourites. The locally caught halibut is wonderfully fresh and there are other great seafood options. Ciopinno, an Italian fish stew, is an indulgent medley of beautifully cooked seafood in a herbed tomato broth. The herbs and greens for the kitchen are grown organically in the little greenhouse within sight of the dining room. Ask your server for recommendations. There are also good Nova Scotia cheeses available either as appetizers or as a dessert alternative — wonderful with some port before walking back to your room or cottage only steps away. Down the road, a young couple have poured their hearts into extensively renovating and refurbishing an old restaurant building and have opened it under the name The Finer Diner. The menu includes comfort food favourites like grilled cheese sandwich, fish and chips and a great club sandwich with lobster.

Trattoria della Nonna, Lunenburg

In Lunenburg, choose accommodations in Old Town so you'll be close to two of Nova Scotia's best restaurants. Trattoria della Nonna brings Italy to this side of the Atlantic. The dark woods used for the décor, combined with bright yellow runners and punches of red, create a warm and cozy ambience. A wood-burning oven used to bake terrific pizzas and breads gives warmth and wonderful aromas to some otherwise chilly Lunenburg nights. The restaurant may be far from Italy, but the food is far from ordinary. Sophisticated combinations of flavours are rendered from local produce, seafood and meats. Wines can be paired to the dishes with the help of the knowledgeable sommelier. Trattoria also serves an interesting brunch on the weekends.

Fleur de Sel is Lunenburg's other top restaurant. A strong commitment to using local ingredients in traditional French cuisine is its *tour de force*. In 2004 Fleur de Sel was included in *en Route* magazine's top ten new restaurants in Canada, and it has continued to maintain stellar standing among its clientele. Fleur de Sel's offspring, the nearby Salt Shaker Deli, is a popular, informal spot for a tasty lunch.

For a Nova Scotia beachside experience, the

Fleur de Sel, Lunenburg

Quarterdeck Grill at Summerville Beach on the South Shore is a funky surf shack with fabulous fresh seafood. The building hangs out over one end of the long white sand beach and is filled with an eclectic mix of brightly coloured chairs and tables in a kitschy décor. Cedar-planked salmon has been a popular choice on the menu summer after summer. There are great choices of haddock and halibut, with lobster and scallops filling out the menu.

Close to the ferry dock in Digby is the Annapolis Room, the fine dining restaurant at the Digby Pines Golf Resort and Spa. It affords a spectacular view over the Annapolis Basin, where the scallop fishing boats can be seen coming and going. This is *the* place to savour world-famous Digby Scallops or the other great innovative dishes on the menu created by Executive Chef and Sommelier Claude Aucoin.Wolfville, in the Annapolis Valley, has a reputation for excellent restaurants. Tempest is currently the brightest star in town. Michael Howell has brought his experience from urban centres across North America to this small town, and has impressed upon it a wide range of world cuisine.

Dining on the patio at The Port Gastropub, Port William

Chef Howell achieves his philosophy of supporting sustainability in fishing and farming practices by sourcing meat, seafood and produce from local suppliers. Indian Butter Chicken is made using local free-range poultry, haddock is line caught and many dishes are served with organic vegetables. Port Gastropub in nearby Port Williams is another Michael Howell creation. The upscale brew pub.specializes in high quality "beer cuisine" utilizing local product in its slow food menu. Also in Wolfville is Acton's, a town favourite for many years.

Cast Iron Seared Deep Ocean Scallops with Beetroot Beurre Blanc and Mango Salsa at Tempest Restaurant, Wolfville

Not far from Wolfville, on the way to Halifax, is Windsor's Woodshire Inn, a beautiful old building with a small dining room — Cocoa Pesto Bistro. The food is fresh and often experimental. An applewood-fired smoker is used to flavour their Annapolis Valley pork dishes; the ribs are sensational.

In Cape Breton, be sure to try the dining room at The Normaway Inn. The Normaway is tucked away in the Margaree Valley, just off the interior section of the Cabot Trail. The food is made with some of the produce from their gardens, and is self-described as "country cooking." The spectacular scenery of the Margaree Valley, combined with some of the best cooking the island has to offer, followed by local live music in the evenings makes the Normaway a quintessential Nova Scotia experience. Some of the province's many good wines are available to complement dinner. On the other side of the Cabot Trail overlooking St. Anne's Bay, Chanterelle Country Inn and Cottages specializes in "Cape Breton Fresh" cuisine prepared according to slow food traditions using organically,

Acton's, Wolfville

Cocoa Pesto Bistro in Windsor

locally produced food. The dining room, listed in *Where to Eat in Canada*, offers a vegetarian, non-vegetarian and seafood entree with seasonal vegetables and freshly baked artisan bread every evening. The Purple Thistle Dining Room at Keltic Lodge Resort and Spa at Ingonish maintains a longstanding reputation for dining excellence. A varied menu is masterfully prepared by award-winning chef Dale Nichols. Local seafood is the specialty.

The traveller will encounter the village of Baddeck either at the beginning or the end of the Cabot Trail. There are a number of very good dining options in Baddeck. At Auberge Gisele Country Inn an award-winning European-trained chef prepares delightful specialties with a French flare. Herbs picked right outside the door, local produce and good wines contribute to a fine dining experience.

In the more populace area of Cape Breton, a small but elegant and excellent dining room can be found at the Gowrie House Country Inn at North Sydney, handy the ferry to Newfoundland. Superb food, service and setting have earned Gowrie House awards and accolades. About halfway between Cape Breton and Halifax, in

Roast Breast of Pheasant in Dried-cranberry Jus, Stories Restaurant at Halliburton House Inn, Halifax

Guysborough, is the DesBarres Manor Inn. An elegantly restored old manor house, it provides modern luxury and exceptional dining. The chef, Shaun Zwarun, uses some of the area's specialties, such as Aspy Bay oysters, redfish and partridgeberries, to create dishes that have been described as "contemporary Canadian cuisine with an East Coast flair." Other ingredients come right from the Manor's organic garden.

Gio in the Prince George Hotel, Halifax

In Halifax, choose carefully, since the best places are not the ones that spend the most on advertising or court reviews in local publications. Stories, at the Halliburton, offers an intimate and exceptional dining experience in the quiet ambience of an old Halifax home that is now an inn. Creative dishes with fresh ingredients are attentively served in small dining rooms. There is also a great backyard patio for summer nights.

The RCR Hospitality Group, already well known in Halifax for Onyx, has recently opened Cut Steakhouse next to the Marriott Courtyard. Aspiring to compete with the great steakhouses in cities across North America, Cut has not failed to impress. The beef is USDA prime grade A, dry aged on-site. The friendly and knowledgeable servers will explain the process and why it produces such a great result.

DesBarres Manor Inn, Guysborough (below) and Rack of Lamb with Barley Pilaf, Spring Vegetables and edible flowers from the Manor's organic garden (bottom)

Gio at the Prince George Hotel is considered to provide the best dining

experience in the city. Chef Bee Choo Char leads and inspires a small group of some of Canada's brightest and most innovative young culinary talents to create outstanding menu selections. Recently, two young chefs from Gio won the top two places in a "black box" cooking competition. This dining room has been given descriptions rarely seen in Halifax: "sexy," "high-style modern" and "chic." Gio offers creative cuisine with phenomenal presentation and attentive service.

Award-winning chef Ray Bear, who was responsible for establishing Gio's illustrious reputation, has recently opened his own restaurant, Bear, on Barrington Street within an easy walk of many downtown hotels. Chives Canadian Bistro, also on Barrington Street, has been a favourite of Halifax diners since it was opened in 2001 by chef/proprietor Craig Flinn whose menu changes frequently to reflect local products, in season and at the peak of freshness. Unni and Geir Simensen's Saege Bistro on Spring Garden Road above the Public Gardens is the latest of the legendary family's culinary successes. Beautifully presented dishes are meticulously served in an urban garden atmosphere. Jane's on the Common on Robie St. offers imaginative, inexpensive dining in a diner format.

Available at tourist information centres, the current issue of *A Taste of Nova Scotia* will have dining room hours, addresses and contact information for these and many other notable restaurants. Also useful is *Maritime Flavours*, a cookbook and guidebook from the Maritimes' finest inns and restaurants by Elaine Elliot and Virginia Lee. Individual websites are also a good way to view sample menus and find out more about a specific restaurant. A more extensive list of fine restaurants can be found in the *Dining* listings in this *Colourguide* on page 179.

Basil Pesto Crusted Sea Bass with Charred Cherry Tomatoes and Pine Nuts, Chives Canadian Bistro, Halifax

The interior of Jane's on the Common

Festivals & Events

Jodie Noiles

With more than 500 celebrations each year, it's small wonder that Nova Scotia is known as Canada's festival province. Festivals are *the* place to enjoy the best of Nova Scotia: spectacular landscapes, relaxing sea coasts, sumptuous food and wines and soul-stirring, foot-stomping music. Nova Scotia culture, shaped by the soul of the Old World and the spirit of the new, comes alive at events across the province — and you are invited.

Nova Scotia hosts a number of world-class events that are worth planning a vacation around. The Royal Nova Scotia International Tattoo, held in Halifax the first week of July, features more than 2,000 world-class Canadian and international military and civilian performers. The Tattoo is one of the world's premiere cultural and entertainment events. On the South Shore of the province in early August, the Mahone Bay Classic Boat Festival, Canada's largest classic boating event, celebrates Mahone Bay's heritage as a wooden-boat building community. The festival features events for all ages, including a parade of sail, re-enactment of the burning of the *Teazer* and fireworks. The Annapolis Valley Apple Blossom Festival, the springtime celebration of agricultural heritage in the Annapolis Valley held in late May, is one of the oldest family festivals in the province.

A wide variety of festivals and events across the province feature Nova Scotian, Canadian and World music. The skirl of the pipes, the beat of the drums and the sounds of the city scene will immerse you in Nova Scotia culture. Cape Breton Island is a well-known destination for music enthusiasts and home to many internationally acclaimed

Harald Haugaard of the Danish duo Haugaard & Høirup at Celtic Colours

39

Nova Scotia Tattoo Parade

performers. The Cape Breton International Drum Festival, held the last weekend of April, features international artists sharing their love of percussion, rhythm and music. The Celtic Colours International Festival is held in October to coincide with Cape Breton's spectacular fall foliage. It is a unique celebration of music and culture, with concerts, education programs and community events held all over the island for nine days each year.

For visitors seeking an urban experience, Halifax plays host to great jazz, blues, pop and rock events. The TD Canada Trust Atlantic Jazz Festival — where the groove kicks in and the city comes alive with an eclectic mix of Jazz, World Beat, Blues and Urban Groove— takes place in July. One of the city's newest events, the Halifax Pop Explosion, features the best in new music fused with unique exhibitions of art, media and pop culture in October.

X-stream cardboard boat race for teens; Mahone Bay Classic Boat Festival

If you are travelling to the Northumberland Shore, the New Glasgow Riverfront Music Jubilee at the end of July

is a celebration of music from Country to Celtic, held in a premier outdoor amphitheatre overlooking the New Glasgow riverfront. In mid-August at the deCoste Centre in Pictou, the Hector Festival celebrates Celtic heritage and music. For five days visitors can enjoy outdoor concerts, main stage performances and highland dance and pipe band competitions.

As much as

Nova Scotians enjoy their pipes and drums, folk and soul music are equally appreciated. The Stan Rogers Folk Festival held in early July is a musical tribute to the great Canadian singer/songwriter. In September,

Wolfville hosts the Canadian Deep Roots Festival, which celebrates Nova Scotia's rich and diverse musical traditions — blending the music of founding cultures with modern roots music from around the world. And the Lunenburg Folk Harbour Festival early in August offers visitors an intimate experience of traditional music by the sea.

Oxen boat launch, Mahone Bay Classic Boat Festival

Smaller community festivals and events give you the chance to get to know the people and places of Nova Scotia. Shelburne's Whirligig and Weathervane Festival in September, the Pumpkin Regatta in Windsor in October, and the annual Old-Fashioned Christmas in Sherbrooke in November are a sampling of many great opportunities to

experience the uniqueness of Nova Scotian towns and villages and to celebrate with local residents. Visitors are warmly welcomed at the many community events across the province. Afternoon teas, craft fairs, quilt shows, community concerts, potluck suppers, strawberry socials and kitchen parties all enhance a visit to Nova Scotia.

Busker Festival Halifax (above) Joel Plaskett on the Wharf stage at the Lunenburg Folk Harbour Festival

Hike the Highlands Festival, Cape Breton

There are hundreds of community concerts and live performances that take place around the province in public parks, local pubs, on waterfront stages and in community centres. Highlights include the Antigonish Ceilidhs, every second Saturday at Piper's Pub; the Sherbrooke Village Courthouse Concert Series (a mix of country, folk and Celtic music); the Pictou Summer Musical Showcase outdoor waterfront concert series held in July and August and featuring local artists; and Music and Martinis on Thursday evenings in July and August at the Grand Pré Winery outdoor pergola.

If you'd like to take a little bit of Nova Scotia home with you, visit one of the arts and crafts events. Among the most popular are the Lunenburg Festival of Crafts in July, Nova Scotia's Gem and Mineral Show in August and the Nova Scotia Folk Art Festival, also in August.

There are events for outdoor adventure and nature buffs as well. The Hike the Highlands Festival in September features ten days of guided hikes in northern Cape Breton, Cape Breton Highlands National Park and other parts of the Cabot Trail, plus presentations and other activities. For both avid and amateur birders, the Birding and Nature Festival held in March in one of the primary birding areas of the province, Shelburne County, features birding tours of the region, including Cape Sable Island, plus nature presentations and exhibits. In June, the annual Tern Festival takes place in West Pubnico with nature walks, presentations and entertainment. These events are a great opportunity to visit some of the best nature and adventure destinations in Nova Scotia and to learn about the province's natural heritage from local experts.

In "New Scotland," naturally, there are many Scottish celebrations. In Pictou, New Scotland Days, a Living Heritage Festival, is held at the Hector Heritage Quay each weekend from July to September. There's also the Gathering of the Clans in Pugwash on Canada Day, Festival of the Tartans in New Glasgow in August, the Halifax Scottish Festival in July and the Antigonish Highland Games, also in July. The Federation of Scottish

Clans in Nova Scotia is a good source of information on Clan Gatherings and Scottish events in the province.

Nova Scotia's rich cultural heritage has inspired many other festivals around the province celebrating the unique history of each region. Privateer Days in Liverpool in July recreates the privateering era in Nova Scotia. The Festival Acadien de Clare is Canada's largest and oldest Acadian cultural festival, from July to August. The Nova Scotia Multicultural Festival takes place in Dartmouth in June and features more than 25 ethno-cultural groups.

Nova Scotia is also known for superb cuisine, especially seafood, and more recently fine wines. There are numerous events celebrating the fisheries, local fare and regional flavours. The Pictou Lobster Carnival in July, started in 1934, celebrates the lobster and fishing heritage of the Northumberland Shore region. Events include lobster dinners, lobster fishing competitions, a midway and great live entertainment for three days. Note also the Louisbourg Crab Festival; Digby Scallop Days and the St. Mary's Chowderfest & Sherbrooke Shindig, both in August; the Bear River Cherry Carnival in July; and the Valley Pumpkin Fest in October. Fall travellers might enjoy the Discover the Wines of Nova Scotia Fall Festival, with more than 35 event venues across the province at wineries and select restaurants, featuring wine tastings, grape stomps and classes paired with fabulous cuisine from the province's finest chefs.

For more information on festivals and events in Nova Scotia check www.novascotia.com or pick up a *Festivals & Events Guide* at tourist information centres in the province. It is wise to check event details in advance as sometimes dates and times change. Smaller community events are not always promoted in the tourism guides, but are often great fun. When travelling around the province, check for event posters in towns you visit. If there is anything happening during your stay (and there more than likely is), you're sure to find out at the community tourist bureau or town hall.

The Royal Nova Scotia International Tattoo

Golf

Dale Dunlop

4th hole at Highlands Links Golf Course

Golfing in Nova Scotia is one of the best ways to enjoy the great variety of scenery and different topography found throughout the province. Perhaps reflective of Nova Scotia's Scottish heritage, the game is played with a passion at no less than 65 courses open to the public. Even better, the greens fees are among the most moderate in North America. But what about the quality of the courses?

Look no further than Highlands Links, located in Cape Breton Highlands National Park, for the answer. This is the ultimate in traditional golf – quite simply the best course designed by Canada's foremost golf architect, Stanley Thompson. It is regularly rated the #1 public course in Canada and among the top 100 in the world. In a recent publication, *1001 Golf Holes You Must Play Before You Die* by Jeff Barr, Highlands Links has no less than six holes selected, as many as Pebble Beach and one more than Augusta National and the Old Course at St. Andrews. Unlike Augusta National, you can actually play the Highlands Links, and unlike Pebble Beach and St. Andrews you can afford to play it. Greens fees are less than $80.00

Lunenburg Golf Course, overlooking the harbour

and resort packages start at under $150.00. Dedicated golfers come from all over the world just to play this sensational layout, which features a combination of seaside, riverside and highland holes in an unbelievably beautiful setting.

However, if travelling to Nova Scotia just to play one course is not for you, don't worry: the Highlands Links is one of the "Fab Four" courses in Cape

Chester Golf Club, overlooking the islands of Mahone Bay

Breton that are often played in sequence by visitors and locals alike. Bell Bay outside Baddeck is an immaculately groomed design by Tom McBroom, which is rated #40 in Canada and continues to host many top flight national and international events. Dundee Resort, on the shores of the Bras D'Or Lakes, has exceptional views of these famed waters with a lot of elevation changes to make up for its relatively modest yardage of just under 6,000. Finally, Le Portage in Cheticamp offers an Acadian slice of golf on a plateau overlooking the Gulf of St. Lawrence, from which whales and fishing boats are a common sight.

On the mainland the choices are equally appealing. In the Halifax area, Glen Arbour is a must play. This 6,800-yard layout by Graham Cooke is rated #24 in Canada and is tough enough to have hosted the 2005 LPGA Canadian Open. It is pricey by Nova Scotia standards, but worth it. Also worth playing in the metro area are Granite Springs near the shores of Shad Bay and the very scenic River Oaks, a 27-hole layout alongside the Musquodoboit River, with greens fees under $40.00.

The Annapolis Valley has enough good courses to keep a golfer happy for weeks. Among the best is Digby Pines, another Stanley Thompson classic, which has hosted golfers for more than 80 years, including Babe Ruth and Canada's own Mike Weir. In New Minas, Ken-Wo is a challenging tree-lined course that is always in great shape, as is Paragon outside Kingston.

Golfers who take the Lighthouse Route won't be disappointed either — many consider the Chester Golf Club to be the most scenic in the province, with a number of holes directly alongside the shore of Mahone Bay. It has commanding view of many islands, the ferries and yachts that regularly traverse the bay and the mansions that overlook the harbour. Farther along is Osprey Ridge, a Graham Cooke design that takes full advantage of the rolling landscape outside Bridgewater. Although only 9 holes, the White Point course outside Liverpool falls into

the must-play category by reason of having holes 3 to 6 directly beside the crashing waves of the open Atlantic, with sensational views of beautiful White Point Beach.

Two municipal courses that are definitely worth playing are Truro, which is more than 100 years old and has hosted many national events, including the 2003 Senior Men's Match Play, and Amherst, which overlooks the Tantramar Marsh from a ridge just outside the town. Almost always windy, both Truro and Amherst provide a stern test for the average golfer. Still in the Northumberland Strait region, there is a chance to play a real hidden gem — Northumberland Links. Designed by Bill Robinson, this course has views of all three Maritime provinces, as well as the Northumberland Strait, from 16 holes. The par 3 fourth, which features a fishing boat embedded behind the green, may be the most scenic and unusual in the province. A true links layout for its first six holes, the wind can drive the average golfer to distraction, only to be remedied by the stunning views.

Highlands Links Golf Course (top) Dundee Resort and Golf Club (middle)

One final course of note, Fox Harb'r, is only for those with deep pockets. This 7,200-plus yard course was designed by Graham Cooke, received the nod as Canada's best new course in 2001 and is currently rated 25th in the country. Located along the shores of Northumberland Strait, it is the private fiefdom of Ron Joyce, the founder of the Tim Horton's coffee chain, who hails from nearby Tatamagouche. The course operates as an ultra exclusive resort, with upscale condos and a marina, so if you get a chance to play it will be costly, but many are willing to pay the price to play a course this highly rated.

Glen Arbour

All of the information needed to plan a golfing vacation in Nova Scotia can be found on two convenient websites. The first is www.golfnovascotia.com, which is run by the province and features a downloadable guide to golf in Nova Scotia, as well as many play and stay packages. The second is www.nsga.ns.ca, the official site of the Nova Scotia Golfing Association. It has contact information on all of the province's courses and direct links to their websites. See also the *Golf* listings at the back of this *Colourguide* on page 202

Golf may have originated in Scotland, but it is just as much fun to play in new Scotland — Nova Scotia.

Cycling

Dale Dunlop

Nova Scotia has long been recognized by cycling aficionados as one of the premiere cycling destinations in North America. A good place to start planning a cycling trip to Nova Scotia is by visiting the Atlantic Cycling Club website at www.atlanticcanadacycling.com. There you will find a wealth of information on Nova Scotia routes, trips and support services. Every year the club offers an 8 to 10 day tour of mainland Nova Scotia, a week-long tour of Cape Breton Island and, in the fall, a three-day assault on the Cabot Trail. The accommodation is based in campgrounds, resulting in a very inexpensive and healthy

French Mountain, Cabot Trail

Touring group with *Bluenose II*, Lunenburg

way to see some of or the entire province. The trips are led by Nova Scotians and are family friendly.

For those who want to plan their own trip or are looking for shorter excursions, the club publishes *The Nova Scotia Bicycle Book* by Gary Conrod, which details some 39 routes around the province and is described as the most comprehensive guide ever published for the cyclist in Nova Scotia. When considering where to cycle, any one of the province's signed scenic routes is a good place to start. The Lighthouse Route along the South Shore is popular because it follows the coast very closely and has many interesting historic towns such as Chester, Mahone Bay and Lunenburg at which to spend the night. The portion of the Evangeline Trail that traverses the Annapolis Valley is equally popular for its gentle pastoral landscape, elegant inns and fine dining. Those looking for a real challenge will consider the Cabot Trail, which is strenuous but rewards strong legs and lungs with spectacular seascapes and highland valleys. The loop around the small island of Isle Madame, linked to Cape Breton Island by a bridge, provides a complete contrast of gentle cycling and captivating scenery.

For a real off-the-beaten-path cycling experience, Marine Drive follows a twisting and rolling route along the coast from Halifax to Cape Breton Island, passing through some of the most remote and well-preserved fishing villages in Canada. Another undiscovered gem is the Sunrise Trail, starting near the New Brunswick border. From Amherst to the historic town of Pictou, this route follows the shores of the Northumberland Strait, offering many grand oceans views, tidal estuaries teeming with bird life and interesting villages such as Pugwash and Tatamagouche, both rich in history and fun to explore. Also not to be overlooked is the Glooscap Trail between Truro and Parrsboro, where the Bay of Fundy is always on the left and there is a chance to see traditional fishing weirs, the spectacular Five Islands and other unusual rock formations associated with the legendary Mi'kmaq demigod Glooscap.

Those who prefer to plan their cycling in day trips from a central base have two outstanding choices in Nova Scotia. Lunenburg, a UNESCO World Heritage Site, offers not only a great base to come home to each night, but an amazing number of interesting coastal peninsulas to explore on day trips. For more than 100 years, the Blue Rocks peninsula has been a favourite with artists and photographers who delight in its tiny colourful fishing shacks that perch upon the unusual blue polished-slate shoreline. In contrast, First Peninsula and Second Peninsula are more pastoral, with tranquil coves in a time-forgotten setting. The Lunenburg

Bike Barn (www.bikelunenburg.com) on Blue Rocks Road offers a variety of rentals and plenty of suggestions for day trips in the area.

On the other side of the mainland lies the college town of Wolfville, from where many paved roads radiate out through the countryside. In late spring, the apple blossoms are in full bloom and a trip through the rolling hills of the Gaspereau Valley, just outside town, will provide a memorable day's outing. Those who are up for a more strenuous day can consider biking up North Mountain to the Look-Off for amazing views of the Minas Basin and the patchwork quilt of fields and orchards far below. Others may opt to tour one of the many wineries in the region or visit historic Grand-Pré, which tells the story of the Acadians who once populated this area.

Those who prefer to let others do the planning might consider Freewheeling Adventures (www.freewheeling.ca), a small Nova Scotia-based company that has been building a solid reputation for many years as experts in Atlantic Canadian cycling tours. Freewheeling provides not only dedicated cycling tours, but also combination tours that may include hiking and kayaking as well as cycling.

For those who prefer to cycle off-highway, Nova Scotia offers plenty of opportunities, particularly on the many completed portions of the Trans Canada Trail. Most of the sections of this trail follow old railbeds, so the cycling is easy and car-free. Just outside Halifax there are a number of excellent cycling opportunities, including the St. Margarets Bay area, which offers great views of this lovely bay; the Salt Marsh Trail, which traverses a large tidal estuary near Dartmouth; and the Musquodoboit trail system, which offers some really nice picnic spots. Outside the Halifax area, other great sections of this trail can be found near Pictou, Guysborough and Mabou in Cape Breton.

Touring cyclists near Cheticamp

Hiking

Dale Dunlop

Hiking in White Point, Cape Breton

Nova Scotia, with more than 7,000 kilometres of coastline, two national parks and more than 100 provincial parks and wilderness areas, offers a wide variety of trails for hikers of all levels of skill and experience. Over the past decade, the number of kilometres of trails has increased dramatically, particularly with the opening of large portions of the Trans Canada Trail. Hiking as a recreational pastime is exceeded perhaps only by sea kayaking as a sector of rapid growth in Nova Scotia's tourist industry. Hiking, whether over the rugged granite outcrops on the Atlantic coast, atop the heights of highland Cape Breton or at the base of the fantastic seascapes of the Fundy coast, is an extremely popular way to enjoy the delights of outdoor Nova Scotia. A book of this size can't begin to describe all of the trails, but here are some of the best.

Hiking the Cabot Trail

Cape Breton Island offers a myriad of hiking opportunities. In particular Cape Breton Highlands National Park, one of Canada's oldest parks, offers more than 25 trails of varying length and difficulty. It is hard to recommend just a few, but Middle Head Trail, which starts right behind Keltic Lodge and winds its way to the tip of Middle Head, provides great views of the sea and highlands in all directions. Also of note are the Skyline Trail, which climbs high above the waters of the Gulf of St. Lawrence; the Coastal Trail, which explores hidden coves and a waterfall

along a gentle portion of the park; and Franey Mountain
Trail, which climbs very steeply to one of the best
viewpoints in the province. Here, eagles and hawks often
soar hundreds of metres beneath you as they rise up in the
thermals from the valley below. Not to be overlooked are
the Mabou Highlands and Cape Smokey Provincial Park,
which provide trails and vistas as good as those in the
national park, but with fewer people.

On the Eastern Shore's Marine Drive at Taylor Head
Provincial Park, a series of trails leads out to rugged,
windswept headlands overlooking the clear, cold waters of
the Atlantic. On the South Shore, the trail to St. Catherines
River Beach at Kejimkujik National Park Seaside Adjunct,
recently lengthened, crosses a coastal barren to arrive at a
spectacular white-sand beach where seals and seabirds
frolic just offshore. Inland, Kejimkujik National Park offers
a great number of trails, including a few that traverse some
of the last remaining old-growth forests in Nova Scotia.

On the Fundy Shore, there are a number of great hiking
sites, including Cape Chignecto Provincial Park, which is
located in one of the most remote areas of the province.
This park features strenuous wilderness trails that make
their way up and over coastal hills to secluded valleys,
deserted settlements and tiny coves not accessible along the
shore. Serious hikers can make a triangular loop of the park
that can take up to a week. Those less daring might prefer
to hike along the beach to Red Rocks and other very
unusual and rare rock formations. At Five Islands Provincial
Park, trails follow the top of the Fundy Cliffs to a series of
look-offs over such well-known landmarks as the Old Wife
and Red Head. In the Annapolis Valley the very popular
Cape Split trail follows the spine of a peninsula that juts out
into the Bay of Fundy to its very tip, from where the
tremendous force of the tides can be viewed first-hand.

Aside from the coastal hikes, Nova Scotia has some
great hiking to waterfalls, including Economy Falls and
Ward Falls in the Bay of Fundy area and Uisge Bahn,
Beulach Bahn and Mary Ann Falls in Cape Breton.

Those who prefer their hiking on the less strenuous
scale can choose from a number of venues, many on
reclaimed railbeds that now form part of the Trans Canada
Trail system. These trails are uniformly flat and well
maintained to the point that some of them are suitable even

Eagle's Nest in Bedford gives a beautiful view of the harbour.

for strollers. Some of the best sections of these railbed trails are the Mabou Harbour Trail in Cape Breton; the Musquodoboit Railway Trail on the Eastern Shore; the Salt Marsh Trail, which starts just outside the Halifax metropolitan area; and the St. Margarets Bay Trail, which skirts the bay of that name between Halifax and Hubbards. All in all, there is something for everyone on the hiking trails of Nova Scotia.

Those with a serious interest in hiking have a number of guidebooks from which to chose, including two by Michael Haynes, whom most consider the dean of Nova Scotia hiking. His *Hiking Trails of Nova Scotia* and *Hiking Trails of Cape Breton* are revised regularly and provide detailed descriptions of more than 70 trails. On the Internet there are a number of sites, the best of which is Trails Nova Scotia (www.trails.gov.ns.ca), which has up-to-date information on the Trans Canada Trail as well as descriptions of dozens of trails in all parts of the province. There are also a number of local and international companies that feature hiking tours of Nova Scotia. One reputable Nova Scotia company that has been in business for many years is Scott Walking Tours (www.scottwalking.com).

Beaches

Nova Scotia is a seaside adventure. Visitors come to be invigorated by the fresh salt breeze, to be soothed by the murmur of the waves and to savour that sand-between-the-toes feeling. You can't get a much closer saltwater experience than at one (or several) of the 400-odd accessible beaches that scallop the 7,400-kilometre coastline of this "almost-island" province.

Nova Scotia's beaches are as varied as its geography. There is a beach experience for every age and inclination.

Junior geologists and paleontologists will have a heyday at beaches along the shores of the Minas Basin, where gemstones, minerals and fossils are constantly liberated from the cliffs by the famous Fundy tides. Rockhounding on the shores at Blomidon Provincial Park and Scots Bay may yield agates and amethysts. In the Parrsboro area, where Jurassic Age dinosaur bones have been discovered, you might see a real dig in progress on the beach at Wasson Bluff.

At Five Islands, you can dig up some lunch. Clam digging is great fun for the whole family — watch for a squirt,

Inverness Beach

The mud flats at Five Islands

Keji Seaside Adjunct

then dig like fury. If you brought a camp stove along, you can steam or grill the clams on the spot. On the same shore at Economy, when the Fundy tide is out — and it goes waaay out — you can walk for what seems like miles on the ocean floor. The cool, red sand flats are great therapy for the foot-weary. The Fundy tides come in very swiftly, so make sure you can get safely back to terra firma ahead of them.

Small children can amuse themselves for hours observing starfish, jellyfish, sea urchins and periwinkles in sun-warmed tide pools at Crescent Beach on the South Shore, Bayswater on the Aspotogan Peninsula and Rushton Beach near Tatamagouche. Big kids, too, like to pick up shells, pretty pebbles and interesting bits of driftwood. Mavillette Beach on the Acadian Shore is a good place to beachcomb for lovely shells deposited on the shore by the tide.

Bird watching is another bona fide beach activity. The beach at Gulf Shore Provincial Park on Wallace Bay is a good starting point to observe the more than 160 bird species recorded in the area. Hirtles Beach and others have signs marking nesting grounds of the endangered piping plover. During nesting season, stick to boardwalks or marked paths and you may be rewarded with a glimpse of this rare little shorebird.

The ocean is capricious and can turn from calm to choppy in pretty short order. Some revel in the excitement of wild seas and whitecaps. When the surf's up, local and itinerant surfers head for Lawrencetown Beach, just outside Dartmouth (which, incidentally, has several supervised beaches on lakes within its boundaries). If you insist on being a traditionalist and must swim in the ocean, there are actually some very fine beaches ideally suited to that purpose, with change houses, lifeguards and, most importantly, warm water. Melmerby Beach, not far from

New Glasgow on the Sunrise Trail, is a great place to break the journey enroute to or from Cape Breton. It is apt to be relatively crowded on weekends, but the Northumberland Shore sports many other warm-water (and less peopled) beaches, including supervised Heather Beach and Blue Sea Beach near Malagash. On Cape Breton Island, the beaches along the Ceilidh Trail also benefit from the warm waters of the Gulf of St. Lawrence. There is a nice supervised beach at Inverness.

The seashore at at White Point Beach Resort

On the Eastern Shore the waters are bracing but the beaches are spectacular. Martinique has almost 5 kilometres of fine white sand, and you might be the only soul in sight. In mid-August, you can participate in the annual Clam Harbour Beach Sandcastle and Sculpture Contest — or simply stroll the beach and judge for yourself. This lovely fine-sand beach is supervised and has full amenities. Along the South Shore there is a whole string of gorgeous beaches with fine white sand — including Summerville, Rissers, Cherry Hill and Crescent Beach at Lockeport.

Some beaches are the reward at the end of a pleasant hike, like St. Catherines River Beach at Kejimkujik Seaside Adjunct, a naturalist's dream. While touring Nova Scotia, there is no better place to stretch the legs and clear the head than a beach — and there is sure to be one handy. There are dozens of little provincial and community parks with picnic tables and a beach. These are well indicated with signs on the highways. Many accommodations offer front-row beaching. The Quarterdeck at Summerville Beach and Salty Rose at Rose Bay are good examples. MacLeod Cottages at Petite Rivière and White Point Beach Resort have been favourites with families for generations.

If you fancy camping at the beach, there are many provincial beach parks with camping facilities. Thomas Raddall Park at East Side Port L'Hèbert, with secluded campsites and white sand beaches, and Caribou and Munroes Island Park near Pictou, with its red sand and warm water, are good choices. For RVers, there is a great spot right across the road from Louis Head Beach near Sable River on the Lighthouse Route. To find and book

Crystal Crescent Beach

beachside accommodations, check the *Nova Scotia Doers' and Dreamers' Guide* or call 800 565-0000.

There are beautiful beaches within a short drive of metro Halifax, including Conrad Beach and Rainbow Haven outside Dartmouth, Crystal Crescent Beach just beyond the fishing village of Sambro and Queensland Beach on St. Margarets Bay.

A few cautionary words — never underestimate the power of the ocean. Do not swim where yellow signs warn of dangerous currents. Strangers to the seaside may not be aware that on foggy or hazy days at the beach, the sun can still scorch the skin, so sunscreen and wide-brimmed hats are a good idea, as well as shirts for the children. For a complete list of supervised beaches, contact the Nova Scotia Lifeguard Service at 902 477-6155.

Take a dip, take a hike, take a break at Nova Scotia's beautiful beaches. And take home a healthy glow, a relaxed body, and a little salt water in your veins from Canada's ocean playground.

Conrad Island Beach

Sailing

Michael Ernst

As a sailing destination, Nova Scotia offers thousands of kilometres of beautiful, natural, accessible coastline, dotted with innumerable small harbours, sheltered coves and uninhabited islands. "The sailing here is better than Chesapeake Bay," commented one of our sailing companions. It was a sunny day, winds steady at 12 knots, beautiful scenery, clear waters with just a few boats on the horizon. A typical Nova Scotia summer day. Yes, the sailing is good!

Nova Scotia is renowned for its many and varied sea birds, and sailing is a great way to observe them, along with seals, porpoises and if you are lucky — whales. Our summers are usually dry and warm with steady southwesterly winds, and we can sail comfortably from June to early October. And after the day's sailing? There are fine onshore amenities including quality accommodations, restaurants and unique cultural experiences.

Nova Scotia's history has been written by the sea. It is a rich mixture of maritime commerce, sea battles, shipwrecks, privateers, buried treasure and ghost ships. Nova Scotians have been linked to the sea since the province was first settled. The Paleo Indians arrived almost 10,000 years ago, lived on the coast during the summers and travelled the coastal waters by birchbark canoe. The first European visitors may have been Vikings, a Scottish prince named Henry Sinclair in 1398 or John Cabot in 1497. Permanent European settlements were established in the early 17th century, and over the next hundred years the province changed ownership between the French and English four times. During the American Revolutionary

Chester Race Week on the waters of Mahone Bay

The Bluenose II in Lunenburg Harbour (top) and in full sail (above)

War and the War of 1812, many battles were fought along Nova Scotia's coast. It has provided a haven for naval ships, fishing fleets, traders, ship builders and privateers, but has also seen thousands of tragic shipwrecks.

Sailing is part of the Nova Scotian culture: it is in our bones and blood. Recreational sailing started in Nova Scotia in the early 1800s and yacht clubs are scattered throughout the province to provide locals and summer residents with high-quality competitions and onshore amenities. The number of visiting yachts increases annually and marina facilities are being developed to keep pace with the demand. The majority of visitors on cruises are from the United States and Canada, but Nova Scotia is also being recognized internationally as a sailing destination. These visitors are attracted by the quality of our sailing areas, the warm summers, fair winds and our rich and diverse culture.

Any visitor who wants to sail can enjoy our wonderful province in a variety of environments and sailing craft. Sailing operators offer a wide range of activities that will meet practically all tastes.

Visitors who have never sailed before but yearn to try can cruise with an experienced skipper, letting someone else do the work while they savour the salt air and the scenery,

Mahone Bay

or they may want to take an active role in sailing the boat.

Some providers will offer sailing lessons to those who are going to stay in Nova Scotia for a short vacation. Visitors who plan to spend the summer or several weeks at one location should check out the availability of lessons for adults or kids at the nearest yacht club. For more information on sailing clubs contact the Nova Scotia Yachting Association at www.nsya.ca.

Whatever option you choose,

Wooden Boat race in Lunenburg

being properly equipped is important. Hat, sunblock, sunglasses, summer clothing, sweater, rain jacket and nonslip shoes are essential items. Being properly prepared will make for a more pleasurable sailing experience.

Nova Scotia is approximately 34,000 square kilometres in area — about the same size as Belgium. With approximately 7,400 kilometres of coastline, the numerous sailing locations are widespread. This is a brief summary of what visitors can expect.

Halifax, with the second-largest natural harbour in the world, has very strong links to the province's maritime history. Learn about this history and such famous events as the sinking of the *Titanic*, the Halifax Explosion and sea battles of both world wars at the Maritime Museum of the Atlantic, located on the city's waterfront. There are three sailing operators near the museum that provide a great way to explore the harbour. The largest of the three is the tall ship *Silva,* a three masted schooner owned by Canadian Sailing Expeditions. Murphy's on the Water operates the 23-metre wooden ketch *Mar II.* A unique historical experience is offered by *Liana's Ransom*, a privateer schooner complete with a Letter of Marque and four black-powder cannon. Also based in Halifax is the *Caledonia* (Canadian Sailing Expeditions) offering cruises under sail throughout Atlantic Canada.

In Hubbards, at the head of St. Margarets Bay, you'll find the schooner, *Peer's Fancy.* A variety of charters are available for exploring this lovely area of Nova Scotia's coast.

Just an hour southwest of Halifax lies Mahone Bay, which shares its name with the scenic village located at its headwaters. Beautiful scenery, sheltered waters, fair winds and warm summer weather make the bay a sailor's paradise. This area was a haven for privateers during the many wars between France and England in the 17th and 18th centuries. Local legends tell of raids, buried treasure and ghost ships. There are almost 100 islands in Mahone Bay. Many are publicly owned or uninhabited and have small beaches — great stopping places for picnics and exploration. The most famous is Oak Island, where the longest on-going treasure hunt in the world has been taking place since 1795.

Three sailing schools affiliated with the Canadian Yachting Association operate in Mahone Bay, providing cruises and instruction. Sou'west Adventures and Discovery Sailing Charters, both based at the Oak Island Resort, offer CYA cruising qualification courses. Discovery Charters will provide a live-aboard cruising experience on

The sloop *Seneca* during Chester Race Week

its 11-metre yacht. Sail Mahone Bay offers single-day introductory and improver sessions, as well as the multi-day CYA courses.

Two annual boating events in the area are Chester Race Week, the largest keel-boat regatta in Eastern Canada, and the Mahone Bay Classic Boat Festival. The festival is a celebration of Nova Scotia's shipbuilding industry through music, water- and shore-based activities — great fun for sailors and landlubbers alike.

In nearby Lunenburg, there are sailing cruises of this historic harbour on the *Eastern Star*, a 14-metre ketch. These tours leave from the wharf near the Fisheries Museum of the Atlantic — a must see for anyone interested in boats and the sea. The *Bluenose II*, a replica of Canada's most famous sailing vessel, is based in Lunenburg but moves around the province during the summer and offers sailing cruises to the public. The schedule changes every year, but information can be found at www.bluenose2.ns.ca.

Sailing near Seabright

On Cape Breton Island, a three-hour drive from Halifax, the Bras d'Or Lakes claim to offer the finest

sailing in the world. This warm, inland saltwater sea is approximately 600 square kilometres in size with breathtaking scenery, sheltered waters and islands — and no fog. Visiting yachts can access the lakes through the historic St. Peters Canal. Those who want to explore the lake by sail can do so on the schooner *Amoeba*, which is based in Baddeck.

The freedom of the sea, the excitement of a lively boat responding to a brisk wind, the challenge of navigation and learning every time you sail — these are a few of the rewards of this great sport. Whether you are an old salt or a novice, Nova Scotia can offer great sailing opportunities. The serenity of our waters, the beauty of the environment, the encounters with wildlife, the sense of exploration and knowledgeable professional guides will provide memories that will make you want to return to Nova Scotia and sail again.

Sea Kayaking

Scott Cunningham

Sea kayaking has become increasingly popular in recent years, and Nova Scotia — with its countless harbours and headlands, inlets and islands — offers a world-class destination. Our meandering shoreline is extensive (more than 7,000 kilometres), access is easy (nowhere are you more than 55 kilometres from the sea) and the contrasts are exceptional. Within a short time you can travel between paddling venues as diverse as the rugged Atlantic coast and the sandy beaches of the Northumberland Strait, or between the highlands of Cape Breton and the tides of the Bay of Fundy. There is something for paddlers of every taste and skill level. You will find protected day trips for the beginner as well as challenging multi-day routes, and everything in between. And you can explore all this in relative solitude — with so much waterfront there is plenty of space to find a spot for yourself.

Kites and Kayaks Festival at Pictou Lodge

The Atlantic Coast

My favourite realm, and my home, is along the rugged Eastern Shore, where an isolated band of

islands stretches from Clam Harbour to Canso. This forgotten wilderness forms a compelling mix of natural and human history. Some of these outposts are just tiny specks, scarcely breathing air at high water, while others are huge forest-covered expanses that dominate the horizon and beckon to the inquisitive traveller. Explore abandoned lighthouses and shipwrecks, uncover those vanishing signs of our own transient history or camp on a deserted isle where your only companions are the seals and the sea birds. There are no bridges or ferries to this archipelago, and few fishing or pleasure craft — only a dramatic and pristine isolation far from the summer bustle. Tangier is an ideal place from which to start. This is where Coastal Adventures, the pioneer in sea kayaking in the province, is located and offers day trips, extended tours and courses.

Heading out on a foggy morning

At the other end of the province, near Yarmouth, the glacier-sculpted Tusket Islands are very different from the resistant bedrock outposts of the Eastern Shore. Fishermen still use them as a base during lobster season, much as their ancestors did for centuries. At other times they are deserted (except for frequent visits by meandering fog banks). Elsewhere along the South Shore there are dozens of idyllic

Paddling amongst the sailboats, Mahone Bay

places to put in and explore, including the Kejimkujik Seaside Adjunct, the LaHave Islands, Blue Rocks, Mahone Bay and Prospect. There are a number of operators to help you out, such as Rossignol Surf Shop, Mahone Bay Adventures, East Coast Outfitters and

Sea Sun). Even Halifax, with its eclectic waterfront and harbour islands, merits a visit by kayak.

Cape Breton Island
On Cape Breton Island the paddling possibilities are also numerous, both along its rugged east coast where Rising Tide Expeditions operates, and on the more protected Bras d'Or Lakes, where you'll find Kayak Cape Breton. However, the gem is certainly the Highlands. This majestic plateau occupies the northwestern tip of the island, where it rises abruptly from the Gulf of St. Lawrence, and it is particularly imposing when viewed from the perspective of a sea kayak. Sea spires, caves and a colourful geology decorate the perimeter, while the Cabot Trail winds out of sight and sound far above. Rich deciduous valleys alternate with barren vertical cliffs washed by waterfalls. Here you will certainly spot bald eagles and seals. If you are lucky you will also paddle with the whales as I have done many a time. By mid-summer the water can warm up considerably (to 20°C), but this is an open coast and experience is advised. Outfitters offering trips along the Highlands include Cape Breton Sea Coast Adventures, Coastal Adventures, Eagle North Canoe & Kayak and North River Kayak Tours.

Fundy
The Bay of Fundy is perhaps our most distinctive region. The highest tides ever recorded on earth wash the these shores, sculpting cliffs and inundating massive salt marshes and mud banks with surprising speed. Experience is essential, but novices can take advantage of a knowledgeable outfitter (Coastal Adventures and Hinterland Adventures run tours here). Cape Chignecto, which juts into the bay separating the Minas Basin from Chignecto Bay, is the jewel of Fundy. This is the boundary where Africa was thrust up against North America eons ago, and where the story of a cataclysmic upheaval can be read in rock strata of the exposed escarpment. Even for those with little knowledge of geology, the striking

Ingonish Harbour

melange of colours, textures and forms is fascinating. The abrupt cliffs, numerous pinnacles and sea caves, combine with tides exceeding 12 metres to create a spectacular land and seascape. In the remote river valleys, remnants of a lost era play hide-and-seek among the shifting gravel. This is where some of our largest wooden vessels were constructed during the "Age of Sail." Elsewhere in the bay, along the Minas shore, the layered sandstones and dark basalt of the Five Islands and Economy Mountain offer another intriguing destination.

The Northumberland Strait Shore

If you arrive early in the season, when the Atlantic coast may be draped in fog, or if the Highlands and the Fundy are too exposed for your taste, you should try the province's North Shore. Along our Northumberland Strait you will be treated to the warmest salt water north of the Carolinas (or so the tourist propaganda runs) and, after numbing your toes in the Atlantic, this can be a real pleasure. Fog has been banned and the miles of sandy shores and saltmarsh estuaries offer protected paddling for the entire family. Kayakers are not the only ones who enjoy soaking up a few summer rays here, and this shore has become a mecca for the vacation crowd. However, secluded corners can still be found. Outfitters along this coast include Coastal Spirit Expeditions.

There are many other exciting areas of our coastline to entice you and your sea kayak. A comprehensive guide, *Sea Kayaking in Nova Scotia*, is available at most bookstores and will help with detailed descriptions of more than 40 routes. Bring your own boat and paddle on your own, or accompany a local outfitter (other than those mentioned, the *Nova Scotia Doers' and Dreamers' Guide* lists more than 20) who can introduce you to the biology, geology and human history of this fascinating environment where the land meets the sea. Happy paddling!

Seakayaking at sunset

Surfing

Lesley Choyce

Surfing at Martinique Beach

Surfing in Nova Scotia has exploded in recent years. When I first moved to this province in 1978, there were about twenty people who surfed on a regular basis. Now there are more than a hundred hard-core surfers and more than a thousand weekend summer surfers. And this despite the fact that Nova Scotia has some of the most challenging surf conditions found anywhere in the world.

The most challenging aspects are the inconsistency of the waves — from dead flat to huge storm waves — and the fact that the water is cold. In the winter the sea temperature drops to 0° Celsius, and in the summer it can hover around 8 or 9° for days or weeks at a time. A recent map put out by the province displays a somewhat misleading picture of a young man in board shorts and no wetsuit venturing out into the waves of the Atlantic. There are days when you can surf without a wetsuit but they are exceedingly rare. Yet when the waves are good, they are really good and cold water can't stop diehard surfers.

Calm days are okay for beginners and amateurs but as the waves build, novices should be very wary — the seas here can be treacherous. If you are new to surfing, you are advised to rent quality wetsuit gear and a beginner board, and you should definitely take lessons from one of the surf shops and surf schools that exist here. In Halifax, there is Da Kane Surf and at Lawrencetown Beach, Kannon Beach Surf Shop in the MacDonald House, where you can rent gear. A little farther along Route 207 is Happy Dude's Surf Emporium and, in the summer, the Dude has a surf shop

open near Martinique Beach as well. In neighbouring Three Fathom Harbour, contact One Life Surf School for instruction from their excellent women surf instructors. On the South Shore is Rossignol Surf Shop in Port Joli, where you can find both boards and instruction. Be sure to rent a long board — 8 foot (2.5 metre) or over for starting out.

Riding a wave at Lawrencetown Beach

When learning to surf, pick some easy breaking waves along sandy stretches of beaches like those at Lawrencetown, Martinique or Hirtles Beach. It is also important to have respect for other surfers in the water. More advanced surfers will be checking out the point breaks — waves that wrap around the point of headlands, and there are many roadside and remote point breaks on the Atlantic-facing shores of Nova Scotia.

Lawrencetown is probably the most popular (and most crowded) surf spot in the summer, but for the skilled and adventurous, there are endless possibilities for finding isolated and excellent waves, both beach break and point break. Along the beaches, watch out for rip currents that can pull you out to sea, and be especially sure to avoid Stoney Beach at Lawrencetown, where a river current runs out to sea that has taken the lives of swimmers who get pulled from the shallows. Always be sure to talk to local surfers if possible to find out about local dangers. The one thing you don't have to worry about though, is sharks. I've never heard of a shark attacking a surfer or swimmer in Nova Scotia.

If you are trying to make the full surf surfari, you might want to log some time at White Point on the South Shore, then on to Lawrencetown and Martinique and then Point Michaud, a stunning crescent of a beach on Isle Madame in Cape Breton.

Just keep in mind that conditions change — sometimes quite quickly — with a change of wind direction or the approach of a storm. Also, many surfers travel to Nova Scotia looking for waves, only to encounter a flat spell lasting for several weeks at a time. Be sure to have a backup plan for other forms of outdoor adventure. But it could go the other way and you could luck onto some clean, clear North Atlantic tubes that you'll remember for the rest of your life.

Birding

Joan Waldron

Nova Scotia has endless beaches, tucked-away fishing villages, hundreds of years of culture and a special natural beauty. With its rich marshlands, forests and lakes at every turn it has perfect habitats for all kinds of birds. Whether the birds visit your backyard feeder, scurry around you on the beach or add to the sounds of nature on a stroll through the woods, you may wonder what kind they are, and whether they are local or just visiting. Some 305 birds have been listed in the province, about 50 of them noted as regular strays or seldom seen. The avid birder may seek these rarities. For example, the rare Bicknell's thrush spends its summers in the Cape Breton Highlands; and Canada's only breeding American oystercatchers have spent the past few years with their families on Cape Light, just off the fabulous birding area on Cape Sable Island. Visiting birders may want to see birds that Nova Scotians take for granted, such as the magnificent osprey, the provincial bird, which is commonly seen around beaches and harbours. Seabirds abound off Nova Scotia's endless shoreline. Puffins breed off Cape Breton Island, and on sea-bound trips one can spot shearwaters, phalaropes and storm petrels and, with luck, a jaeger or skua as well. It's a treat to see these birds feeding alongside huge whales.

As in most places, Nova Scotia's birds have a time and a place. A winter birding trip can produce visiting seabirds such as the tiny dovekie, murres, and glaucous and Iceland gulls. And if you want to spend a quick weekend in winter ogling eagles, scores of bald eagles can be seen during the

Shorebirds at Evangeline beach

Osprey

Sheffield Mills Eagle Watch in the Annapolis Valley at the end of January (www.eaglens.ca).

Spring and early summer birding offers the sounds of warblers. Their sounds are so varied you often wonder what bird you are hearing. The ovenbird, for example, yells "teacher-teacher." Twenty-two species of warblers breed in Nova Scotia, which is filled with woodland roads and parks, both national and provincial. The national parks have birding lists and may offer field trips. The *Atlas of Breeding Birds of the Maritimes*, by Anthony J. Erskine, will help pinpoint where particular birds can be found. Also, in late springtime, a careful walk on a quiet beach might give you a glimpse of the breeding endangered piping plover that Nova Scotians are trying so hard to protect. Late July features more than 20 species of shorebird, which stop in Nova Scotia to fatten up on the way south from their northern breeding grounds. Fall is delightful, with scores of bird species coming and going, and there's always the chance that one of Nova Scotia's edge-of-the-continent weather surprises can bring a rarity or two or three.

Birders of all feathers flock to Shelburne County in March for the Birding and Nature Festival. This annual event brings birding and nature enthusiasts together for excursions, presentations, demonstrations, displays and jolly good fun (discovershelburnecounty.com/birdfestival.html). The Tern Festival in West Pubnico in June is another good opportunity to commune with birds and birders.

In addition to the actual excitement and anticipation of birdwatching, most birders enjoy the homework they must

Eagles at Sheffield Mills in the Annapolis Valley

do before a trip. Information about birding in all parts of Nova Scotia is available online, but if a computer is not yet part of your life, write a letter requesting information to the Nova Scotia Bird Society, c/o Nova Scotia Museum, 1747 Summer Street, Halifax, Nova Scotia, B3H 3A6. The Society's website, www.nsbs.chebucto.org, offers a

Birders on the beach

range of information, including contacts throughout the province and recommended reading. If you are in Nova Scotia for a Bird Society meeting, join some local birders. Nova Scotians are very friendly, particularly the binocular-wearing species. The dates and meeting topics are included online, as are upcoming field trips, to which visitors are most welcome. Try to let the leader know you are joining the group.

An important part of the society's website includes links to other birding websites. Birders can browse various sites and plan their birding locations. The Cape Sable Island Important Bird Area website includes wonderful photos of the shorebirds you can expect to see at this location. Ted D'Eon's homepage has great photos and shows his achievements in helping to preserve the endangered roseate tern. *The Classic Birds of Nova Scotia*, by Robie W. Tufts (in print again), is also linked to the site.

A visit through cyberspace will offer thousands of websites linked to birding in Nova Scotia. The Birding the Americas website (www.birdingtheamericas.com), maintained by Blake Maybank, includes trip reports from Nova Scotia that will give visiting birders a sense of what they can expect to see. Blake also maintains the Nova Scotia rare bird alert site at group.yahoo.com/group/NS-RBA.

Many bird reference books and field guides are available. A handy reference guide to keep in your pocket or on the kitchen counter is *The New Formac Pocketguide to Nova Scotia Birds*. In Mahone Bay, For the Birds Nature Shop carries all the best birding supplies, including reference books, field guides, binoculars and scopes.

A chestnut-sided warbler

Lighthouses

Peggys Cove

Lighthouses are part of the history, the lore and the mystique of a province whose life, growth and prosperity have been shaped by the sea. The first lighthouse in Canada, a circular stone tower built by the French between 1731 and 1734 at Louisbourg, was gutted by fire in 1736 and rebuilt, only to be laid to ruin by the British in 1758. It was replaced in the 1840s. The present octagonal tower, built in 1922–1923, is now part of the Fortress of Louisbourg National Historic Site.

Originally lit by whale and seal oil, then by kerosene and finally by electricity, several hundred lighthouses have guided ships past the dangers off Nova Scotia's complex and perilous seacoast. Many lights were isolated, and the keepers and their families were often the only inhabitants on desolate islands. Totally automated today, many of the remaining 150 lighthouses and range lights (pairs of towers aligned to direct vessels into port) are being replaced with modern towers of fibreglass or metal. Others have been replaced by buoys, self-guiding harbour sector lights or skeleton towers, as modern vessels rely increasingly on satellite navigational systems. The Sambro Light is the oldest operational lighthouse in North America.

About 80 lights are accessible (with varying degrees of difficulty) on the Nova Scotia mainland, and 12 of them are open to visitors. More than a dozen others invite you to picnic in their shade. Many other lighthouses can be viewed as you tour the coast.

A few lights have been incorporated into public or historic parks by local community groups and are open seasonally. One of the most photographed lighthouses in North America is the classical tapering tower at Peggys Cove. First erected in 1868 at the entrance to St. Margarets Bay, the original light was replaced with the present octagonal tower in 1915.

At Burntcoat Head on the Bay of Fundy, a lovely little park incorporates a replica of the keeper's house surmounted by a lantern. At Port Bickerton on Marine Drive along the rugged Eastern Shore, the Nova Scotia Lighthouse Interpretive Centre houses photographs and memorabilia in a restored 1930s keeper's home with roof-mounted light. Another roof-mounted light at Gilbert's Cove near Digby has also been restored by a local group.

Kidston Island Lighthouse, Baddeck

One of the most common designs for lighthouses along our shores is the wooden tapered square or pyramid style, commonly referred to as a "pepper shaker." The non-operational restored light at Walton Harbour, situated in a quiet little park with commanding views of the Bay of Fundy, is open to the public. A similar light graces the waterfront in Annapolis Royal. The small Five Islands lighthouse, moved several times due to constant shoreline erosion, can be seen in a local campground. Another tapered-design light has been relocated to the Historical Acadian Village in West Pubnico. The little light tower overlooking the Bay of Fundy at Spencers Island is now a heritage property. Famous as the homeport of the ghost ship *Mary Celeste*, this tiny village is nestled along a gravel beach. At Margaretsville, a viewing platform surrounds the base of its lighthouse. The beauty of Neils Harbour, with its colourful fishing boats and the wharf below its lighthouse, is the subject of many a photograph.

The unique "apple core" tower at Cape Forchu, near Yarmouth, is perhaps out-photographed only by the rock-mounted light at Peggys Cove. Although the Forchu light isn't open to the public, the keeper's house displays artifacts of a bygone era. A replica of the Seal Island light

Lighthouse at Cape D'Or

is open seasonally in Barrington, while the lovely setting of the uniquely designed lighthouse at Fort Point in Liverpool makes it a popular attraction. The Cape d'Or light near Advocate Harbour isn't unusual, but its location is dramatic, hugging the edge of a steep cliff. The tower at Cape George, north of Antigonish, is reminiscent of the one at Peggys Cove and offers a sweeping view of the Canso Strait.

Detailed information about lighthouses in Nova Scotia is available on the website of the Nova Scotia Lighthouse Preservation Society at www.nslps.com.

Gardens

Jodi DeLong

Annapolis Royal Historic Gardens

A bridge at the Harriet Irving Botanical Gardens

From the rose borders along Yarmouth's waterfront to the more formal plantings of Halifax's Public Gardens, most towns and villages in Nova Scotia have summer plantings to welcome visitors and cheer the eyes. There are also a number of destination gardens throughout the province, some open year-round, others more seasonal in nature.

Our province has had a long and varied history with formal gardening since the arrival of French settlers in the early part of the seventeenth century. The finest public garden space in the province, the Annapolis Royal Historic Gardens offers a sense of that history. Since 1981 the Gardens have welcomed visitors from all over the world. There's a world of difference between the formal layout of the 18th-century Governor's Garden and the joyous abandon of the perennial borders. Visitors flock to the gardens throughout the year, but especially in late May to enjoy the flowering of the rhododendron and azalea collection, mostly bred in Nova Scotia. Another ideal time to visit is between late June and early July, when the immense Rose Collection begins its spectacular bloom period. An Acadian cottage, complete with thatched roof, hosts a generous-sized potager or kitchen garden, featuring numerous edible and medicinal plants that would have been used by the Acadian settlers whose culture remains a rich part of Nova Scotia's heritage.

The Harriet Irving Botanical Gardens at Acadia University in Wolfville focus primarily on the native plants and ecosystems of Nova Scotia and showcase nine different types of habitats and the plants they host, from

deciduous woodlands and coastal headlands to sand barrens and bogs. There's a medicinal and food garden as well as an experimental planting, where researchers test out growing conditions and challenges, as well as a conservatory. The Gardens are open year-round at no charge.

Harriet Irving Botanical Gardens at Acadia University

The historic Blomidon Inn offers three acres of garden surrounding that property — visitors are welcome year-round. In nearby Grand-Pré, history buffs can enjoy the traditional Acadian potager and plantings at Grand-Pré National Historic Site and then meander the herb and perennial plantings at Tangled Garden, a local business featuring organic herbal jellies, vinegars and other products.

Truro holds another jewel in the province's gardening crown with two remarkable gardens at the Nova Scotia Agricultural College. The Alumni Gardens feature an extensive perennial border, many unique trees and shrubs, a magnificent pergola and gazebo and a wonderful herb and medicinal garden featuring a woven willow fence. The must-see attraction is the recently developed Rock Garden, created with hundreds of tons of native rock. There's a dry creek bed, a niche garden featuring troughs of succulents and alpines and wonderful displays of plants designed for growing in drier conditions.

Lupin (below) The Tangled Garden, Wolfville (bottom)

History meets contemporary times at the Halifax Public Gardens, designed and built in 1867 and witness to many epic moments since that time. The Gardens remain a unique tribute to the heyday of Victorian gardening. With tropical plantings, carpet bedding and many heirloom or heritage species of roses and other plants arranged around statuary, fountains, ponds and a bandstand the Gardens are a tranquil sanctuary in the heart of a bustling city.

In Cape Breton the Alexander Graham Bell National Historic Site features wonderful gardens of shrubs and flowering plants. The Fortress of Louisbourg, another National Historic Site in Cape Breton, also features numerous gardens, geometrically laid out and primarily focusing on the useful species that residents would have grown.

Nova Scotians are great gardeners, and there are "open gardens" at private homes, where anyone may visit. The Nova Scotia Association of Garden Clubs (www.nsagc.com) provides information on garden-related events happening throughout the year, from workshops to garden tours to flower shows.

Nova Scotia
by Region

Halifax Metro

Halifax has emerged as one of Canada's most attractive cities to visit. It's a relatively small city in an appealing setting, offering a variety of attractions. Halifax is at its best in summer and fall — and fall lasts longer here than in the rest of Canada, with many beautiful days in October and even into November.

Halifax Harbour

The waterfront area has become the most popular place to spend time in the summer. It's a long, vibrant boardwalk along the harbour, with many attractive cafés, bars and restaurants, street entertainment, the Maritime Museum of the Atlantic, Historic Properties and culminating at its southern end with Pier 21 National Historic Site. The city's best bargain, and one kids love, is the ferry trip across the harbour to Dartmouth. All this, together with the added thrill of the occasional container ship, navy vessel or cruise ship passing by, appeals to residents and visitors alike. Almost every visitor makes the trip up to the Citadel, a historical attraction with wonderful views of the harbour. The Spring Garden Road area rivals the waterfront for friendly, low-key street life and its variety of shops, bars and restaurants.

Entrance to the harbour boardwalk

Within 40 minutes' drive of downtown there are beautiful ocean beaches at Crystal Crescent and Lawrencetown, fine for warm summer afternoons when small children (and hardy adults) don't mind the relatively

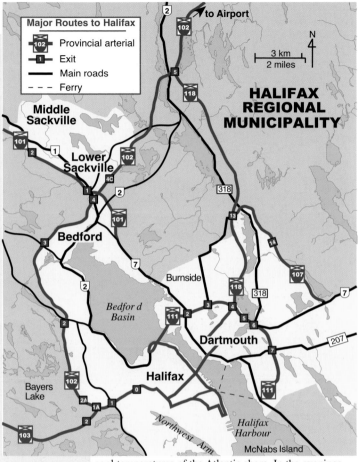

Major Routes to Halifax

- **102** Provincial arterial
- **1** Exit
- Main roads
- - - - Ferry

HALIFAX REGIONAL MUNICIPALITY

Middle Sackville

Lower Sackville

Bedford

Burnside

Bedford Basin

Dartmouth

Halifax

Bayers Lake

Northwest Arm

Halifax Harbour

McNabs Island

to Airport

3 km
2 miles

cool temperatures of the Atlantic shore. In the evenings, Halifax offers a surprisingly wide range of entertainment options, and that is one of the reasons why most visitors to Nova Scotia make a point of including the city on their itinerary.

There are many good hotels in the downtown core. Visitors may be well advised to book in advance, especially if there is a major event (like a Rolling Stones concert) scheduled. While rooms may be at a premium online, a call directly to the hotel will most likely yield accommodation in the downtown. On the outskirts of the city there are

Angus L. Macdonald Bridge

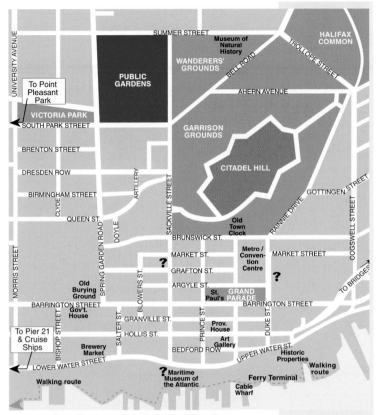

many hotels and older motels that some travellers may prefer. Halifax also has some excellent inns and B&Bs.

Halifax sits atop a great slab of slate that rises from the harbour. There is precious little topsoil. It was the harbour that attracted the Mi'kmaq for centuries and the British in 1749. The harbour extends inland about 16 kilometres from its seaward approaches, spanned by two bridges connecting Halifax and Dartmouth, through the Narrows and into Bedford Basin. Except for an occasional freakish episode, it remains ice-free — a point long stressed by those interested in steering winter ship traffic the way of Halifax.

Recreational sailors happily coexist with shipping in the harbour. During the summer months, Bedford Basin is flecked with hundreds of colourful sailboats. The Northwest Arm, on the southwest side of the Halifax peninsula, is also a yachting haven.

Summers in Halifax tend to be mild, with sunny days made fresh by sea breezes. Winters are cool and snowy. Although there are days in January that are cold enough to draw wisps of sea smoke off the harbour, Haligonians are accustomed to winter temperatures around the freezing point. Nice spring days are cherished because they are few. But autumn — Nova Scotia's finest season — flatters Halifax. Then the days are crisp and bright, and the city's

View from York Redoubt

tree-lined streets blush with colour.

Halifax was established in 1749 to counter the military threat posed by the French Fortress of Louisbourg. During the last century, the city's magnificent harbour served as a marshalling area for North Atlantic convoys during two world wars. Halifax's economic fortunes have historically flowed during conflict and ebbed with peace.

Today, the Citadel in the heart of the city and the historic fortifications at Point Pleasant Park and York Redoubt are celebrated aspects of Halifax's military landscape, but there is also a contemporary military presence to go along with those reminders of the past. Warships regularly ply the harbour and helicopters fly overhead. A substantial number of military personnel are stationed here and sailors from the NATO fleet are regular visitors.

A view from Citadel Hill

Despite the steady thrum of naval activity, Halifax is no longer primarily a military town. In post-war Halifax, rapid growth in the research, technology and public service sectors has turned

the old garrison town into a vital commercial and government centre. This is Atlantic Canada's largest city. The provincial legislature is here, and a substantial federal bureaucracy works out of the city. There is a thriving alternative scene, and the city's five universities, including Nova Scotia College of Art and Design University (NSCAD) provide much of the impetus for it.

Halifax serves up some startling contrasts. The same city that annually hosts the popular Royal Nova Scotia International Tattoo, with its regimental bands and drill teams, also stages the Halifax Fringe Festival — alternative theatre that scandalizes the city's conservative element. The military is here, but so is Vajradhatu, the headquarters for an international network of Buddhist meditation centres. Burgers and draught beer or sushi and chai tea — the downtown pubs and bistros cater to a city with multiple personalities.

A walk along Hollis Street, one of the city's oldest, tells some of the story. Government departments and law offices operate cheek by jowl in high-rises that stand along the street's northern end.

You can explore the downtown area by foot, as the heart of the city extends for just a few — but very hilly — blocks.

The Grand Parade, framed by Argyle and Barrington Streets, sits between Citadel Hill and the waterfront. Special activities, like the Remembrance Day service and the New Year's Eve party, take place here, and Halifax City Hall is situated on the north side. On mild nights, people collect at the Grand Parade as they go from bar to bar, and summer days see business people patronizing hot dog vendors in the square.

Completed in 1750, St. Paul's Anglican Church still occupies the south side of the Parade. It was patterned on James Gibbs' design for St. Peter's on Vere Street in London. Gibbs apprenticed with Christopher Wren, and his work includes the beautiful St. Martin-in-the-Fields on Trafalgar Square. St. Paul's is the oldest Protestant church in Canada. Local legend has it that the profile of the vicar

1st Battalion Middlesex Regiment at Halifax Citadel

The Art Gallery of
Nova Scotia

who died in the Explosion of 1917 can still be seen in one
of the upper windows on the Argyle Street side of the
church. Church tours are available in summer. St. Paul's
Cemetery (the Old Burying Ground) on Barrington Street
was the town's original cemetery. Information on the
headstones is available at the church.

Nearby, on Hollis Street, is Province House, the seat of
provincial government. Opened in 1819, it is a fine
example of the Palladian style. During a visit to Halifax in
1842, Charles Dickens described it as "a gem of Georgian
architecture." The building really is beautiful —
remarkably so, given that as far as anyone can tell the plans
were drawn up by John Merrick, a local contractor. Tour
guides are on hand to take you through the building's
splendid interior. Highlights include the Red Chamber, with
its tall windows and ornate plasterwork, where you can see
the oak table from the Beaufort, the ship that brought
Edward Cornwallis to Halifax in June of 1749. The
Legislative Library, complete with hanging staircases and a
three-sided balcony, is also magnificent.

The city's turn-of-the-century commercial success is
reflected in the Barrington and Granville streetscapes.
Many of these buildings were of steel beam construction, a
new technology that emerged in the wake of the Chicago
Fire of 1871. The walls of these structures were not load
bearing, so they were often built high with lots of windows
and decorative arches. Contemporaries questioned their
extravagance, but millionaires like George Wright could
afford the best. The Wright Building still stands at 1672–74
Barrington Street. (Wright was one of 33 millionaires to go
down with the *Titanic* in 1912.)

This area is also the old stomping ground of Anna
Leonowens, immortalized in the Rodgers and Hammerstein
musical *The King and I*, and several movies, including the
film *Anna and the King* starring Jodie Foster. In 1876
Leonowens moved here with her daughter and son-in-law.
Soon after, she was actively involved in establishing
libraries, reading clubs and a Shakespeare Club. Today,
NSCAD University represents the culmination of
Leonowens's interest in the local artistic community.

Halifax jewellers and graphic designers — and there are many — share in her legacy.

The Art Gallery of Nova Scotia, a modern facility located in a heritage building on Hollis Street, houses a collection of historic and contemporary art, and an acclaimed folk art collection. Paintings by Nova Scotian artists can be purchased at the Art Sales and Rental Gallery.

Unique Nova Scotian wares can also be found in Barrington Place and the shops at Granville Mall, adjacent to the Delta Barrington Hotel.

Continue south on Hollis to the Brewery — Alexander Keith's Nova Scotia Brewery, that is — the oldest working brewery in North America. (Keith's beer, now brewed by Labatt, is still sold in Nova Scotia's liquor stores). Year-round brewery tours feature stories and songs and, of course, beer sampling. The brewery is frequently held up as an example of what can be achieved by preservation-minded developers. Its arches and gothic windows provide a comfortable setting for one of Halifax's better restaurants, Da Maurizio's.

Farther south, walk up Bishop Street to Barrington. Here is Government House, another example of a beautiful Georgian building in the Palladian style. When John Wentworth became Lieutenant-Governor of Nova Scotia in 1792, he sought to upgrade his accommodation. A member of a well-connected family, who knew royalty on the most intimate terms, he was probably justified in doing so. The cornerstone of Government House, the Wentworths' new residence, was laid in 1800. It has served as the Lieutenant-

Alexander Keith's Brewery (above) and St. Mary's Cathedral Basilica, Spring Garden Road (below)

Shopping on Spring Garden Road (above and below)

Governor's residence ever since. Although it is normally not open to the public, the Lieutenant-Governor continues a long-standing tradition of hosting a New Year's Day levee, when everyone is invited inside for a look (and a glass of sherry).

Backtracking on Barrington, you come to Spring Garden Road. There are a number of fine boutiques and craft shops in the Spring Garden Road area. The Halifax Folklore Centre provides the city's best introduction to the traditional music of Nova Scotia. Jennifer's of Nova Scotia sells everything from small souvenirs to the prized works of some of Nova Scotia's best artisans. Fine foods and wines are available at Pete's Frootique, Port of Wines and the Italian Gourmet on Doyle Street. There are also a number of good apparel, book and coffee shops along the city's most fashionable street. Nearby, on the other side of the Public Gardens, the Museum of Natural History features the natural wonders of Nova Scotia's land and sea — whales, fossils, dinosaurs and birds, along with a number of other permanent and temporary exhibits.

Jennifer's of Nova Scotia

The Halifax Citadel, a national historic site operated by Parks Canada, is Nova Scotia's most visited attraction.

Built between 1828 and 1856, the fortification is the fourth to occupy the hilltop site, with its commanding view of Halifax Harbour. The present Citadel was built through the semi-divine intervention of the "Iron Duke," Arthur Wellesley. The Duke of Wellington, a strong proponent of colonial defenses at a time when opinion was sharply divided, used his prime ministerial authority to push approval for the project through the British Parliament. In his view, a strong fortification was needed to defend against the American threat, which remained palpable in the wake of the War of 1812.

The fort was designed to prevent a land-based attack on the naval dockyard. It was left to the harbour defenses to repel an attack from the sea. Whether the Citadel was a necessary discouragement is open to debate — no attack ever came. The Citadel's smoothbore cannons were never fired in anger.

During the summer months, Citadel staff re-enact the fort's military routines as they were carried out during the years 1869–71. At that time, the Citadel was manned by soldiers from the 78th Highlanders and the Royal Artillery, along with sailors of the Naval Brigade. Today, students take on these roles, drilling according to instructions laid out in the 1860s manuals, hoisting the signal flags and standing watch at the sentry posts. The firing of the noon gun is heard throughout downtown Halifax year-round. The signal flags flying above the ramparts once told civilians what ships were in the harbour and where they were docked. They were also used to send messages to the other harbour fortifications. At one time, it was thought that a series of signalling stations could be used to reach as far as Quebec!

Tour guides help explain the Citadel's rituals and exhibits in French or English, adding anecdotes about the fort's colourful past. "The Tides of History," a 40-minute audiovisual presentation, takes visitors on a dramatic tour through Halifax's military history. Visitors to Halifax are encouraged to find time for the Citadel, where they will

The entrance to the Citadel

Re-enactors parade down Sackville Street

The Old Town
Clock at sunset

discover why it held pride of place for much of the city's long life as a garrison town. And the view of downtown Halifax and the harbour is often reward enough for making the steep climb up Citadel Hill. The Old Town Clock has marked the time at the base of Citadel Hill since 1803. Unperturbed by such cataclysmic events as the Halifax Explosion in 1917, the clock has undergone restoration to ensure that it will remain, in the words of Joseph Howe, "a good example to all the idle chaps in town." From the Citadel, looking east and north, you see Halifax's North End and the area demolished in the explosion. Nearby, there are some fascinating historical buildings.

The Little Dutch (Deutsche) Church was originally built to accommodate German settlers who were brought to Halifax not long after its founding. Across the street is the beautiful St. George's Round Church, largely reconstructed after a disastrous fire several years ago. It is one of Prince Edward's many round-shaped buildings in the city. Several handsome 19th-century townhouses still stand along Brunswick Street. Farther from the Citadel in the North

Walking along the
boardwalk

End is the Hydrostone area, known to Canadian town planners as the first example of 20th-century urban renewal (and a much better precedent than what came later). By the MacKay Bridge is Seaview Park, site of Africville, which was razed by Halifax City Hall in the 1960s in a relocation scheme meant to better living conditions for the Black community. The residents were opposed to the plan, a vital community was destroyed and Africville is mourned to this day.

While not exactly Vegas, the casino overlooking Halifax Harbour offers a taste of all the usual fare — gaming, slots, entertainment and dining. Moving south along the

The Cable Wharf

waterfront are the Historic Properties, a 1970s restoration project that revitalized the downtown core. The Privateers' Warehouse, one of 10 buildings from the Georgian and early Victorian periods, is the most storied. Early in the 19th century Enos Collins, a wealthy Halifax merchant, used the building to warehouse booty that he seized during legalized privateering raids off the New England coast. Today, these buildings house a variety of shops and services. Handsmith sells lovely crafts made by artisans from across Canada. The Lower Deck offers lively Celtic entertainment. The food court offers casual dining, including a microbrewery, pizza and seafood, with a view of the harbour.

More shops and restaurants can be found on the boardwalk along the harbour's edge to Cable Wharf, named for the transatlantic cable ships that once docked here. NovaScotian Crystal, home of Canada's only mouth-blown, hand-cut crystal, has a window that gives visitors a peek at the glass blowers at work.

Boats operating from Cable Wharf are available for private charter or cruises featuring fishing, sightseeing and whalewatching. *The Harbour Queen I* and the *Haligonian III* offer historical commentaries during their harbour cruises. *Theodore Too*, a full-sized replica tugboat from the

Theodore Too tugboat

popular TV series gives Big Harbour tours designed for children. A private ferry will take you to McNabs Island, where grassy trails lead to secluded coves, overgrown forts and rocky beaches.

Farther along the boardwalk from Cable Wharf is the Maritime Museum of the Atlantic. The museum houses more than 20,000 maritime artifacts and features an exhibit that gives a complete account of the Halifax

Model of RMS *Titanic*, Maritime Museum of the Atlantic

Harbour Explosion of 1917. There are also exhibits on shipwrecks and lifesaving, the *Titanic*, the Navy, steamships and sailing ships. The William Robertson & Son ship chandlery has been restored, and there are lots of boats — about 70 in all.

Since the blockbuster movie Titanic, the museum has mounted a permanent display of its fine collection of artifacts from the doomed ship. Halifax's connection to the *Titanic* disaster came about because the city was the nearest large port to the site of the sinking. It was from Halifax that efforts were organized to search for the wreckage and to recover the bodies of the victims. Funerals were organized, and many of the dead lie in graves in Halifax. Crew members on the ships sent out to the wreck site collected memorabilia (a deck chair, for example), and many of these items gradually found their way into the museum's collection.

Items in the exhibit also reflect the work of scientists from the Bedford Institute of Oceanography, who were more recently involved in expeditions to the wreck site, and who conduct research on the deep ocean environment.

Though modest in size, the *Titanic* exhibit is informative and appealing to visitors of all ages. It has become the museum's leading attraction and is well worth a visit. Note that there is a tourist information centre at Sackville Landing behind the museum. Farther south is Bishop's Landing, a complex of upscale restaurants, boutiques, residences and a spa.

Continue south on the boardwalk to Gateway Park, a fine spot from which to watch the comings and goings on the harbour. Beyond the boardwalk is an up-and-coming art and culture district with studios, galleries and the Nova

Halifax Ferry with cruise ship at Pier 21 in the background

Scotia Centre for Craft and Design on Marginal Road, where the work of many of the province's best craftspeople and designers is displayed. Nearby is the recently opened NSCAD Port Campus.

Pier 21 on Marginal Road, now a National Historic Site, was the last immigration shed in Canada; a million immigrants and refugees passed through here to their new country. Multimedia presentations, live performances and genealogical records tell their stories.

One of the easiest and least expensive ways for visitors to get out on the water is to take a trip on the Halifax Harbour ferry. In Dartmouth, Ferry Terminal Park affords outstanding views of the Halifax waterfront. The World Peace Pavilion on the Dartmouth waterfront displays historical rocks and bricks from countries around the world, including pieces of the Berlin Wall and the Great Wall of China.

Halifax waterfront, near the Maritime Museum

Restaurants near the boardwalk

The beginning of the Shubenacadie Canal is nearby. Following the old Mi'kmaq canoe route cross-country from the Bay of Fundy, the canal took more than 30 years to build. Shortly after it was completed in 1861, the new Intercolonial Railway made it obsolete, but the canal workings remain a source of fascination. More of the canal, including locks 2 and 3, can be seen at Shubie Canal Park, off Waverley Road.

Up by the MacKay Bridge in Dartmouth, the Bedford Institute of Oceanography is one of the world's largest oceanographic establishments. Models and tours explain to

Shubenacadie Canal

Anchor from aircraft carrier (below)
Point Pleasant Park (bottom)

visitors the institute's research of fishery science, oceanography and hydrography. On Main Street (Route 7) at Cherrybrook Road in Dartmouth, the Black Cultural Centre for Nova Scotia preserves the history and culture of Black Nova Scotians with a library, auditorium and exhibits on life dating back to the 1600s.

The Cole Harbour Heritage Farm is also worth a look. Right in the middle of the suburbs, this 1-hectare farm includes heritage buildings, farm animals, archival materials, gardens and a tearoom. Special events are held here throughout the year.

On February 1, 1793, a 22-year conflict began with the French declaration of war against Britain. A year later, Prince Edward, son of George III and, eventually, father to Queen Victoria, arrived to take command of the garrison in Halifax. He set to work strengthening the town's fortifications. Martello towers were all the rage, and Edward built three of them. Two of these, one overlooking the western approaches of the harbour at York Redoubt, and the Prince of Wales Tower (which Edward named after his favourite brother) in Point Pleasant Park are national historic sites. Both locations are worth visiting, for their scenic as well as historical value. York Redoubt is a perfect spot for a picnic, affording a wonderful view of the harbour.

Point Pleasant Park covers 75

hectares in Halifax's South End and is leased by the city from the Crown for a shilling a year. From the park, ships entering the harbour or sailboats tacking across the Northwest Arm can be seen. A series of walking paths makes Point Pleasant ideal for an afternoon stroll, passing by a number of interesting ruins (see the map in the parking lot at the western entrance). From the Chain Rock Battery, a chain boom once stretched across the water to defend against enemy warships. During the First World War, mines were laid between the Point Pleasant Battery and McNabs Island, leaving a narrow channel lit by searchlights. A steel anti-submarine net was added later.

Victorian craftsmanship

Returning from Point Pleasant Park towards the downtown, you pass through Halifax's South End. Here are many of the city's grandest old homes and a wonderful collection of unique Victorian townhouses built of wood and painted bright colours.

From Young Avenue (which becomes South Park Street), you can explore the Victorian South End by turning east along any one of the streets that run between Inglis and Spring Garden. Of course, the Victorian streetscape is regularly interrupted by clumsy, unappealing post-1945 construction, including high-rise apartments, but many of the original buildings remain and there are wonderful architectural details to notice in these houses' porches, windows, gables and trim.

For visitors curious about Halifax's royal past, a small park along the Bedford Highway has a wonderfully romantic origin and a beautiful small building to

Walking in Point Pleasant Park

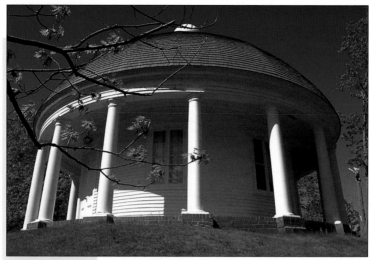

Music building, Bedford Highway

Public Gardens

appreciate. Three months after Prince Edward arrived, his beautiful French mistress followed. Governor John Wentworth lent them his country estate along the shores of Bedford Basin. The only building still standing is a round ornamental garden temple that is similar in design to several buildings that had been constructed at Kew Gardens, Edward's childhood home. Visible from the Bedford Highway, the building is not open to the public, but visitors are welcome to stroll through Hemlock Ravine opposite the rotunda. The pond in the 75-hectare park is heart-shaped and known as Julie's Pond in honour of Edward's mistress. Legend has it that the paths that once meandered through the estate spelled out her name.

Many of Halifax's parks evoke a sense of Victorian times, when Halifax "society" took leisurely

Public Gardens

strolls through Point Pleasant Park and picnicked on McNabs Island. The Royal Nova Scotia Yacht Squadron held regular regattas. By the 1880s, skating parties were held regularly at the rink in the Exhibition Building. In 1882, the Wanderers' Amateur Athletic Association Club was established to foster the growth of cricket, football and hockey. After a purifying workout on the Wanderers' Grounds, participants could cross Sackville Street and take a relaxing stroll through the Public Gardens.

These formal Victorian gardens are the oldest in North America. Originally owned by a group of prominent Haligonians who constituted the Nova Scotia Horticultural Society, the 7-hectare gardens were opened to the public in 1867. In 1874, the society sold them to the city, which still maintains them. The Public Gardens were to serve a threefold purpose: they would improve the physical and mental health of the working classes, provide material for polite discourse among the more refined and be a source of civic pride for all.

Canada Day fireworks over the harbour

The gardens are outstanding. Pathways wander among beautiful weeping trees, formal flowerbeds and subtropical plantings. They lead across classical bridges and past cast-iron fountains to the elaborate central bandstand. During the summer months, Sunday afternoon concerts are held there. On Saturday afternoons, brides, grooms and attendants can be seen posing for photographers. If you need a break from the demands of travel, the gardens are a fine oasis.

Across the Northwest Arm from Point Pleasant is Sir

The Dingle Park

Sandford Fleming Park, or "the Dingle." Fleming, creator of Standard Time Zones and engineer for the Canadian Pacific Railway, donated the park to Halifax in 1908. The 38-hectare park features the Dingle Tower, a sandy beach, a frog pond and an extensive walking trail system.

On the other side of the harbour in Dartmouth the Trans Canada Trail, connected to the trails in Shubie Park, winds from Sullivans Pond along Lake Banook and Lake MicMac for 7 kilometres. The paths are wide and wheelchair accessible.

Throughout the summer months, Halifax and Dartmouth host a wide range of festivals and events. What follows is only a small sampling. Dates vary, so call the province's Information and Reservation Service (800 565-0000), or consult the *Nova Scotia Festivals and Events Guide* for details.

Busy waterfront during the Busker Festival

The Royal Nova Scotia International Tattoo, which draws military bands from around the world, runs for a week each July at the Metro Centre. The International

Armdale Yacht Club

Busker Festival, held in August on the Halifax waterfront and along city sidewalks, is very popular with both locals and visitors. Children especially enjoy the clowns and jugglers. The Atlantic Jazz Festival is a first-rate event. Held in July, mainstage and late-night concerts make for crowded downtown bars. The annual Africville Reunion brings together former residents of the Halifax community that was razed in the 1960s. Visitors are welcomed, and the reunion provides a good opportunity to learn about the Black community of Halifax.

At the city's fine restaurants, not surprisingly, seafood is a ubiquitous specialty. Check the Dining section of the listings at the back of this book for recommended dining spots.

For a lively pub night, try the Lower Deck in the Privateers' Warehouse or the Old Triangle on Prince Street. Live Celtic music is a regular feature at both. The Economy Shoe Shop on Argyle Street is a mecca for the cultural set.

The Old Triangle

Along the South Shore: Lighthouse Route

Peggys Cove lighthouse at dusk

Peggys Cove is a 30- to 40-minute drive from Halifax on Route 333. About 15 kilometres before Peggys Cove, the 18-hole Granite Springs golf course at Bayside, a member of Golf Nova Scotia, makes tee time available to visitors.

Peggys Cove, with its vivid, pitched-roof houses perched atop a mass of granite overlooking the snug harbour, has been captured on miles of film and acres of canvas. It has become the postcard profile of an East Coast fishing village.

It became the focal point of tragedy in 1998 when a Boeing MD-11, Swissair Flight 111, plunged into the ocean and all 229 persons aboard perished. Rescuers, families and the media flocked to Peggys Cove in the aftermath. Two memorials are found nearby.

Swissair III Memorial

Canadian journalist J. F. B. Livesay discovered the village in the 1920s, and his book *Peggys Cove*, based on a summer visit in 1943, was published posthumously a year later. Livesay presented an unabashedly romantic view of the village: "The Cove on that first glance was still quite perfect, nothing to be added and nothing to be taken away, a little pulsing human cosmos set in the uneasy sea."

What Livesay's prose did for Peggys Cove in the 1940s, the

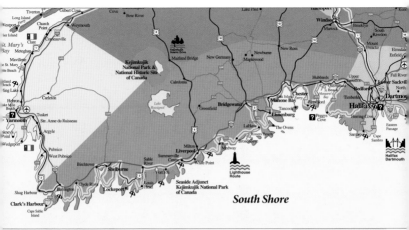

South Shore

photographs of W. R. MacAskill had been doing since 1921. In that year, MacAskill's "Quiet Cove" appeared. Tourism promoters seized the opportunity afforded by MacAskill's beautiful photography. Peggys Cove was close enough to Halifax to offer visitors to the city a chance to encounter the "essential" Nova Scotia — the desolate boundary where land meets sea.

The successful promotion of Peggys Cove has led to a curious irony. You are exhorted to discover the unspoiled beauty of Peggys Cove in the company of dozens or even hundreds of other people. A mass of glacier-scarred granite cuts an impressive profile against sky and sea, but here you will also find air-conditioned coaches from all over North America. There is a busy restaurant and gift shop (the Sou'wester), and the old lighthouse now serves as a post office. The postcard you mail home will bear a postmark of the lighthouse itself. For an impressive view of the cove from seaward, the Peggys Cove Express offers daylong tours from the Halifax waterfront.

But something truly elemental is still revealed at Peggys Cove — something about the human spirit in the face of adversity. William deGarthe, one of many artists

Peggys Cove

who have lived here and drawn inspiration from the rugged beauty of this place, immortalized Peggys Cove with a 30.5-metre sculpture of local fishermen and their families, carved into a huge wall of granite behind his home. The deGarthe Gallery exhibits a good representation of the artist's paintings and sculptures.

From Peggys Cove Route 333 continues along through the picturesque villages that dot the eastern shore of St. Margarets Bay.

DeGarthe sculpture
Peggys Cove

Oceanstone Inn & Cottages serves up the South Shore experience at Indian Harbour, with fine seafood dining and seaside activities.

Route 333 rejoins Route 3, which leads either back to Halifax or farther along the South Shore towards Chester and Mahone Bay. It passes popular Queensland Beach and eventually comes to the village of Hubbards, a popular vacation destination for Haligonians since the mid-1800s. The Shore Club's lobster suppers and Saturday night dances are legendary. There are cottages, inns, B&Bs and restaurants within easy range of Hubbards Beach. Route 329 around the Aspotogan Peninsula is a scenic diversion that will reveal the quintessential Nova Scotia; it rejoins Route 3 at East River.

Nova Scotia's South Shore is a storied stretch of shoreline. In colonial times, privateers — American, French and Nova Scotian — plied these waters with letters of marque from their governments, licensing them to plunder enemy ships. Later, rumrunners unloaded their illicit cargoes in secluded coves and bays. Tall ships once crowded South Shore harbours, and today coastal towns like Chester and Mahone Bay have retained the romantic aura of earlier days. Their harbours are still boating havens.

St. Margarets Bay
at dawn

The village of Chester lies across three fingers of a peninsula that overlooks Mahone Bay, a sailor's paradise. Local lore has it that there are 365 islands in Mahone Bay (one for each day of the year). However, 100-odd islands appear on the charts today. The village itself is a New England coastal town that just happened to end up in Nova Scotia.

Appropriately, Chester's first settlers (it was called Shoreham then) sailed from Boston in 1759. Much of the rest of the Mahone Bay area was colonized by Germans, French and Swiss. Although Chester is also increasingly the haunt of yachtsmen from Halifax, Toronto and beyond, its

Mahone Bay Harbour

predominantly Cape Cod–style architecture and the Yankee accents of many of its summer residents still give the town an unmistakable New England flavour.

Throughout the 19th century, many wealthy Americans discovered Chester. They came to sail, fish and get away from it all. Students from Yale came to Chester to unwind following their studies, and the town's magnificent Front Harbour and Back Harbour provided a scenic refuge for yachtsmen and retired naval brass. American admirals joined their Canadian counterparts, as did bankers, doctors and oilmen from Boston, Baltimore and Pittsburgh. Their houses are among Chester's main attractions, especially those along the peninsula at the western boundary of Front Harbour. In the early days of the 20th century, American families would travel by steamer from Boston and Philadelphia to Yarmouth, Halifax or Digby, where they would catch a train or take another boat to Chester. Several gruelling days later, their chauffeurs would arrive with their fancy cars. Of course, this annual pilgrimage changed Chester. Chesterites, who traditionally fished and farmed, began working as guides on the trout and salmon streams and crewed on splashy sailboats.

Visitors who arrive at Chester by boat will find a range of yachting services without equal in Atlantic Canada. South Shore Marine, in nearby Marriotts Cove, is the region's largest marina. Chester Race Week, held in early August, is the height of the summer social season. Then, the Front and Back harbours are filled with sleek yachts. This prestigious regatta provides world-class racing and watching. The parade grounds off South Street, site of the Yacht Club, a bandstand, a war memorial and a saltwater swimming pool (the Lido), provide the best vantage point for non-sailors who are interested in viewing the races.

Chester Playhouse

A 45-minute ferry trip (for pedestrians only) from the government wharf takes you to Big Tancook, the largest island in Mahone Bay, and then to Little Tancook. The ferry is a great way to enjoy the beauty of the bay and views of Chester. The islands have many lovely walking trails where you might see unique flora.

Chester offers a number of landward diversions. Just outside the village, an 18-

Lido, saltwater swimming pool in Chester

hole golf course is characterized by its short, tight fairways and wonderful views of the ocean and nearby islands. Live theatre and concerts are presented at the Chester Playhouse year-round. Next door at Nicki's Inn you can enjoy a fine dinner before the theatre. The Kiwi Café is the hot spot for lunch. Those who like to shop can visit the Warp and Woof on Water Street. Nova Scotia's oldest gift shop sells local art and prints, handcrafts and table accessories.

Between Chester and the nearby town of Mahone Bay, on the old road, Route 3, the Seaside Shanty at Chester Basin serves up a great chowder lunch. You soon pass Oak Island (now joined to the mainland by a causeway), reputed to be the hiding place of Captain William Kidd's treasure. Since 1795, when a pit was discovered on the island, fortune-seekers have sought in vain for the booty. And for just as long, people have tried to explain the ingenious method by which the famous pirate is thought to have hidden his treasure in an elaborate network of underground tunnels. The story is well told by Mark Finnan in *Oak Island Secrets*, and by Graham Harris and Les MacPhee in *Oak Island and its Lost Treasure*; both are available in local bookstores and gift shops. The Oak Island Resort and Spa is a good jumping-off point from which to explore the area.

Tancook Island view of the ferry

The road dips and winds its way along the shore until a

long, sweeping bend brings one of Nova Scotia's most recognizable landscapes into view. Colourful buildings and wharves, monuments to Mahone Bay's seafaring past, line the waterfront of the town's near-perfect harbour. Sailboats and other pleasure craft are moored offshore, and three fine 19th-century churches — United, Lutheran and Anglican — stand side by side at the head of the harbour. These heritage churches are the venue for classical music concerts, Music at the Three Churches, every second Friday night in summer. The pretty drive to Indian Point (turn left before the bridge) is worth the few minute's detour. The Indian Point Mussel Farm is the focal point of a Mussel Festival in May.

The area's original inhabitants were Mi'kmaq. The Mushamush River on the edge of town bears the name of an early encampment. The present town was

established by "Foreign Protestants" in 1754. The Settlers' Museum, on Main Street, tells their story.

Three churches in Mahone Bay

Mahone Bay was also a haven for French fishermen and pirates. The name Mahone is believed to be derived from the French *mahonne*, a low-lying vessel that kept French pirates hidden from their prey.

Mahone Bay had its own encounters with American privateers. During the War of 1812, the *Young Teazer* was chased into Mahone Bay by a British warship. One of the privateer's crew was a British deserter. Rather than risk capture, he set fire to the ship's powder magazine; 28 died in the explosion that followed. A re-enactment of the burning of the *Teazer* is a feature of Mahone Bay's Classic Boat Festival held the first weekend of August. Inaugurated in 1990, the festival is one of Nova Scotia's best. The quality of craftsmanship of many of the boats displayed at the festival upholds Mahone Bay standards. The Great Scarecrow Festival and Antiques Fair held in early October swells the small town with hundreds of amateur photographers and treasure seekers.

Mahone Bay was once a flourishing shipbuilding centre. Many Main Street businesses now occupy buildings formerly used in the trade. On the second floor of the Settlers Museum, the town's shipbuilding heritage is revealed. It is also visible in the architecture of Mahone Bay. A walking-tour brochure is available at the museum and will steer you towards some of the beautiful Cape Cod, Georgian and Victorian homes that used to belong to local shipbuilders. After the three churches, Mahone Bay Bed & Breakfast, with its lovely wrap-around porch, is probably the most photographed structure in Mahone Bay. It is one of many heritage bed and breakfasts in the area.

Fine shops abound — the kind of shops that have given way to malls in so many other places. Birdsall-Worthington Pottery on Main Street has an international reputation for its distinctive wares made of Nova Scotia clay. Across the road is Amos Pewter, where boats were once built. An interpretive workshop allows visitors to see artisans at work fashioning pewter items — vases, candleholders, annual Christmas collectible ornaments, earrings and pendants. Still on Main Street, but away from the water, Suttles and Seawinds is one of Mahone Bay's most successful enterprises. Vicki Lynn Bardon is responsible for the collection of colourful, quilt-inspired home decor and gift items. The jewel-hued quilts in the adjacent Barnstorm must be seen. The traditional craft of rug hooking is fostered by

The Teazer gift shop

two studios exhibiting and selling beautiful rugs, kits and supplies. Trees Gallery, P'lovers and Joanne's Market celebrate nature and sustainability in art and living.

Several local restaurants attain the same high standard as Mahone Bay's shops. The Innlet Café, with a harbour view that includes the three churches, emphasizes stylish seafood dishes in casual surroundings. The Cheesecake Gallery serves artful entrees amidst local art. For good pub fare and 13 beers on tap (and sometimes Saturday night bands), try the Mug & Anchor. The Biscuit Eater is an Internet café with good coffee, good books and good vibes.

With the possible exception of Annapolis Royal, Lunenburg is the province's prettiest and most interesting town. Its architectural integrity has been preserved to a remarkable degree. Lunenburg's "Old Town" — first laid out by the province's chief surveyor in 1753 — has been

Amos Pewter

designated a National Historic District by the Government of Canada and a World Heritage Site by UNESCO.

Lunenburg's beautiful harbour, its outstanding architecture, its seafaring tradition and its proximity to Halifax have attracted many visitors over the years. Some have stayed. Lunenburg is home to a vital artistic community and

Colourful buildings along Main Street in Mahone Bay

has long been at the centre of Nova Scotia's fishing industry. The demand for wooden ships has declined, but waterfront companies continue to outfit and repair local boats.

Lunenburg represents the second attempt made by British authorities to colonize Nova Scotia (Halifax was the first). This site had a number of advantages. It offered the best agricultural land along Nova Scotia's Atlantic coast, some of which was already cleared — though not nearly as much as was promised. There was a fine harbour, the narrow peninsula could be easily defended by a palisade, and the site was close to Halifax and far from the French settlements at Ile-Royale (Cape Breton) and along the Bay of Fundy.

In 1753, a group of German-speaking "Foreign Protestants" (French, German and Swiss) arrived by boat from Halifax. These labourers and farmers had been recruited by British authorities to populate their colony. Surveyor General Charles Morris measured off blocks and streets in a gridiron pattern along the slope overlooking the harbour. The Old Town was a 48-block rectangle with rows of six blocks running parallel to the shore and columns of eight blocks running up the hill. A central core of four

Classic Boat Festival, Mahone Bay

Lunenburg, home port of the *Bluenose II*, below

blocks was reserved for public purposes.

The settlers overcame the adversities of hostile French and Mi'kmaq in the area, and their endeavours eventually flourished. Surpluses of timber, boards and root vegetables were sent to Halifax. Settlement reached southwest as far as West Berlin, and northeast to Mahone Bay and beyond. Prime land along the banks of the LaHave River drew people farther and farther upriver, from Bridgewater to New Germany.

It was inevitable that some of the new settlers would turn to the sea for their livelihood. Towards the end of the 18th century, the inshore fishery began to flourish. Cod, mackerel, dogfish, salmon, herring and gaspereaux were easily caught from small boats close to shore.

Lunenburg's waterfront still reflects the importance of its shipbuilding industry and the fishery. At the eastern end of Montague Street, Scotia Trawlers has been outfitting and repairing fishing vessels since acquiring the Smith and Rhuland boatyards in 1976. Smith and Rhuland, established in 1900, built both the *Bluenose* (1921) and the *Bluenose II* (1963). Lunenburg shipbuilders were renowned long before the *Bluenose* was launched, but it was this 285-ton racing schooner, never defeated in Nova Scotia waters, that won them international recognition. In addition to the *Bluenose II*, the same shipyard also launched replicas of *HMS Bounty* (1960) and the *Rose*.

The fishery spawned other industries. The buildings of the old Adams & Knickle outfitting company can still be

seen. Farther west on Montague Street, the Fisheries Museum of the Atlantic occupies buildings that were once a part of the National Sea Products processing plant. The museum, one of Nova Scotia's best, has many excellent exhibits relating to Lunenburg's

fishing and shipbuilding heritage. The aquarium of Atlantic fish is especially popular with children; adults may find the rum-running display more to their taste. An exhibit on the Banks fishery and the Age of Sail includes meticulously crafted models. Various demonstrations take place throughout the summer. Moored alongside the museum's wharf, the *Theresa E. Connor*, a salt-bank schooner, and the *Cape Sable*, a steel-hulled trawler, welcome visitors aboard. The *Bluenose II* may also sometimes be berthed here (she sails out of Halifax and other Nova Scotia port towns as well).

In recent years, careful planning has preserved Lunenburg's architectural character. Before that, good fortune was largely responsible. Lunenburg's failure to industrialize in areas other than the fishery is one explanation for the absence of major fires in the downtown area. And significant redevelopment in the Old Town was averted when the "New Town" was established in 1862. With a few minor exceptions, Old Town remains remarkably similar in both form and function to Morris's 1753 plan. Public buildings still stand where they did in the settlement's early days. St. John's Anglican Church, built

Lost sailors memorial

Historic buildings in Lunenburg

between 1754 and 1763, was the tragic victim of a Halloween fire in 2001. The second-oldest Anglican Church in Canada, it has been faithfully restored to its former magnificence. The house of worship is also a home of classical music. Lunenburg's courthouse was built in 1775, and is now used by St. John's parish as a church hall. Predictably, the new courthouse, built in 1902, also stands on the Grand Parade in the centre of town.

There are a number of other 18th-century structures. Typically, these are one-storey Cape Cod–style houses or two-storey dwellings in the British Classical tradition. Knaut-Rhuland House Museum, a designated heritage property (c. 1793) on Pelham Street, has one of the most intact original Georgian interiors in Nova Scotia.

Nineteenth-century buildings dominate Old Town. Although architecturally conservative, Lunenburgers permitted themselves one extravagance in the latter half of the 19th century: Scottish dormer windows were added to British Classical houses. Over time, these were moved down the slope of the roof until they hung over central doorways. The "Lunenburg Bump" can be quite ostentatious, and probably was a reflection of the town's success in the salt fish trade. Many of the

The Lunenburg Academy

interesting buildings in Old Town are now antique-decorated B&Bs.

Built just before the turn of the 20th century, the second Lunenburg Academy (the first was destroyed by fire in 1893) is one of the town's architectural gems. It stands outside Old Town, atop Gallows Hill, and the four towers that jut from its mansard roof are visible for miles. Young Lunenburgers are still educated at the academy.

Lunenburg hosts a series of first-rate festivals during the summer. Its growing reputation as a centre for arts and crafts is reflected in the quality of work displayed at the Lunenburg Festival of Crafts in mid-July and the Nova Scotia Folk Art Festival in early August. At the Lunenburg Fishermen's Reunion and Picnic in August, fishermen's competitions, including dory racing and scallop shucking, are hotly contested by highly skilled participants. A highlight of the summer festival season, the Lunenburg Folk Harbour Festival in August features top North American performers, as well as some from farther afield, and attractive waterside venues.

The town boasts a number of fine shops and galleries, and across the harbour you can shoot nine holes of golf at the Bluenose Golf and Country Club, while enjoying the spectacular view. There are several good restaurants serving, not surprisingly, lobster and fish dishes. Fleur de Sel on Montague Street provides an elegant, upscale interpretation while its offspring, the Salt Shaker Deli, is one of several excellent cafés in the downtown. Sweet Indulgence is a treat for the sweet tooth.

To the south of Lunenburg, the privately run Ovens Natural Park has a series of coastal caves. A cliff-side hiking trail leads down a concrete stairway to the mouth of Cannon Cave — so named because of the dramatic boom created by the surge of waves into the narrow cavern. Zodiac tours of the caves are available between late June and early September, weather permitting.

Follow the coastline south to the LaHave River, and then go upriver on Route 332 to Bridgewater, a thriving town that prides itself as the main street of the South Shore. Bridgewater offers its visitors numerous services and conveniences, including restaurants, accommodations, bustling malls, banks, a regional hospital, a library, museums, recreational facilities and a visitor information centre.

Built in 1860, the Wile Carding Mill displays machines that once carded wool for spinning and weaving. The

The bridge at Bristol Avenue, crossing the Mersey River, Liverpool

DesBrisay Museum relates the history and development of Lunenburg County through documents, exhibits and artifacts, including a beautiful Mi'kmaq quillwork cradle. Bridgewater hosts its rural neighbours each July at the South Shore Exhibition and International Ox Pull.

A pleasant drive down the western banks of the LaHave River (Route 331) leads to the dock where a cable ferry provides a transportation link across the river. Nearby is the Fort Point Museum, a former lighthouse keeper's house, and site of the Fort Sainte-Marie-de-Grâce National Historic Site, where Isaac de Razilly, the first governor of New France, landed with his settlers in 1632. At Rissers Beach, a popular white-sand beach at Petite Rivière, supervised swimming, picnic areas and change facilities are provided.

More excellent beaches and inviting villages can be found at such shoreline communities as Broad Cove, Cherry Hill and Beach Meadows.

Situated at the estuary of the Mersey River, Liverpool was settled by New England Planters in the 1760s. These settlers were invited to Nova Scotia by Governor Charles Lawrence to take up lands made vacant by the expulsion of the Acadians and to bolster the loyal British population of the province.

Much of Liverpool's colonial past has been popularized in the historical fiction of Thomas Raddall. Raddall was far and away Nova Scotia's best-selling novelist, with millions of copies of his books sold in the United States, Great Britain and Canada. In *His Majesty's Yankees*, he told the powerful story of a fictional Liverpool family caught up in the events surrounding the American Revolution. To give his novel life, Raddall relied heavily on the diaries of an 18th-century Liverpool merchant, Simeon Perkins.

Perkins' diaries give a unique account of colonial Nova Scotia. They describe the dilemma faced by the Planters, who had spent most of their lives as New Englanders, when the American Revolution polarized loyalties. Perkins was among those community leaders who eventually called for armed resistance to the attacks of American privateers.

Today, Perkins House on Main Street is one of Liverpool's chief attractions. Built in 1766, the house was acquired by the Queens County Historical Society in 1936 and is now a part of the Nova Scotia Museum. Like Raddall's novels, Perkins House and the adjacent Queens

County Museum tell a romantic story of Liverpool's tumultuous early days. Much is made of privateers — hardly surprising in a town that styles itself as the "Port of the Privateers." Liverpool hosts a Privateer Days celebration at the end of June. The town also stages a summer program of concerts and plays at the beautiful Astor Theatre, once the town hall. This is also the venue for the Liverpool International Theatre Festival, a biennial springtime series of high-calibre performances.

Logging has been the backbone of Liverpool's economy almost from the town's beginning. Some of the lumber was used to build ships, which often took on additional lumber for export to Great Britain.

In the 1920s, the forest industry in Queens County was given a major boost by the decision of Yarmouth-born financier Izaak Walton Killam to build a pulp and paper mill at Brooklyn, on the north side of Liverpool Bay. Completed in 1929, the Mersey Paper Mill got off to a slow start, but soon picked up speed. When Killam died in 1955, he held approximately three-quarters of the company's common stock and his estate was valued at around $200 million. The Killam trusts are still used for university endowments and the construction of public buildings across Canada. Bowater Mersey continues to be the major employer in the Liverpool area.

The Sherman Hines Museum of Photography and Galleries, located in Liverpool's historic town hall, is the only photographic museum east of Montreal. It features artifacts and vintage photographs by the likes of Karsh and MacAskill. Another one-of-a-kind attraction, the Rossignol Cultural Centre on Church Street is a museum and gallery complex that illustrates many natural and social aspects of the area's past. The former Liverpool train station is now the Hank Snow Country Music Centre, honouring the Queens County-born country music legend. The centre has rotating displays and memorabilia from well-known Nova Scotia musicians, interactive exhibits, railway memorabilia, workshops and a gift shop. In August, the Friends of Hank Snow Society hosts a weekend of classic country music at the exhibition grounds in Bridgewater.

Perkins House

Nova Scotia's fourth-oldest surviving lighthouse is the centrepiece of Fort Point Lighthouse Park. Once a welcome sight for seafarers entering Liverpool's busy harbour, the lighthouse now contains an exhibit area with models, interpretive panels and an audiovisual presentation. Lane's Privateer Inn offers good accommodation and dining in a restored building (more than 200 years old) with lovely grounds on the edge of the Mersey River.

South of Liverpool, Route 3 leads to White Point Beach Resort; its wide-ranging facilities include a playground, pool, spa, nine-hole Canadian PGA-rated golf course, tennis courts, freshwater paddling and, of course, a long stretch of fine, white, sandy beach (warm-water enthusiasts will prefer the pool for swimming). Farther along Route 3 are some of the province's best beaches. Summerville Beach Park, with its saltwater lagoon, is a great spot for a picnic and swim. The Quarterdeck Beachside Villas & Grill is situated along this white-sand beach. The villas offer all the amenities, including full kitchen facilities, jacuzzis and fireplaces.

For a more secluded setting, drive on to Carters Beach at South West Port Mouton. The beach is actually three crescent-shaped stretches of the finest white sand imaginable. It's worth the trouble to ford the small stream that separates the last two of these beaches from the first. Here, you will find magnificent dunes and unmatched views of Port Mouton Bay.

The endangered piping plover has also taken advantage of the relative seclusion of this coastline. Kejimkujik National Park's Seaside Adjunct protects key nesting areas between Port Mouton and Port Joli. Two hiking trails lead to

isolated beaches, sections of which are closed from late April to late July, so that nesting birds remain undisturbed. Both hikes offer spectacular coastal views. There are still more wonderful beaches at Lockeport, just off Route 3. Crescent Beach, one of five in the area, is a fully serviced 1.5-kilometre-long stretch of fine, white sand. It is a short drive from here up the indraft of Jordan Bay and across the peninsula to Shelburne.

Shelburne is Nova Scotia's Loyalist town. Drawn by the outstanding harbour — one of the largest in the world — thousands of Loyalists settled along the shores of the

Roseway River estuary in 1783. Within a year, nearly 10,000 people were there, making Shelburne the largest town in British North America.

Carters Beach

A number of Loyalist-era structures have survived in Shelburne. Ross-Thomson House and Store, now part of the Nova Scotia Museum, was built in 1785. The store was soon occupied by business partners and brothers Robert and George Ross (Robert Thomson would become their clerk). The old store has since been refurbished with 18th-century furnishings and merchandise. The comfortable, solid building, no doubt the work of a shipbuilder, is impressive in itself.

The Cooper's Inn, on Dock Street, is one of several waterfront restoration projects that grew out of the visit of the Prince and Princess of Wales to Shelburne in 1983. The former owners received an award from Heritage Trust Nova Scotia for their work on this Loyalist home, dating from around 1785.

South on Dock Street, the Shelburne County Museum tells more of the Loyalist story. A walking-tour brochure available at the museum points out several other Loyalist buildings in town. Most points of interest are along the waterfront, on or near Dock Street. Treat yourself to a wonderful meal prepared by chef Roland Glauser at Charlotte Lane.

Like other fishing communities along the South Shore, Shelburne also has a rich shipbuilding heritage. The town is renowned for its dories. In 1877 Isaac Coffin Crowell, a native of nearby Barrington, invented and patented a metal clip for joining the floor futtocks with those on the sides of the dory. In Lunenburg, dory builders continued (and continue) to use naturally crooked tamarack roots for the job. A debate still rages as to whose method is better, but Crowell's clip allowed Shelburne builders to undersell their Lunenburg competitors.

Loyalist days, Shelburne

At one time, Shelburne had seven dory shops. The Dory Shop, a going concern from 1880 to 1970 and now part of the Nova Scotia Museum, demonstrates the building and outfitting of a Shelburne dory and explains the crucial role that these boats played in the fishery. The Dory Shop Museum has a dory builder at work several days a week.

Between Shelburne and Yarmouth lies Barrington. Just four years after Barrington was founded by Planter families from Cape Cod in 1761, the new township had a New England-style meetinghouse. Now part of the Nova Scotia Museum, the unadorned structure that served both religious and secular purposes is Canada's oldest extant

Loyalist re-enactors

nonconformist place of worship.

Nearby, the Barrington Woolen Mill, built in 1884, is also operated by the museum. The mill houses original machinery and includes exhibits on sheep raising and wool processing. The Seal Island Lighthouse Museum was constructed in Barrington to commemorate the light and its keepers, who steered countless sailors past Seal Island's notorious shoals for 160 years. Built in 1830, the lighthouse was automated in 1990. The exhibits relate to lighthouse life. There is a good view of Barrington Bay from the top of the five-storey lighthouse tower.

Reached by causeway from Barrington Passage, Cape Sable Island in Barrington Bay is also steeped in maritime lore. The island was home to Ephraim Atkinson, who first built the boat that became the workhorse of the North Atlantic lobster fishery. Typically, Cape Islanders are about 12 metres long with a 3- to 4-metre beam. You'll find them in working harbours throughout Atlantic Canada. Learn more about the Cape Islander and this storied fishing community at the Archelaus Smith Museum in Centreville.

At West Pubnico (founded in 1653), the oldest Acadian settlement still inhabited by descendants of its founders, Historic Acadian Village honours the perseverance and generosity of the Acadian people. Original structures and artifacts donated by local residents were used to create vintage Acadian buildings, including houses, a forge, a barn and a lobster peg mill. Guides in period costume welcome visitors to a reception centre, a restaurant serving traditional Acadian dishes and an arts and crafts shop. Museé Acadien illuminates Acadian history and culture and hosts kitchen parties featuring traditional music throughout the summer.

Loyalist Days, Shelburne

Take a stroll through the town of Yarmouth and you'll be struck by the houses. On the slope rising up from the

ferry terminal are lavish 19th-century homes — Georgian, Gothic and Italianate, among others. Some have costly frills, like the one on Parade Street, not far from the Yarmouth County Museum, which is trimmed with wooden rope and comes complete with portholes.

Barrington Meeting House

Fish-processing plants along the waterfront attest to a fairly healthy fishery (a rarity in Nova Scotia these days) and the town is well serviced, but there are few clues as to where the extravagant wealth came from that built these homes. That is because Yarmouth's century was the 19th — first as Nova Scotia's most prosperous "wood, wind and sail" community, and then as a thriving industrial centre.

The excellent Yarmouth County Museum is a good place to begin a tour of the town. Here, there are many paintings of the fleet, commissioned by Yarmouth captains in ports like New York, Belfast and Hong Kong.

During the middle of the 19th century, Yarmouth families like the Killams and Lovitts, who traced their roots back to the New England Planters who first settled Yarmouth in the 1760s, became powerful shipping magnates. Their ships, flush with lumber and salt fish, made for the West Indies. There they laded rum, sugar and molasses bound for Boston, then returned to Yarmouth with manufactured goods. They reinvested the profits in shipping. For a time, Yarmouth boasted the largest per capita concentration of registered shipping tonnage in the world. By the 1860s, huge ships were being built for the international bulk trade. Yarmouth's wealthiest families entered into partnerships to finance their construction. All along the French Shore — the string of Acadian communities between Yarmouth and Digby — shipyards were kept busy.

The Killam Brothers Building, part of the Yarmouth County Museum and located along the waterfront, attests to the wealth of the ship owners. Look for the hand-worn grooves in the cash tray of the huge, stand-up chestnut desk.

And then, so the story usually goes, sail was replaced by steam, and it was over. The worldwide slump in trade in 1873 is often cited as the turning point. The golden age of wooden ships and iron men had passed. Yarmouth's mercantile class was left to languish in the face of progress.

But that's not what really happened. A visit to Yarmouth's excellent Firefighters' Museum on Main Street provides some insight into the real story. Among the exhibits is a horse-drawn hose reel that was built in Yarmouth by the Burrill-Johnson Iron Company in 1891. The threat of fire was real because Yarmouth industry boomed until the turn of the century. In addition to the Burrill-Johnson foundry,

The Dory Shop

which had been expanded during the 1880s to supply more products to national and international markets, the Yarmouth Duck and Yarn Company was started in 1883. It was one of several cotton mills established in the Maritimes to take advantage of the federal government's National Policy.

That policy, implemented in 1878, sought to stimulate the

Canadian manufacturing sector by slapping tariffs on foreign manufactured goods, while allowing certain raw materials, including cotton, to enter the country duty-free. So, Yarmouth merchants did not suddenly abandon shipping in a fit of panic. Rather, they scaled back operations in light of the advent of steam and sought to take advantage of the new technologies by investing in land-based manufacturing. The National Policy provided the economic stimulus, and the newly completed Western Counties Railway linked Yarmouth to the national market.

But regional manufacturers could not compete with their central Canadian counterparts. The transfer of local capital to larger Ontario and Quebec interests was a problem experienced in all of Nova Scotia's industrial towns. Yarmouth's decline was as dramatic as its rise. By 1900 little industry was left. The cotton mill was still around, but was soon controlled by outsiders.

Today, there are some wistful reminders of Yarmouth's heyday. But there is a bright side to the story. The town still thrives as the service centre for southwestern Nova Scotia and a key entry point for the province. Bay Ferries operates a speedy car ferry, the Cat, to Yarmouth from Bar Harbor and Portland, Maine.

The Yarmouth Arts Centre (Th'YARC) stages a variety of entertainment, including summer theatre, in its 380-seat theatre on Parade Street. The Art Gallery of Nova Scotia maintains a presence here in a refurbished building on Main Street. Dory races are a highlight of Seafest, a weeklong community festival held each July.

For the most part, Yarmouth offers hotel/motel-style accommodation, but there are notable exceptions. Harbour's Edge Bed & Breakfast is an elegantly appointed heritage property. The beautifully restored Charles C. Richards House is another notable B&B. The impressive Guest-Lovitt House B&B, with its widow's walk, speaks of Yarmouth's former shipping wealth. The Manor Inn, in nearby Hebron, features all the amenities (dining room, pub, tennis courts and more) on about 4 hectares of attractively landscaped waterfrontage. Still in the Yarmouth area, Trout Point Lodge in Kemptville features a rustic decor (with all amenities) on a large river- and lakeside acreage.

CAT ferry

Rudder's Seafood Restaurant and Brewpub is the centre of activity on the Yarmouth waterfront; it offers good food, house-brewed beer and lively entertainment.

Yarmouth's lobster fishery still flourishes. Along the scenic drive out to the lighthouse at Cape Forchu, between the spring and fall lobster seasons, you'll see thousands of traps piled along the roadside.

Annapolis Valley & Acadian Shore: Evangeline Trail

The Annapolis Valley is an area of peaceful beauty. The North and South Mountain ranges provide shelter from heavy winds and Fundy fog. The valley is blessed with more sunshine than anywhere else in Nova Scotia. The fertile soil has been farmed since the Acadians settled the land early in the 17th century. Stately elms and beautiful willows (an Acadian favourite) impart a sense of timelessness to the valley. Is it any wonder that you can find a village named Paradise here?

The Annapolis Valley is an ideal setting for a tragic romance. And history obliged with a suitable cast of characters, the Acadians — French farmers who were Nova Scotia's earliest European settlers. Unable to retain their neutrality in the struggle between France and Britain for supremacy in the New World, the peaceful Acadians were expelled in 1755 for refusing to take an unconditional oath of loyalty to the British Crown — their lands, houses and livestock were all confiscated. All that was needed was for someone to write their story.

Henry Wadsworth Longfellow's epic poem *Evangeline* was published in Boston in 1847. It was immensely popular, running through five editions in its first year. Other publications followed, which further aroused the curiosity of New Englanders in the "Land of Evangeline."

A rail link between Halifax and Yarmouth, completed in 1891, provided a convenient way of getting here. The Yarmouth Steamship Company added a new ship to its Boston run, and the Windsor and Annapolis Railway inaugurated the "Flying Bluenose." Since then, the valley has been a popular destination for visitors from New England and beyond.

Approaching the Annapolis Valley from Halifax, Highway 101 passes Mount Uniacke, where Richard John

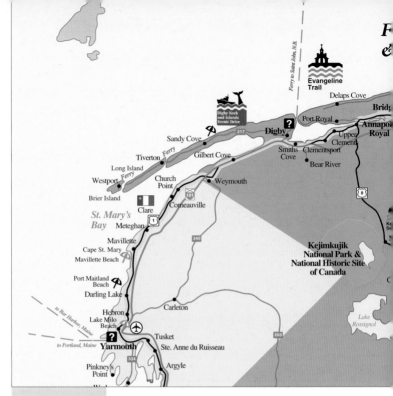

F
&

Ferry to Saint John, N.B.

Evangeline Trail

Delaps Cove

Bridg

Port Royal

Annapo Royal

Digby

Upper Clement

Sandy Cove

Digby Neck and Islands Scenic Drive

217

Smiths Cove

Clementsport

Tiverton Ferry

Gilbert Cove

Bear River

Long Island Ferry

Church Point

Weymouth

Westport

101

Brier Island

Comeauville

Clare

St. Mary's Bay

Meteghan

1

Kejimkujik National Park & National Historic Site of Canada

Ke Se

340

Mavillette

Cape St. Mary

Mavillette Beach

Port Maitland Beach

Carleton

Darling Lake

Lake Rossignol

to Bar Harbor, Maine

Hebron

Lake Milo Beach

203

Tusket

to Portland, Maine

Yarmouth

Ste. Anne du Ruisseau

Pinkney's Point

334

Argyle

Uniacke built an impressive Georgian mansion, Uniacke House, in 1813. After fighting on the rebel side of the American Revolution, Uniacke bounced back nicely, becoming one of Nova Scotia's wealthiest and most influential men. As Attorney General and Advocate General to the Admiralty Court during the War of 1812, he made a fortune — a chunk of which went into building his country home. The Uniacke Estate Museum Park is now part of the Nova Scotia Museum, and features many original furnishings and Uniacke family portraits. Many kilometres of walking and hiking trails have been developed throughout the landscaped grounds and natural woodlands.

Grape stomping at Sainte Famille Winery

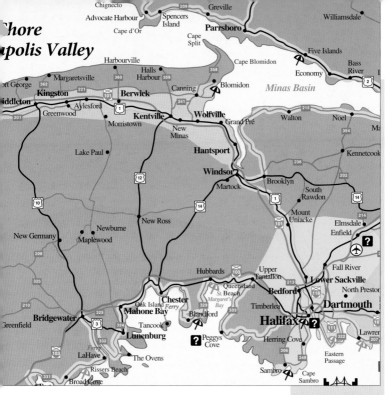

On the continuing journey toward Windsor, the lush valley landscape makes a dramatic appearance. Spread out before you are the rich farmlands that skirt the Avon River. If the tide is out, the river is an expanse of red mudflats. Remnants of Acadian dykes are here, although it is impossible to distinguish the originals from later reconstructions. Windsor is the hub of the whole Minas Basin. Route 215 follows the Noel Shore (Glooscap Trail), while Highway 1 or 101 parallels the Fundy Shore all the way to Digby and thence to Yarmouth.

Windsor is a service centre for Hants County farmers. The town was also home to Thomas Chandler Haliburton, the Nova Scotian humorist who created the character Sam Slick, the Yankee clockmaker with an acerbic wit.

Haliburton House, a provincial museum, features Victorian furnishings and an attractive 10-hectare estate. Shand House, another provincial museum, is a state-of-the-art Victorian home with all of the modern conveniences of the time. Windsor is the home of the late Howard Dill,

Valley apples

Apple Blossoms

the farmer who developed the "Atlantic Giant" pumpkin that has produced specimens weighing more than 650 kilograms. Visitors flock to the Dill farm on College Road, particularly in late summer and early fall, to marvel at the monster vegetables.

The Dill farm is also the site of Long Pond, where students at King's College School played the first-ever game of hockey. Downtown, the Windsor Hockey Heritage Centre tells the story of how Canada's great winter sport began.

Close by, at Falmouth, the Saint Famille Winery, which provides tours, and the well-kept greens and fairways of the Avon Valley golf course attest to the fine Annapolis Valley weather.

Hantsport, once a prosperous shipbuilding centre, is now home to a busy pulp and paper products industry, and serves as a depot for the export of gypsum to all parts of the world. As you travel west, fields and orchards appear, reminders that agriculture has always been the mainstay of the area. During harvest season, roadside stands and U-picks do a brisk business as locals and visitors load up with fresh fruit and vegetables.

In late May, the Annapolis Valley is in full bloom — orchards of apple trees are laden with delicate pink and white blossoms. Since 1932, valley residents have celebrated the start of the growing season with an Apple Blossom Festival. Before the mid-19th century, there was not much of an apple industry in the area. Poor roads and contrary winds made the shipment of perishable goods a dubious enterprise. Railways and steamships changed all that. By the 1880s, apples from the Annapolis Valley were being regularly shipped to Great Britain. The British gobbled down more apples than any other people in the world. By the 1930s, Britain regularly consumed three-quarters of Nova Scotia's commercial crop.

When that market suddenly dried up with the outbreak of war, the problem was thought to be temporary. It was not. A sluggish post-war economy forced Britons to severely limit the number of pounds that they could convert for purchases made in dollars, and apples were not a high priority.

The British market for Annapolis Valley apples never recovered. Now, much of the crop is processed locally into juice, applesauce and pies for world markets. Relatively few apples are grown for export.

Gaspereau Vineyards

But there are plenty of apples for the local market. In early fall, roadside stands brim with apples — old favourites like Cortland, McIntosh, Gravenstein and Delicious, as well as the newer Royal Gala and Jonagold. Visitors can spend an idyllic afternoon at one of the valley's many U-pick orchards.

Between Windsor and Wolfville is the Grand-Pré National Historic Site. Hundreds of Acadians were deported from the area in 1755, and the village of Grand-Pré became the setting for Longfellow's *Evangeline*. The grounds of the historic site are beautiful, with gardens and winding paths shaded by old willow trees. A memorial church built in 1922 houses an exhibit, and a new interpretive centre explains the history of the expulsion. Bilingual tours are provided.

In recent years the Valley has become as well known for wine as for apples. There is a thriving winery in the village of Grand Pré, with a restaurant and inn on site. Nearby in the Gaspereau Valley is Gaspereau Vineyards — a newer winery operated by the Jost family, who started the winemaking industry in Nova Scotia at Malagash.

Wolfville is the cultural and academic centre of the Annapolis Valley. Acadia University, established as Acadia

Blomidon Inn

View from the look-off

College in 1838, is situated on one of Canada's prettiest campuses. The 2.4-hectare Harriet Irving Botanical Gardens of native plants is part of the university's new K.C. Irving Environmental Sciences Research Centre.

In addition to being the valley's cultural centre, Wolfville is also one of its loveliest towns. Beautiful Victorian homes line elm-shaded streets. The visitor information centre at Willow Park, on Main Street, will provide you with a brochure for the Heritage Home Walking Tour.

Several of Wolfville's grandest homes are now among the province's best tourist accommodations. The Blomidon Inn features 28 rooms in a lavish 1877 mansion. The entrance and public spaces are especially impressive, as are the Blomidon's best rooms. Blomidon Inn's House of Gifts has a wide selection of handcrafted items and kitchenwares. The Tattingstone Inn is a special place — you'll find four-poster beds and marble-tiled bathrooms, but also a swimming pool. There is a carriage house and a cottage for honeymooners. Victoria's Historic Inn and Carriage House Bed & Breakfast (1893) is another registered heritage property. The main house includes five honeymoon suites, complete with jacuzzis.

Wolfville offers fine dining as well. Two restaurants in particular — Tempest, world cuisine with locally sourced ingredients, and Acton's, where a popular lunch buffet features fresh Valley produce and Fundy seafood — make dining out in Wolfville a pleasure.

The town's Robie Tufts Nature Centre provides summer visitors with a rare spectacle. From May to late August, chimney swifts gather here for a startlingly acrobatic descent down a chimney. (Tufts's bird books are available at most Nova Scotia bookstores.)

Randall House, a Georgian-period Wolfville farmhouse, features a collection of historical materials relating to the Planters — New Englanders invited to Nova Scotia to take over the lands made vacant by the Expulsion of 1755 — who settled Mud Creek before it became Wolfville. Across the street, a path leads to a series of dykes that are ideal for walking and offer great views of the town and surrounding countryside.

In an area renowned for its agriculture, it may surprise you to learn that many of Wolfville's elegant homes, including the Blomidon Inn, were built with wealth earned from the shipping trades. Nearby Kingsport, Hantsport and Port Williams were all important shipping centres. After

Cape Split

1928, some independent growers shipped local apples directly from Port Williams. Three kilometres away, at Starrs Point, Prescott House was built in 1815 by Charles Prescott, a businessman and horticulturist who introduced several varieties of apples, including the Gravenstein, to Nova Scotia. The house, now part of the Nova Scotia Museum, is filled with period furnishings, and the perennial garden and grounds are especially attractive. Today, visitors can enjoy a sunny early-fall afternoon picking their fill of apples at U-picks in Starrs Point and many other locations throughout the valley.

Back at Port Williams, Route 358 continues north across Acadian dykes, through Canning (where there is yet another winery — Blomidon Estate) then on to the Blomidon Look Off. From high atop Cape Blomidon you can survey the Minas Basin and 6 river valleys. In autumn, the view is made even more beautiful by the fall foliage that spreads out beneath you.

At the end of Route 358, hikers can carry on to the end of Cape Split (the continuation of Cape Blomidon) along a 13-kilometre marked trail that yields spectacular views of the Bay of Fundy. Farther along Route 358 is Blomidon Provincial Park, which has many hiking trails offering amazing views of the Minas Basin and

Oaklawn Farm Zoo

The tasty delights
of Halls Harbour

opportunities for rockhounding for the amethysts and agates that are constantly being exposed along the cliffs and beaches by the massive Fundy tides.

Kentville services the richest farming area in the valley and has been a long-time leader in the apple industry. The Agriculture Canada Research Station assists fruit growers with an ongoing program of scientific research. Blair House is an on-site museum with exhibits relating to the history of the apple industry and the research station's involvement in it. In town, the Old Kings Courthouse Heritage Museum on Cornwallis Street devotes much of its space to the social history of the area — especially to the arrival of the New England Planters in the 1760s. A good walking-tour brochure is available from the visitor information centre. The tour lasts about three hours and will take you past several outstanding heritage homes.

Back towards Wolfville, the Ken-Wo Golf Club is one of the valley's best courses. The sheltered fairways are well maintained, and the casual atmosphere makes green-fee players feel more than welcome.

Villages and towns run into one another as you continue west through the valley along Route 1. Road-weary travellers can choose from the many rural bed and breakfasts in places like Berwick, Middleton and Lawrencetown. Century Farm Inn and Falcourt Inn in the Middleton area are gracious old establishments. At Aylesford, families will enjoy the Oaklawn Farm Zoo, which features more than 100 species of mammals and birds. The 18-hole Paragon Golf Course at Kingston is usually less crowded than other courses in the valley, and is almost always drier (a nuisance at the height of summer, but a blessing at other times). Its wide-open fairways make it a forgiving course for novices.

A short side trip over North Mountain takes visitors to picturesque fishing villages hugging the shores of the Bay

Port Royal
Habitation

of Fundy. At places like Halls Harbour, Harbourville, Margaretsville or Hampton, fishing boats dramatically demonstrate the rise and fall of the tides, as they alternately ride high at their moorings or sit on the mud flats awaiting the next rising tide. Stop for fresh lobster at the pound in Halls Harbour. For a few days stay right on the Fundy Shore, there are housekeeping cottages with lovely gardens at Margaretsville. If you have time, take a detour through Bridgetown and see for yourself why it is billed as "the prettiest little town in Nova Scotia." A self-guided walking tour highlights Bridgetown's heritage homes and history. Bridgetown was the setting for Ernest Buckler's *The Mountain and the Valley*, probably the best work of fiction to come out of Nova Scotia.

The communities along the shores of the Annapolis Basin are a treasure trove of history. All Nova Scotia school children know the story of the arrival of Sieur de Monts and Samuel de Champlain at Port Royal in 1605. They also learn how a second Port Royal, established on the opposite shore of the basin in 1635, became Annapolis Royal in 1710 and served as the seat of British colonial government in Nova Scotia until Halifax was established in 1749. Here was the first successful European settlement in what is now Canada — and the genesis of British rule in Nova Scotia.

Off Route 1, about 10 kilometres southwest of Granville Ferry, is the reconstructed Port Royal Habitation. Close by, de Monts and Champlain established a fur-trading post in 1605. The reconstruction is based on Champlain's sketch of the site. Like Normandy farms of that time, buildings form a rectangle around a central courtyard.

A good deal is known about the French stay at Port Royal through the writings of Champlain, Marc Lescarbot and Father Pierre Biard. Lescarbot, a disenchanted lawyer with literary aspirations and an ebullient personality, wrote extensively about his year at the habitation. His frivolous Neptune pageant, now celebrated as Canada's first theatrical presentation, was played out along the shores of Port Royal in November 1606. Even Champlain, no great fan of Lescarbot, was entertained.

The winter that followed was a relatively mild one, made even more bearable by Champlain's Ordre de Bon Temps (Order of Good Cheer). Champlain sought to ward off the ravages of scurvy and the monotony of winter by promoting feasting and fellowship among the order's members.

Fort Anne National Historic Site

In 1607, de Monts' fears were realized when his monopoly was revoked; the habitation was abandoned until 1610. Father Biard, a Jesuit priest, arrived the following year. His frequent clashes with the Biencourts, the father and son who now ran the habitation, and the difficulties he encountered in his mission work with the Mi'kmaq, were well suited to Biard's acid pen. When Port Royal was sacked by a group of Virginians led by Samuel Argall in 1613, Biard may well have breathed a sigh of relief had he not been wrongfully accused of complicity in the raid by the younger Biencourt. (Elizabeth Jones provides a lively narrative history of the Port Royal years in *Gentlemen and Jesuits*.)

The present-day habitation evokes Canada's first European settlement. Costumed interpreters, employed as 17th-century artisans, go about their tasks. Visitors can imagine Marc Lescarbot scribbling away in his reconstructed dwelling. Other buildings at the site, which include the Governor's House, the Priest's Dwelling, the Chapel, the Blacksmith's Shop and the Trading Room, may well inspire 17th-century reveries.

At Granville Ferry, pause long enough to look across the river at the Annapolis Royal waterfront. On a calm, clear day this is one of Nova Scotia's special views. Also worth a look is the fine collection of Georgian furniture, ceramics, glass and silver housed at the North Hills Museum.

At the Annapolis River Causeway, there is a prototype tidal power installation. An on-site interpretive display shows how the generators work, but the power house itself is underground and off-limits to the public. From here, Route 1 leads directly into Annapolis Royal.

Beautiful Annapolis Royal, on the shores of the Annapolis Basin, is a showcase of heritage restoration. A reconstruction project launched in 1979 spruced up some of the town's fine old buildings, attracting both business and tourists. Before the project, visitors to Annapolis Royal had to leave town to get a good meal. Today, there are several good local restaurants. Leo's Café is situated in the Adams-Ritchie House, built by a New England merchant in 1712. The fine dining at Garrison House Inn has been recommended in *Where to Eat in Canada*. The Queen Anne Inn is one of several grand old mansions that now accommodate tourists in fine style. The restored King's Theatre hosts a summer theatre festival during July and

August. The work of local artists and artisans, many of them recent arrivals to Annapolis Royal, can be seen in waterfront shops and galleries.

In the centre of town, the Fort Anne National Historic Site represents the fourth and last fort built by the French at this location. Governor Subercase's powder magazine (1708) is the only extant building from the French era. The story of the struggle for supremacy between the French and English is told in the museum building, which was constructed as officers' quarters by the Duke of Kent in 1797. A stroll along the earthworks affords some beautiful views of the Annapolis Basin.

Historic Gardens, Annapolis Royal

The Annapolis Royal Historic Gardens were opened in August 1981 as part of the heritage restoration project. Abutted by reclaimed marshland and a 20-hectare wildfowl sanctuary, the stunning 4-hectare gardens display much of the area's natural history. Among the more than 200 varieties in the Rose Garden are several that were grown by Acadian settlers in the area in the 17th century (the roses are at their peak from late June until August). Next to the replica of an Acadian cottage, willow and apple trees shade an Acadian potager, or vegetable garden, wherein can be found the makings of an outstanding pot of soup. Other highlights include the Governor's Garden, which was modelled after 18th-century gardens in southern New England, and the carefully ordered Victorian Garden with its 300-year-old elm tree. A nice lunch can be had at the on-site café.

Annapolis Royal bustled during the late 18th and 19th centuries. Ships left waterfront wharves loaded with apples, potatoes and lumber, and returned with sugar, molasses and rum from the West Indies. Packet boats from Digby, Saint John and Boston made Annapolis Royal a regular port of call. The town was a popular overnight stop.

Today, the O'Dell Inn Museum, dating from the 1860s, recreates the cosmopolitan atmosphere of a busy 19th-century inn. It catered to well-off travellers, the nicer

Bear River

rooms going for $1.50 a night. The museum also houses
collections of Victorian costumes and furnishings, artifacts
of childhood, as well as the ubiquitous relics of a
shipbuilding past. Sinclair Inn National Historic Site, built
in 1710, offers a fascinating insight into construction
techniques spanning nearly three centuries, from the
Acadian clay walls to modern wood panelling.

Several other outstanding Georgian and Victorian
structures are along or just off St. George Street. The
deGannes-Cosby House, built in 1708, is thought to be the
oldest wooden house in Canada. "Stroll Through the
Centuries," a brochure put out by the Historical
Association of Annapolis Royal, provides an interpretive
walking tour of the town. During the summer months, on
Mondays, Wednesdays and Thursdays, the association
offers regular guided tours from its headquarters at the
lighthouse on Lower St. George Street.

From Annapolis Royal, Route 1 meanders along the
shore of the Annapolis Basin towards Digby.
(Alternatively, Highway 101 provides a faster, but less
scenic, route.) At Upper Clements, the 10-hectare Upper
Clements Park is popular with children. The flume ride,
roller coaster and carousel are special favourites, as is the

Digby Pines Resort

large waterslide. Across the highway, the Upper Clements

The scallop fleet at Digby

Wildlife Park offers visitors a chance to see native Nova Scotian animals — lynxes, cougars, porcupines, foxes, groundhogs, skunks, deer and moose — along winding, wooded trails.

To the southwest, Route 1 eventually crosses Bear River into Digby County. The work of Nova Scotia artisans, many from Bear River, is showcased at Flight of Fancy on Main Street. Featured downstairs are striking bird paintings on stone, Mi'kmaq crafts, sculptured hardwood burls, pottery, weaving, jewellery, stained glass and carved birds. The upstairs gallery displays paintings, photographs and sculptures by well-known Nova Scotia artists. The First Nations Heritage and Cultural Centre interprets the history of the Mi'kmaq of the area. Bear River is stunning in autumn, when the hardwood hills on either side of the river are ablaze with colour.

Back on the main drag is the community of Smiths Cove. Outstanding views of the Annapolis Basin and Digby Gut can be enjoyed from Smiths Cove, where good accommodation can be found — the Harbourview Inn is exceptional. From there, it is a short drive to Digby, home of the world's largest scallop fleet. Scallops and Digby chicks (smoked herring) are served in local restaurants. From the deck of the Fundy Restaurant on Water Street, you can enjoy Digby seafood with a view of the boats that caught your meal. Golfers rave about Stanley Thompson's championship course at the Digby Pines Resort. The par-71, 18-hole course plays through mature stands of spruce and pine, while affording some beautiful views of the

Annapolis Basin from Fisherman's Wharf, Digby

Balancing rock,
Tiverton Long
Island

Annapolis Basin. The hotel, built in 1929, features a
Norman-style chateau and 30 cottages strung out along a
bluff that rises from the shores of the basin. There are a
number of excellent inns and bed and breakfasts in the
Digby area. Dockside Suites offers modern conveniences
right on the waterfront. Whale- and seabird-watching tours
are just some of the reasons to enjoy a drive and two short
ferry rides along Digby Neck to Long Island and Brier
Island. Along the way there are spectacular panoramas of
rocky headlands that have been carved by the powerful
Fundy tides. At Tiverton on Long Island, a scenic hiking
trail leads to the amazing Balancing Rock. Brier Island
Lodge offers food and accommodation as well as
breathtaking ocean views.

Between Digby and Yarmouth, along the margin of
Baie Ste-Marie (St. Marys Bay), runs a string of Acadian
villages. There is no mistaking Nova Scotia's Acadian
Shore. Every few kilometres, a steeple soars from one of
the magnificent Catholic churches. Colourful houses in
distinctive Acadian style line the road at Mavillette or
Grosses Coques. Yet for generations after their arrival from
France, the original Acadian settlers ignored this area. Most
preferred the fertile land of the Annapolis Valley.

The British paid no heed to Acadian preferences in
1755. The Acadians were deported, their houses and barns
put to the torch, and the lands they had farmed for 100
years were seized by the Crown. Soon after, the governor
began granting these lands to new settlers, the so-called
Planters, many of whom came from New England and
whose loyalty he trusted.

Some Acadians managed to escape deportation. They
withdrew to the forests or fled to remote corners of the

St. Mary's Church, Church Point

province, where they lived as refugees. Many died during that first winter, while others were caught and imprisoned at Halifax, Windsor or Annapolis Royal. Still, there was a group of Acadians in Nova Scotia who somehow persevered. When the Treaty of Paris ended the war between France and England in 1763, these people began to look for a home. Others returned from exile. Sadly, the Annapolis Valley was lost to them.

Eventually, Lieutenant-Governor Michael Francklin responded to their plight. Land was surveyed along St. Marys Bay. In 1768 the Township of Clare, named after the Irish county, was created for settlement by the Acadians. The villages of St. Bernard, Belliveau Cove, Grosses Coques, Church Point and Little Brook fall within the boundaries of that original grant. As families grew and others returned from exile, Acadian settlement extended southward to Salmon River. Today, this entire stretch is part of the Municipality of Clare.

Life along the shore was much different from the life the Acadians had known in the Annapolis Valley. They still kept gardens, although the soil was poorer, but the forest and the sea were irresistible forces. Acadian farmers became woodsmen, shipbuilders and fishermen — jacks-of-all-trades.

Today, their self-reliance is revealed by a drive along Route 1, sometimes called "the longest main street on earth." Family run businesses crowd the shore. U. J. Robichaud and Sons run a lumber business at Meteghan Centre. A. F. Theriault and his sons have a shipyard at Meteghan River. Comeau and Deveau are another two French names that you will frequently see. Comeau's Sea Foods in Saulnierville is a huge operation. The Deveaus have a fish operation at Belliveau Cove and an insurance business at Meteghan. Few businesses along the Acadian Shore are run by outsiders.

The Acadian Shore has long served as a centre for Acadian culture in Nova Scotia. Both in terms of size and population density, it is the largest Acadian region in the province. In

Acadian dancers at Festival Acadien de Clare

villages all along Baie Ste-Marie, people gather each July to celebrate their Acadian heritage during the Festival Acadien de Clare. Festivities are fuelled by Acadian music and food. (For a special treat try rappie pie, a savoury casserole of potato and chicken, at the Cape View Restaurant, overlooking Mavillette Beach.) Mavillette, one of several wonderful beaches in the area, has 5 kilometres of magnificent shore.

In 1890, a group of Eudist priests established Collège Sainte-Anne at Church Point. Over the years, Saint-Anne, which became a university in 1977, has made enormous contributions to Acadian culture in Nova Scotia. The Magasin Campus (campus bookstore) has a wide selection of books on Acadian themes.

A large, fairly homogeneous Acadian population has benefited the people of the Acadian Shore in other ways. The area also has a long tradition of political representation by Acadians, both at the federal and provincial levels. And recent studies have shown that the French spoken in this part of the province has retained more 17th-century features than that spoken elsewhere in Nova Scotia.

But the most visible expressions of the cultural vitality along the shore are the beautiful churches. Acadians pride themselves on their Catholic faith, and parishioners of modest means went to great pains to demonstrate this pride. Hidden behind the graceful exteriors of these churches are surer signs of Acadian faith, workmanship and resourcefulness. Two churches — St. Mary's Church at Church Point and St. Bernard's Church at St. Bernard — should not be missed.

The plans for St. Mary's Church, (Eglise Sainte-Marie) were drawn up in France, but construction of the church was left in the skillful hands of Leo Melanson, a master carpenter from nearby Little Brook. Between 1903 and 1905, he and many others laboured. They must have been in awe of their achievement.

St. Mary's is the largest wooden church in North America. Its steeple rises 56 metres above the community of less than 500 people. It is anchored by 36 tonnes of stone ballast to keep it from blowing off in hurricane-force winds. Other features are also impressive. The interior of the church belies its size. A wooden floor softens the stained glass light, lending a warm and comfortable feeling to the entire nave. The "stone" pillars that support the roof are not stone. They are huge tree trunks that have been lathed and covered in plaster. Overhead, the "marble" arches are wooden as well.

The parishioners of St. Bernard were not to be outdone. They hired an architect from Moncton, New Brunswick, who had visited France. He sent down the plans, but the work was left to locals. Between 1910 and 1942, they built a huge stone church that seats more than 1,000.

Visitors to the Acadian Shore will receive a warm welcome in French or English. All but a handful of the Acadian population speak both languages. However, it is through French, like their magnificent churches, that the Acadians of Clare express pride in their culture.

The Evangeline Trail continues on to Yarmouth.

Along the Fundy Shore:
Glooscap Trail

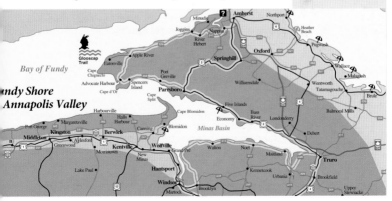

Spectacular views of the Bay of Fundy, where the world's highest tides twice daily move 115 billion tonnes of water, await the visitor to the Glooscap Trail. Named for the mythic cultural hero of the Mi'kmaq and other northeastern Native tribes, the Glooscap Trail starts at Amherst, the border point with New Brunswick, and follows the Fundy Shore to Windsor.

Along the shores of Cobequid Bay, the tide can rise 2.5 centimetres in a minute, and in some areas the difference between low and high tide has been recorded at 16 metres. The explanation for these extreme tides lies in the bay's funnel shape, which serves as an amplifier. The bulge of water that floods up the Fundy is less than 1 metre high at the edge of the continental shelf, but at its mouth it meets a slow-moving wave that continually sloshes up and down

The bay. This wave, reinforced and pushed by the tide, moves up the bay, where it is squeezed by the rising ocean bottom and the narrowing Fundy shores.

This produces some dramatic effects. Tidal bores occur when a rapid incoming tide moves up a river or narrow bay, creating a wave. Depending on the phase of the moon and other factors such as wind direction, the tidal bore can be either a barely detectable ripple or a wall of water a metre high. Tidal bores can be viewed along a number of rivers in the upper Fundy region, including the Salmon River near Truro; the Shubenacadie River at various locations, including South Maitland Village Park and from the Maccan and River Hebert bridges. Several companies offer upriver rafting trips on the Shubenacadie.

The Tidal Bore coming in (above); and people rafting the bore, above right

Join the Glooscap Trail at Amherst, where the shells of old factories and some truly grand homes, especially along Victoria Street, stand as evidence of past industrial glory. Some of these grand old homes are now bed and breakfasts; the Regent B&B is notable. The Cumberland County Museum tells some of Amherst's industrial and labour history. Amherst was one of the towns able to take advantage of the steam-based technologies that fuelled the new industrialism of the 19th century. The town of Amherst boomed, as textile milling, boot and shoe manufacturing, gas-boiler production and railway car construction drew hundreds of people to the town. The Amherst area is a bird-watcher's paradise. The Amherst Marsh, part of the Tantramar Marsh, is an important breeding site for more than 100 species and a migratory bird stopover. At Amherst Point, just south of town, there is a migratory bird sanctuary.

There is a choice of routes from Amherst to Parrsboro. You can either follow Route 302, along a sparsely populated section of the Fundy Shore, or Highway 2, to enjoy a stop at Springhill, which remembers the bustle and tragedy of its coal mining history. Over the years, more than 400 people have died in local mines. The "Springhill Bump" of 1958, remembered more for the miraculous survival of 18 men who spent a week trapped underground than for the 75 who did not make it, brought an end to large-scale mining in the town. But it did not bring an end to tragedy. In 1975, fire ravaged the town's main street business district. Today, retired miners give underground tours at the Springhill Miners' Museum, which is built on the site of a small mine that closed in 1970.

Springhill also celebrates the success of its contribution to the continent's entertainment industry. The Anne Murray Centre pays tribute to the Springhill-born recording artist

and offers a surprisingly candid look at her life.

Those who choose to take the Fundy Shore, following Route 302 to Apple River, will see a part of the province that has long been recognized as a treasure trove of fossils. At Joggins, an old coal-mining town on Chignecto Bay, the Joggins Fossil Centre is housed in a new facility incorporating state-of-the-art green technologies. The Centre offers guided tours of the famous fossil cliffs, now a UNESCO World Heritage Site. Fossil finds, usually plant material, date from the time when Nova Scotia's vast coal deposits were formed about 300 million years ago. The cliffs themselves are off-limits, but they erode so quickly that new fossils are always falling to the beach.

The Anne Murray Centre

At Apple River, continue on Route 209, passing Cape Chignecto Provincial Park, Nova Scotia's largest provincial park — 4,000 hectares of coastal wilderness trails, dramatic cliffs and old-growth forest. This is Nova Scotia's premier hiking destination. A day park offers short hikes and views of the famous "Three Sisters" rock formation. More spectacular views can be enjoyed from the look-off at the Cape d'Or lighthouse (just off Route 209) — east toward the Minas Basin, south across the Minas Channel and west to the Bay of Fundy. A good lunch can be had in the old lightkeeper's house.

Fundy Geological Museum and Joggins Fossil Cliffs

The Bay of Fundy, like most large bodies of water, has its share of marine folklore, and one of these stories, the saga of the *Mary Celeste*, is recounted on a cairn at Spencers Island where the "ghost ship" was built. In December 1872, the brigantine was discovered at sea with sails set and everything in order but no one was on board. It would turn out to be one of the great sea mysteries of all time. More seafaring history of the area can be found at the Age of Sail Centre in nearby Port Greville.

Along the stretch of coastline between Advocate and Parrsboro, the scenery rivals the coastal views along Cape Breton's Cabot Trail. A sea kayaking company out of Advocate Harbour offers tours around the coast of Cape Chignecto Park. Across the Minas Channel, Cape Split and North Mountain loom large on a clear day, and Cape d'Or is just as spectacular.

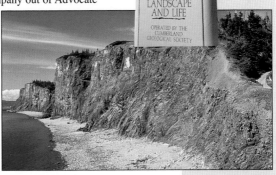

In Parrsboro, the Fundy

Examining a tidal pool on the rocky shore

Geological Museum displays geological treasures and 200-million-year-old dinosaur fossils. The museum conducts geological tours, including sites where some of the oldest dinosaur bones in Canada were found.

Good opportunities for rockhounding are plentiful in the Parrsboro area. The town holds Nova Scotia's Gem and Mineral Show each August. Zeolites — semi-precious stones such as agate and amethyst — are common finds along the beaches and cliffs of the Minas Basin. Eldon George, Parrsboro's most famous rockhound, has a rock shop at the edge of town. In April 1984, George found a rock with some very tiny — and soon to be highly celebrated — dinosaur footprints on its surface.

Parrsboro's Ship's Company Theatre stages innovative productions at a theatre built around the original MV *Kipawo*, a beached ferry boat that once serviced Parrsboro, Kingsport and Wolfville. The acclaimed company features many plays by Maritime writers during a season that runs from mid-June to Labour Day. Gillespie House Inn is one of several good B&Bs in Parrsboro.

The road from Parrsboro to the Trans-Canada Highway at Glenholme offers an opportunity to visit several quaint and historic hamlets such as Economy, Bass River, Portaupique and Great Village. Try your hand at digging clams or enjoy a feed at Diane's in Five Islands. If you stop at Five Islands Provincial Park, you can see where the legendary Glooscap threw handfuls of sod at Beaver, creating Moose, Diamond, Long, Egg and Pinnacle islands. There are a number of hiking trails in the park. Five Islands Lighthouse, a "pepper pot" wooden structure, has a terrific view of the islands. Scenic waterfalls in the region are popular destinations for hikers. A novel opportunity to observe the evolution of nature can be enjoyed at Economy Falls, where a major rock fall changed the appearance of that popular attraction in late 1997. For enjoying a respite from town life, the cottages at Four Seasons Retreat near Economy are ideal.

Truro is the commercial crossroads in the centre of the province and is known as "the Hub of Nova Scotia." Truro is a good stopping place. You can't miss the 13-metre-tall statue of Glooscap at Exit 13A off Highway 102. It marks the entrance to the Glooscap Heritage Centre, where Mi'kmaq culture is interpreted through exhibits, displays and a multimedia presentation. Truro has many shops, restaurants and hotel/motel accommodations. For something different, the John Stanfield Inn is a century house with period furnishings and fine dining. At Old Barns, just outside town, Irwin Lake Chalets offers another alternative.

Truro is also a hub for golf, with several options, including the Truro Golf Club, the oldest club in the

province. Victoria Park is a surprising 405-hectare oasis in the middle of town with shaded walking trails, waterfalls and Jacob's Ladder — about 200 wooden steps that are a challenge for even the fittest legs.

A Blues festival named for Nova Scotian blues legend Dutch Mason, dubbed "the Prime Minister of the Blues," draws big names and thousands of fans to Truro in early August.

From Truro, you can head towards Halifax or continue along the Fundy Shore to Maitland. Route 2 towards Halifax passes Stewiacke, and the pastoral 18-hole Fox Hollow golf course. A little farther along Route 2 is the Shubenacadie Wildlife Park, where most of Nova Scotia's native birds and animals can be seen in natural surroundings. A recent addition to the park is a marsh and wetland interpretative centre.

The cliffs at Cape D'Or

The village of Maitland, located at the mouth of the Shubenacadie River, flourished during the Age of Sail. At one time, 11 shipyards bordered an 11-kilometre stretch of shore near Maitland. Fortunes were made and lavish homes were built. Close to 50 of these have survived and Maitland is designated as Nova Scotia's first Heritage Conservation District. Several heritage B&Bs provide good accommodations from which to explore the Bay of Fundy. The Frieze and Roy General Store, established in 1839, is the oldest continuously operating store of its kind in Canada.

On October 27, 1874, more than 4,000 people gathered in Maitland to see the launching of the *William D Lawrence*, at nearly 2,500 gross tons the largest full-rigged ship ever built in Canada, and named after the man who built her. The village commemorates the event with a Launch Day Festival in September. At Lawrence House, designated a National Historic Site in 1965, the signs of wealth are everywhere. English ironwork radiators are topped with Italian marble. At the back of the house, you can see the huge blocks that were used to step the masts of Lawrence's ships. Not surprisingly, William Lawrence, elected to the Nova Scotia Assembly in 1863, strongly opposed Confederation, and fought for the repeal of the Union Act. The Intercolonial Railway, the linchpin of Confederation and a symbol of future prosperity, would not run through Maitland.

Continuing west from Maitland, along coastal Route 215 toward Windsor, one soon begins enjoying the scenic Noel Shore, one of the prettiest spots in the province when the horse chestnuts are in bloom in late June. At Burncoat Head, during the Saxby Gale of 1869, the highest tides in the world were recorded. There are fully equipped modern cottages at Burncoat. At low tide you can walk the ocean floor at Burncoat Head Park.

Along the Northumberland Shore: Sunrise Trail

The Sunrise Trail follows the Northumberland Shore from
Amherst to the Canso Causeway. With its picturesque
towns, gentle farmland and seaside views, this route is a
recommended alternative to the Trans-Canada Highway.
Several fine beaches and the warm waters of the
Northumberland Strait help make it a popular summer
holiday destination.

From Amherst, Route 366 takes you to Tidnish, a less-
travelled provincial gateway where the visitor information
centre displays information on the Chignecto Ship Railway,
the ambitious 19th-century venture that was to transport

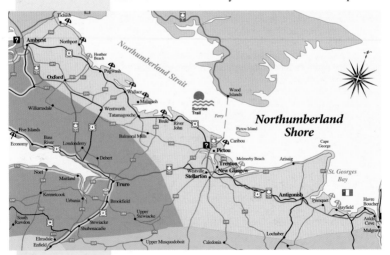

ships from the Bay of Fundy to the Northumberland Strait by rail. A 4-kilometre walking trail follows the remnants of the railbed to Tidnish Dock Provincial Park.

Not much farther, near Lorneville, is the Amherst Shore Country Inn. The inn offers four rooms and four suites, as well as a rustic seaside cottage and memorable dining. In Port Howe, Chase's Lobster Pound offers fresh live and cooked lobsters.

Pugwash, with street signs in both Gaelic and English, is one of several North Shore communities with a rich Scottish heritage. The village holds a Gathering of the Clans Festival in early July.

Jost Vineyards

During the 1950s and 1960s, wealthy Cleveland industrialist Cyrus Eaton hosted a number of Thinkers Conferences at his Pugwash estate, to which he invited Western and Soviet intellectuals. Albert Einstein was among the attendees.

Today, Pugwash is home to Seagull Pewter, Canada's largest manufacturer of pewter giftware, which ships to worldwide markets and has a large retail shop on the main road. Just outside town, serious golfers can enjoy 18 challenging holes on the Northumberland Links. The open, tree-lined fairways are well maintained. Several holes play along the water, and the views of the strait can be quite a distraction.

The views are just as striking at Ocean Links at Brule Point, overlooking Brule Harbour near Tatamagouche. But unlike the Pugwash course, this wide-open, nine-hole round of golf is well suited to beginners.

Wallace Bay is an important waterfowl migration and breeding habitat; a 4-kilometre hiking trail around diked wetlands provides good viewing.

The Josts, one of several German families to settle along the North Shore since the Second World War, have a winemaking operation in Malagash. Tours of the vineyards are provided, and visitors are invited to sample Jost wines at the on-site retail store. Good-quality, inexpensive wines, including some award-winners, are available for purchase. Blue Sea Beach, at the tip of the Malagash peninsula, is one of the finest in an area renowned for its beaches. Nearby there are excellent housekeeping cottages, with all the amenities and a private beach.

Tatamagouche Train Station Inn

In addition to a modest fishery, Tatamagouche is a service centre for local dairy farms. The historic Tatamagouche Creamery has been recently reincarnated as a farmers' market, museum complex, archival and

Balmoral Grist Mill

historical research facility and performing arts centre. Early settlement and agriculture, 290-million-year-old fossils and local giantess Anna Swan are among the museum's features. There are many cottages and B&Bs within easy reach of the many great beaches. Stone Garden Chalets, right in town, has its own beach. For railway buffs, the Train Station Inn is a treat. An eclectic café on the edge of town, Sunrise Mercantile, offers specialty yarns, gifts and gourmet foods.

Farther along, two restored mills give a glimpse of earlier times. The Balmoral Grist Mill Museum, at Balmoral Mills (Route 256), grinds wheat, oats and buckwheat into flour using 19th-century milling techniques. The Sutherland Steam Mill, in nearby Denmark (Route 326), began sawing logs into lumber in 1894 and is now part of the Nova Scotia Museum. On Route 311, between Balmoral Mills and Denmark, is Earltown and Sugar Moon Farm, a year-round Maple Sugar Camp and Pancake House.

Back on Route 6, between Tatamagouche and River John, Beach Lane Lavender Farm soothes all of the senses, with a U-pick, lavender product shop and demonstrations.

The Northumberland Strait is a choice area for the lobster fishery. The season runs from early May to late June, when communities like River John bustle. The village holds frequent lobster suppers during the season, and visitors are invited to take part. The Lismore Sheep Farm and Wool Shop is a working sheep farm where you can see some sheep and learn about wool. You can also buy wonderful wool and sheepskin items, from comforters to slippers, as well as handcrafted birch knitting needles. The many good beaches in Pictou County — such as the one at

The *Hector*

Caribou, northwest of Pictou — attract cottagers to this shoreline. For a shorter stay, you might choose the *circa* 1920 Pictou Lodge Resort on Braeshore Road, just east of the town of Pictou and 4 kilometres from the Prince Edward Island ferry. Stonehame Lodge and Chalets, at nearby Scotsburn, is a good modern alternative.

Pictou's Scottish culture, scenic harbour and fine architecture make it the

North Shore's most popular destination for visitors. And for those Nova Scotians who take great pride in their Scottish heritage, Pictou is a kind of Plymouth Rock. The *Hector*, which landed Nova Scotia's first Scots on the shores of Pictou Harbour in 1773, has been called the "Scottish Mayflower." For a Nova Scotia Scot, having ancestors aboard the *Hector* accords special status.

See highland dancing demonstrations at the Hector Festival

Today, the showpiece of Pictou's waterfront is the replica ship *Hector*, at the Hector Heritage Quay. The 33-metre-long full-rigged ship was reconstructed on-site and is now a floating heritage exhibit. Although no plans for the original *Hector* exist, engineers conducted extensive research to ensure that the reconstructed ship closely resembled its predecessor. The saga of 18th-century Scottish immigration and the Hector voyage is told in the adjacent interpretive centre. The site also includes a carpentry shop, a blacksmith shop and a gift shop — and nearby a pub for a wee dram.

During August, the Hector Festival celebrates the arrival of the ship and the town's Scottish heritage and features Scottish music, dance and food, with Celtic musical performances at the deCoste Centre on Water Street. This venue also serves as northeastern Nova Scotia's centre for the performing arts throughout the year. New Scotland Days, from mid-July through 15 September (the anniversary of the arrival of the *Hector*), feature lots of bagpipes, highland dancing and wooden-boatbuilding demonstrations.

McCulloch House

Next to the Hector National Exhibit Centre, on Old Haliburton Road, is the restored McCulloch House (now a museum), which was built in 1806 with bricks brought over from Scotland.

Pictou's architecture is another Scottish legacy. Throughout the town you can see 19th-century Neoclassical buildings, mostly of stone. Typically,

Pictou's Scottish architecture

these have gabled walls that extend above the plane of the roof at either end of the house. The Scottish dormer, recognizable by its bay window, is another prominent feature. Fine trim and mouldings lend elegance to houses that would otherwise appear stark. Some Pictou streets, especially those with row houses, could easily run through towns in western Scotland. Walking tours of the town, led by guides in period costume, are available throughout the summer.

The tourist information centre, located at the rotary just outside town, can direct you to the town's historic buildings. Several are open to visitors. The Consulate Inn (c. 1810), so named because it housed the American Consulate during the last half of the 19th century, offers bed and breakfast style accommodation in the downtown area. The Customs House Inn on the waterfront has carefully restored rooms in an 1870s brick and sandstone building that also houses a pub. The Braeside Inn, though built this century, also impresses from its hilltop perch overlooking the harbour. The inn offers fine harbour views from its two large dining rooms (seafood is a specialty) and from several of its 20 guest rooms.

Pictou's architecture and landscape also reflect its historic importance as a shipbuilding centre, and the lobster fishery keeps this a working harbour. Here, and in countless other villages along the strait, fishermen spend May and June mornings setting and unloading traps. Since 1934, the town has celebrated this fishery with the Pictou Lobster Carnival, held in early July. Local boat races, a lobster dinner and concerts featuring the best of Nova Scotia's musical talent highlight one of Nova Scotia's premier festivals. The Northumberland Fisheries Museum, housed in an old CN railway station, displays some 3,000 fishing-related artifacts; a lobster hatchery explains lobstering from start to finish.

While in town, you can also visit Grohmann Knives, known to outdoor enthusiasts as the manufacturer of the world-renowned D. H. Russell belt knife. Grohmann offers free factory tours (some restrictions apply), and the gift shop often has good buys on seconds. Nearby gift shops and galleries offer a range of crafts from local artisans.

The Pictou Golf Club, overlooking the harbour, is a fairly easy nine-hole course despite all the downhill, uphill, and side hill lies that you'll encounter. The Jitney Trail, spanning the southern portion of Pictou Harbour, is a scenic 3-kilometre pathway connecting the waterfront to the original landing site of the *Hector*.

Melmerby is the most popular of several good warm-water beaches in the Pictou area. Take Exit 25 off Highway 104 (the Trans-Canada) to get to this 2-kilometre stretch of broad, sandy beach. Melmerby is supervised and offers a canteen, shower and change facilities.

Melmerby Beach

Most of the area's heavy industry sprang up in the towns across the harbour, to the southeast of Pictou. Coal mining transformed the landscapes of Westville and Stellarton. Canada's first integrated metalmaking and metalworking complex did the same to New Glasgow and Trenton. These towns, with their long history of industrial activity, have fascinating stories to tell, including the 1992 disaster at the Westray coalmine.

There was nothing exceptional in the rise of the Pictou County coal industry; similar growth was taking place in Cape Breton and Cumberland County. It was the metals industry that relied heavily on the entrepreneurial spirit of the Pictou County elite. When shipbuilding became unprofitable in the 1880s, New Glasgow's wealthy merchant families began looking for somewhere else to put their money. What they founded — the Nova Scotia Steel and Coal Company — changed Pictou County. The populations of New Glasgow and Trenton exploded as people came to work in one of the country's foremost industrial enterprises. During the First World War, "Scotia" employed close to 6,000 miners and steelworkers. Many other Pictou County operations were busy converting Scotia's steel into a wide range of secondary metal products.

But Scotia's story is a familiar one. During the 1920s, increased freight rates, competition from central Canada and outside ownership led to a rapid decline. Pictou County industry has been teetering on the brink ever since. There were, however, some hardy survivors. Maritime Steel and Foundries Limited marked its 100th anniversary in 2002. Maritime Steel produces steel castings that are

Museum of Industry

exported around the world. The story of industrial boom and bust is told at the Nova Scotia Museum of Industry, just off the Trans-Canada Highway at Stellarton. Exhibits include two of the world's oldest steam locomotives. Children especially enjoy working on the museum's toy train assembly line. Stellarton is also where the Sobey grocery giant was born, and today is home to the corporate office of what is now the second largest grocery retailer in Canada. Westville has been

Festival of the Tartans

celebrating Canada Day in a big way for more than 100 years. Events fill the week leading up to July 1.

New Glasgow was settled by Scots in 1784, and by 1809 the town had been named after Glasgow in Scotland. A strong entrepreneurial spirit was evident even in 1809, when James William Carmichael and George Amos established a trading post and later a shipbuilding company. Today New Glasgow is a Canada Blooms riverside town with impressive Victorian architecture and scenic walking trails. Historic walking tours include one of a pioneer cemetery, the burial site of some of the *Hector* settlers. Three community museums present the history of the area, a military tribute and a sports hall of fame. The Bistro and Hebel's restaurants offer special delicacies in charming settings. On the outskirts of New Glasgow is the poignant Westray Miners Memorial.

In early August, the New Glasgow Riverfront Music Jubilee features East Coast, Canadian and international headliners. Later in August, there is the Race on the River, the Pictou County Dragon Boat Festival and the Festival of the Tartans, complete with Highland dancing and caber tossing. New Glasgow's Abercrombie Country Club is a challenging 18-hole course that punishes wayward tee shots. It is essential to book tee time in advance. Within 10 minutes of New Glasgow are Glen Lovat and Linacy Greens golf courses and Melmerby Beach.

Antigonish, along the eastern section of the North Shore, is home to St. Francis Xavier University and historic St. Ninian's Cathedral. Festival Antigonish presents live professional theatre in the 227-seat Bauer Theatre on the St. FX campus throughout the summer months. The Antigonish Highland Games, held in mid-July, include piping, Highland dancing, heavy events and track and field, making for one of Nova Scotia's best Scottish festivals. Within walking distance of the campus is the elegant Antigonish Victorian Inn. The Antigonish Golf Club is the North Shore's best 18-hole bet for spur-of-the-moment golf. It is rarely crowded on summer weekdays and provides a stiff test, playing 6,100 yards from the men's tees.

If you have time to dawdle, take Route 337 north from Antigonish along the western shore of St. George's Bay. Like many of the roads along the North Shore, this drive takes you off the beaten track. The views from the Cape George Lighthouse grounds are beautiful, and there are more scenic look-offs, good beaches for birdwatching and hiking trails along the way.

Cape Breton Island:
Cabot Trail & Ceilidh Trail
Fleur-de-Lis & Marconi Trails

Cabot Trail

It is a rare thing for a road to become more famous than any of the places it passes through, but that is what has happened with Cape Breton's Cabot Trail. Its hairpin turns and spectacular cliff-side views have been thrilling motorists since the 1930s.

If we take A. S. MacMillan (Minister of Highways during the 1920s) at his word, the decision to undertake the costly and ambitious

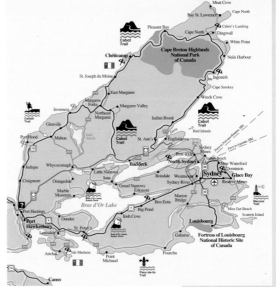

construction of the Cabot Trail was, quite literally, the result of one man's dream. In August 1924, MacMillan went to Cheticamp to look into the possibility of building a road that would extend northward to the community of

Pleasant Bay and beyond. Apparently, the trip along the northwestern shore of Cape Breton left quite an impression on the minister. He recalls, in a 1952 document reproduced in the June 1992 issue of *Cape Breton's Magazine*, what took place upon his return to Baddeck: "Some time near morning I fell asleep and dreamed about a wonderful development that I could see underway, numerous houses, cottages and tourist homes in the many bays and inlets as well as sail boats and all kinds of pleasure craft, apparently everybody enjoying themselves."

MacMillan was inspired and the rest, as he would have wanted it, is history. Today, the 300-kilometre Cabot Trail, named for the famous explorer who reputedly landed on the shores of Aspy Bay in June 1497, is a loop that takes you along most of the coastline of northwestern Cape Breton. Contrary to MacMillan's vision, much of that coastline remains undeveloped. This, however, is a good thing. Cape Breton has been named the most scenic island in North America and fourth in the world. Its unspoiled natural beauty has earned it a rating as the second-best sustainable tourism destination in the world. It is also renowned for the friendliness of its people. The Cabot Trail has become not just a scenic drive but a year-round destination, offering the best in adventure tourism: golf, hiking, sea kayaking, sailing, skiing and beaches — not to mention the stunning scenery. Outdoor adventurers will want to take most of their vacation to explore the beautiful wilderness areas in Cape Breton Highlands National Park. For the not-so-adventurous the scenery is stunning, and accommodations and dining are as good as you'll get anywhere.

Baddeck is generally considered to be the beginning and end of the Cabot Trail. However, the village was attracting summer visitors long before it earned this distinction. In 1879, Charles Dudley Warner's *Baddeck, and That Sort of Thing* was published. Though not very popular with Cape Bretoners — they were mockingly

Graham Bell Museum exhibit

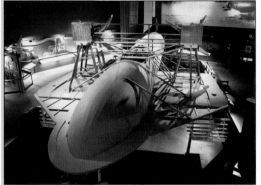

portrayed as backward and primitive for their tepees and Gaelic speech — the book's description of Baddeck's splendid isolation struck a chord with many American readers. Among those was the inventor of the telephone, Alexander Graham Bell. Seeking refuge from the hot summers of Washington, D.C., Bell and his wife,

Mabel, decided to stop at Baddeck on their way to Newfoundland for a holiday in 1885. They fell in love with the place. Eight years later, they built their estate, Beinn Bhreagh (Beautiful Mountain) on a headland overlooking the Bras d'Or Lakes. There, Alexander and Mabel spent many happy summers, until his death in 1922. Their gravesites can be found on the hillside next to Beinn Bhreagh.

Beinn Bhreagh, home of Alexander Graham Bell as viewed from Baddeck

Today, the Alexander Graham Bell National Historic Site, Nova Scotia's finest indoor museum, offers visitors to Baddeck a chance to learn a great deal about the inventor's life. The site's collection of Bell's artifacts, written materials and personal mementoes is the most comprehensive in the world.

Bell was a compulsive inventor. He may have left the Washington heat behind, but Bell brought his passion for invention and experimentation to his summer home. During his last years, the hydrofoil was Bell's special interest. Several models were built and tested in Baddeck, and a full-sized hydrofoil is housed in the museum.

Baddeck's status as a resort and tourist centre has grown since the Bell era. The friendly bustle of the village makes it a popular stopping place for visitors. Baddeck has a population of approximately 1,000 and about an equivalent number of guest rooms; even so, it is advisable to book early. The Inverary Resort has 125 rooms in five main buildings, along with 7 cottages. This full-service resort offers tennis, an indoor pool, private beach, bike rentals and a host of activities. Auberge Gisele's Inn has 75 well-appointed rooms (many overlooking the Bras d'Or Lakes) and a

Fishing on the Margaree

dining room with a select wine list. MacNeil House, on the grounds of the Silver Dart Lodge, has six luxurious suites with jacuzzis, fireplaces and kitchen facilities. Water's Edge Inn, Broadwater Inn and Lynwood Country Inn also offer fine accommodations. Just before Baddeck at Bucklaw, you will be treated like royalty at Castle Moffatt.

Baddeck's shops carry a variety of upscale handcrafts and folk art. Fine wool sweaters are sold at Seawinds Chandlery, on the government wharf. Up from the water, Kidston Landing features a wide selection of Nova Scotian crafts, woolens and country clothing. Blue Heron Gifts offers a wide selection of Nova Scotian and Cape Breton books and CDs. The Outdoorstore sells quality outdoor clothing and camping supplies.

Baddeck is full of summertime activity. Since 1904, the village has held its annual regatta in early August. Throughout the summer months, yachts are berthed at the government wharf or at private anchorages along the shores of Baddeck Bay. You can go for a tour on the Schooner *Amoeba* and view Alexander Graham Bell's stately mansion from the water. Spectacular views and great golf are to be enjoyed at the Thomas McBroom-designed Bell Bay Golf Course.

Some distance inland, near Baddeck Bridge, is Uisge Bahn Falls Provincial Park, one of the prettiest spots in all of Cape Breton. A network of maintained hiking trails leads through hardwood forest to a dramatic gorge and

Fly display at Margaree Salmon Museum

waterfalls. This is a great place for a picnic. (All the fixings for a delicious lunch are available at the Herring Choker Deli & Bakery, 1 kilometre west of the Cabot Trail entrance at Nyanza.)

When leaving the Baddeck area, you have a choice. You can head for Hunters Mountain and the Margaree Valley, which

The Margaree

would take you in a clockwise direction around the Cabot Trail, or you can take the counter-clockwise route along the shores of St. Anns Bay and north to Ingonish.

The clockwise route takes you away from the salt water and through the beautiful Margaree Valley. The Margaree is a Canadian Heritage River. Anglers should not pass it by, especially during August and September. Guides are available for salmon and backwater trout fishing. The Margaree Salmon Museum, near North East Margaree, is one of the best privately run museums in Nova Scotia. If you plan on fishing the river and even if you are not a fisher, drop in for sure. Fly fishers will have heard of John Cosseboom; the Cosseboom fly has fooled many Atlantic salmon. Cosseboom was an ardent disciple of Izaak Walton (*The Compleat Angler*) and spent many summers on the Margaree. His is one of several stories well told by the museum's wonderful collection of fishing memorabilia.

Nearby, along the mysteriously named Egypt Road, is the Normaway Inn, which has catered to anglers and others since the 1920s. The main lodge and 17 cabins (7 with jacuzzis) are within easy striking distance of some of Nova Scotia's best salmon pools. The dining room offers four-course country gourmet dinners, often followed by live traditional music.

The trail follows the Margaree until the river spills into the Gulf of St. Lawrence. There is a small sand beach to the south of Margaree Harbour and a larger sand and gravel beach to the north. The larger beach is part of a narrow sandspit that serves as a natural breakwater for the colourful fishing boats of Margaree Harbour. From here, the road bends to the northeast towards Cheticamp. At Cap Le Moine, one of several tiny Acadian villages that dot this shore, Joe's Scarecrow Theatre has been giving visitors the willies for a number of years. The Mask Making Museum (Centre de la Mi-Carême) in nearby St. Joseph du Moine exhibits locally made masks and explains the history of the winter festival La Mi-Carême still celebrated in this area.

Cheticamp is the largest and oldest Acadian village along this shore. Cheticantins take special pride in the large co-operatives that dominate the waterfront. They represent the culmination of a long struggle for independence.

When the Treaty of Paris forced the French to abandon the Gulf of St. Lawrence fishery in 1763, merchants from the English Channel Islands were quick to take their place. Charles Robin, a French Huguenot from the Isle of Jersey, set up his operation at Le Chadye (Cheticamp). He encouraged exiled Acadians who had spent time near the French port of St. Malo (just to the south of Jersey) to settle in Cheticamp, where they could work for him.

And that's just what they did for more than a century.

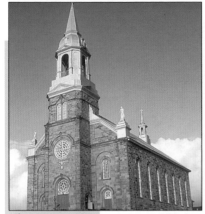

L'Église Saint-Pierre, Cheticamp

The Charles Robin Company ruled Cheticamp. It owned boats and fishing gear. Fishermen were paid in provisions from the company store. Indebtedness to the "Jerseys" was a way of life from the time the Acadians first settled Cheticamp in the 1780s until late in the 19th century.

Then Father Pierre Fiset arrived. He devoted himself to the spiritual well-being of the Cheticantins — Cheticamp's beautiful Saint-Pierre Church was built under his direction — but he also took a special interest in the worldly affairs of his parishioners. Determined to loosen the Jerseys' grip on the community, Father Fiset purchased a store in 1883. He traded in fish and livestock, and in 1888 he built a wharf on the harbour. Five years later, Father Fiset bought Cheticamp Island from the Robins. The extent of his involvement in worldly affairs troubled some clergy, but they did not question his motives.

Fiset died in 1909. Six years later, a group of fishermen founded Cheticamp's first sales co-operative. During the 1930s, they were greatly assisted by another Catholic clergyman, Reverend Moses Coady, a professor at St. Francis Xavier University in Antigonish, who was appointed by the government to help Maritime fishermen organize co-operatives. The so-called Antigonish Movement had its greatest successes in Antigonish County and Cape Breton. Today, there are seven co-operatives in the Cheticamp area — the most in any Acadian region of Nova Scotia. One of the groups to organize a co-operative in Cheticamp during the 1930s was the rug hookers. Rug hooking is an industry with a peculiar connection to the Bells and Baddeck. Cheticamp women had been hooking rugs from old rags for ages when, in 1922, Lillian Burke, an American friend of the Bells, suggested that they would be able to sell their rugs if they switched from rags to wool and began using softer colours. A cottage industry was born. Burke did well selling Cheticamp rugs in New York until 1936, when Alexandre Boudreau, a leader of the local co-op movement, suggested that the women organize themselves.

Now, the Co-opérative Artisanale de Cheticamp Ltée runs the business. Cheticamp rugs are world famous — especially those of Elizabeth LeFort, whose works can be found at the Vatican, the White House, Buckingham Palace and the Dr. Elizabeth LeFort Gallery & Museum at Les Trois Pignons (The Three Gables) in Cheticamp. Rug hooking is still a cottage industry, but it is no longer quaint. The computerized cash system in the Co-op Artisanale attests to that. Some rugs retail for $2,000 dollars. At Le

Cheticamp
hooked rug

Motif, a local gift shop featuring needlework and folk art, there are some original rag-style rugs for sale.

There are plenty more rugs (and a wide selection of Cape Breton and Nova Scotian crafts) at Flora's, one of the province's largest craft shops. But Cheticamp-area artisans do more than hook rugs. Some of Nova Scotia's most interesting folk art is produced here. You'll see colourful whirligigs and gizmos in shops and front yards throughout the Acadian villages along this coast. One of Canada's best folk artists, Bill Roach, works out of the Sunset Art Gallery in Cheticamp. His whimsical, brightly coloured woodcarvings — birds, fish and people among them — are prized by collectors worldwide.

Local artists and artisans draw strength from Cheticamp's rich Acadian culture (Acadian flags are everywhere). Locals still speak French with a 17th-century accent. Cheticantins are justifiably proud of Father Fiset's magnificent church. Saint-Pierre, overlooking the village and the bay, anchors the community. Each August, a special mass is held here during the Festival de l'Escaouette, a summer-long cultural celebration that brims with Acadian food, song and dance.

The waterfront bustles during summer. Several whalewatching cruises, deep-sea fishing charters and water tours leave from the government wharf and the Quai Mathieu waterfront boardwalk. Pilot whales and minkes are frequently sighted (fin whales less often) and the landward views of Cheticamp and the Cape Breton Highlands are spectacular.

There are a number of restaurants along the water side of Main Street that feature Acadian cuisine. Savoury meat pies and rich seafood chowders are served with thick slices of homemade bread at the Restaurant Acadien in the Co-op Artisanale. Fruit pies are made the traditional way, with flaky biscuit crusts. Several establishments on the waterfront boardwalk have outdoor patios where you can enjoy a drink and watch the sun set behind Cheticamp Island.

If you plan an overnight stay in Cheticamp, book well in advance. For the most part, the village offers motel-style

Pilot whales off the coast

accommodation along its busy Main Street. Laurie's Motor Inn has many guest amenities, including a whalewatching cruise. Across the harbour, the Cheticamp Island Resort features two-bedroom cottages with housekeeping facilities and ocean swimming. The resort offers weekly rates and is ideal for those who plan an extended stay in the Cheticamp area. Other good choices for families are Pilot Whale Chalets and Cabot Trail Sea and Golf Chalets. Le Portage, one of the Cape Breton's "Fab Four" golf courses is a good reason to stay in Cheticamp.

Just to the northeast of Cheticamp is the entrance to Cape Breton Highlands National Park. Established in 1936, the park protects about 950 square kilometres of coastline, wooded valleys and barren plateaus. If you plan to hike, cycle, fish or camp in the park, then stop at the Cheticamp Information Centre for permits and advice. Vehicle permits should be purchased at the centre by anyone intending to use park facilities. Exhibits, including interactive games for children, will introduce you to the park. To get better acquainted, visit the centre's well-stocked bookstore.

Hikers, especially, will find useful resources here. *Walking in the Highlands*, a guide to the park's 25 hiking trails, can be purchased at the centre. So can David Lawley's *Cabot Trail,* an interpretive naturalist's guide to hiking in the area. There are hikes well suited to a family stroll (like the Lone Shieling Trail near Pleasant Bay) and those with more challenging terrain (the Franey Trail, near

Carving by Bill Roach of Sunset Art

Plage St. Pierre, Cheticamp

Ingonish Beach, ascends 366 metres in only 4 kilometres). Some offer spectacular coastal scenery (like the Coastal Trail that leaves from Black Brook Beach); others climb to the barren highland plateau (the Lake of Islands Trail, near Ingonish, is a 26-kilometre-long back-country adventure). At the top of the trail, between Cheticamp and Pleasant Bay, is Skyline, the most popular trail (recently upgraded and wheelchair accessible), which affords spectacular ridgeline views. To truly appreciate the grandeur of the Cape Breton Highlands, park the car and go for a walk on any of the 26 maintained trails. Each September hikers unite at Hike the Highlands Festival, a 10-day festival of guided hikes and special events. Some of these trails are groomed for cross-country skiing in winter.

The 106-kilometre stretch of road between Cheticamp and Ingonish is what made the Cabot Trail famous. Soon after entering the park, the roller coaster ride begins — up French Mountain to a height of 455 metres, then down the other side, then another ascent, this time 372 metres to the top of MacKenzie Mountain, and down to Pleasant Bay with look-offs along the way. The view from Fishing Cove Lookoff is breathtaking, as is the 9-kilometre hike into Fishing Cove. You can camp overnight by the beach and running brook. Check with the park for a permit. On a crystal clear day you might be able to spy the Magdalene Islands to the northwest, across more than 80 kilometres of water.

Pleasant Bay, following a serpentine descent of MacKenzie Mountain (you can imagine the difficulty of a landward approach to this community before the road was built), is a scenic fishing village with a variety of visitor services. Whalewatching cruises leave from the Pleasant Bay wharf, and the Whale Interpretive Centre provides a wealth of background information with models, exhibits and interactive displays. The coastline north of Pleasant Bay is spectacular and pristine (a community of Tibetan Buddhist monks is located here); pilot whales, grey seals and bald eagles are regularly sighted. You'll find plenty of whales and seabirds among the beautiful folk art creations of Reed Timmons, a local lobsterman and gill-netter. His Pleasant Bay studio is also filled with colourful roosters.

Cape Breton Highlands National Park

From Pleasant Bay, the trail moves inland towards North Mountain. At the mountain's base is the Lone Shieling, a replica of a Scottish crofter's hut. The hut is the result of an outpouring of Scottish sentiment from a rather unlikely source. Donald MacIntosh, a native of Pleasant Bay, was a geology professor at Dalhousie University in Halifax. When he died in 1934, he left 40.5 hectares at Pleasant Bay to the Crown. His will expressed the desire that the government use the land for a small park where they would construct a cabin modelled after the Lone Shieling on the Isle of Skye. That is how a Skye crofter's cottage came to be tucked among a stand of 350-year-old sugar maples. While the cottage may leave you scratching your head, the massive trees — some are more than 36 metres tall — along the Lone Shieling hiking trail make the stop worthwhile.

From the top of North Mountain (445 metres), the Cabot Trail descends into the Aspy River valley, passing some spectacular gorges along the way. At the bottom, a dirt road leads to Beulach Bahn Falls, an ideal spot for a picnic. Nearby, Arts North is a fine craft store that features the functional and decorative pottery of Linda and Dennis Doyon, and the deceptively simple designs of jeweller Johanna Padelt. The work of other local artisans is on display in the loft.

Fishing boats in Pleasant Bay

If you have time to explore this remote and awesome part of the island, there are some very good B&B

Cabot's Landing Beach

accommodations in the area. Leave the trail here and head still farther north to Cabot's Landing (site of a picnic park and an 11-kilometre-long sandy beach) and Bay St. Lawrence. To boldly go where few tourists have gone, continue along the shores of Bay St. Lawrence to Capstick and follow the winding dirt road to Meat Cove, a drive you'll not soon forget! Watch out for moose along the road. For a landward view of the wild beauty of Cape Breton's northern tip, take a bird- and whalewatching boat tour from either Bay St. Lawrence or Dingwall on Aspy Bay. At Dingwall, Markland Coastal Resort is a luxurious base from which to hike, bike, canoe, kayak or go whalewatching. The Octagon Performing Arts Centre, adjacent to the Markland, has a full schedule of chamber and Celtic music throughout the summer.

Back in the village of Cape North, the Cabot Trail bends to the southeast, towards Ingonish. Not far from

A red fox at Meat Cove

Cape North, turn down Shore Road to reach Eagle North for kayaking excursions in South Harbour. Many prefer the alternative coastal route, which takes you through the fishing villages of Smelt Brook, White Point, New Haven and Neils Harbour. At the end of the village of White Point, there is a hiking trail that gives spectacular views of the Aspy Ridge. At Neils Harbour, the Chowder House restaurant makes good use of the

village's active fishery in its thick seafood chowders. You can see the fishing fleet from the restaurant and walk down to the edge of the Atlantic after your meal.

From Neils Harbour the trail heads south towards Ingonish. On a hot day stop at Black Brook Beach along the way. The water is reasonably warm and there are usually great waves for body surfing and boogie boarding (the left side of the beach is less rocky). There is a waterfall next to the beach.

The Ingonish area is the resort centre on the Cabot Trail's eastern shore. The beaches are wonderful. The challenging Highlands Links Golf Course was recently rated by *SCOREGolf* magazine as the best public course in

Meat Cove

Canada, and as one of the world's top 100 courses by *Golf* magazine. The Middle Head hiking trail runs the length of the narrow peninsula that separates South Bay Ingonish from North Bay Ingonish. Cliff-side views, including an offshore colony of nesting terns at the trail's end, are ample reward for a relatively easy hike. This same promontory is also the site of the provincially owned Keltic Lodge. Other accommodations in the Ingonish area are more modestly priced, but some visitors are willing to pay a premium for the lodge's commanding view of Ingonish Beach and South Bay. The Purple Thistle dining room at the Keltic features fresh seafood and local produce, elegantly presented. The lodge also offers the weary traveller luxury pampering at its Aveda Spa overlooking Ingonish Beach. Sit in the outdoor hot tub and take in the magnificent scenery. There is more fine dining at Castlerock Inn in nearby Ingonish Ferry.

There is ample opportunity to survey the waters of South Bay Ingonish. Whalewatching cruises leave from the ports of Ingonish Beach, North Ingonish and Ingonish Ferry. Minke and pilot whales are frequently sighted, and the coastline is pocked with sea caves and unusual rock formations.

After Ingonish, the Cabot Trail snakes its way up and down Cape Smokey — steel yourself for yet another spectacular view before heading south on the home stretch. Unique gifts and clothing (including period costume) are displayed at Sew Inclined in Wreck Cove. Numerous arts and crafts shops are worth a stop along the North Shore, including glass artisans and woodsmiths. In Indian Brook you can see the creations of one of Cape Breton's best artisans at Leather Works. John Roberts got his start in handmade historic leatherwork when someone from Louisbourg approached him to make reproductions for the fortress.

Several lovely accommodations have sprung up in the St. Anns Bay region in the past few years, including Sea Parrot Ocean View Manor, Cabot Shores Adventure and Retreat Centre and Chanterelle Country Inn. Some are luxury accommodations, including outdoor hot tubs and oceanside swimming.

At the Barachois River Bridge the road forks. Route 312 takes you to Englishtown via a short ferry ride across

The Keltic Lodge

St. Anns Harbour. (While waiting for the ferry you can visit Sea Shanty Antique and Crafts, where the quilts — old and new — are of special interest.) Englishtown was home to Angus MacAskill, Cape Breton's famous 2.4-metre, 193-kilogram giant.

From the Barachois River Bridge, the Cabot Trail twists its way toward South Gut St. Anns. Beginning at Tarbotvale, the road passes several interesting craft shops. Iron Art & Photography is owned by Gordon and Carol Kennedy. Shape Shift Pottery at North River sells beautiful stoneware and porcelain pottery.

The Gaelic College of Celtic Arts and Crafts, the only Gaelic College in North America, teaches traditional Highland music, dance and craft on the shores of South Haven, St. Anns. The Gaelic language is also taught during the six-week summer session. The Gaelic Mod, a festival of Celtic culture, and a festival of Cape Breton fiddling are held here each August.

The Bras d'Or Lakes form Cape Breton's 1,165-square-kilometre inland sea. Two narrow channels — Great Bras d'Or and St. Andrews — and a canal at St. Peter's link this sailors' mecca to the North Atlantic. Numerous islands,

Sew Inclined, Wreck Cove

harbours, coves and saltwater ponds provide shelter from ocean storms, and the region is virtually fog-free.

At the Atlantic entrance to the Great Bras d'Or Channel there are two islands, Ciboux and Hertford. Each summer the "Bird Islands" host Nova Scotia's largest colony of breeding sea birds —

153

Gaelic College of Celtic Arts and Crafts, South Gut St. Anns

razorbills, guillemots, gulls, kittiwakes, cormorants and the feature attraction, Atlantic puffins. Bird Island Boat Tours operates out of Big Bras d'Or, on Boularderie Island. The two-and-a-half hour boat trip skirts the shores of both islands and the Van Schaiks.

Its favourable climate, abundant wildlife and outstanding natural beauty have long drawn people to the shores of the Bras d'Or. The Mi'kmaq have been here for centuries. Today, there are four reserves in the area, including Eskasoni, the largest in the province.

The Bras d'Or Lakes Scenic Drive is a signed series of roads skirting almost the entire coastline of the Bras d'Or. It can be accessed at a number of different points. Setting out from Baddeck, head south on the Trans-Canada Highway. Wagmatcook Reserve, just past Nyanza, has a Culture and Heritage Centre that demonstrates and interprets Mi'kmaq culture and history from early times to the present. It also has a unique native crafts shop. Farther along at Whycocomagh, the Googoo family has been running the Negemow basket shop for more than 30 years. (Before that, baskets were sold door-to-door.) The craftsmanship is exceptional; so is the smell of sweet grass. Follow the signs with the eagle along the south coast, passing through Orangedale, where the railway station immortalized in the song "Orangedale Station" is now a museum. Continue on the Marble Mountain Road through coves and inlets that are the habitat of many shorebirds and bald eagles.

Perhaps the best view of the Bras d'Or is from Marble Mountain, overlooking West Bay. A steep trail to the abandoned quarry (750 men once mined this hillside) starts from the main road, directly across from a small look-off and picnic area. Interesting old workings provide a good excuse to stop and catch your breath on the way up. The view from the top — islet-studded West Bay and the wide-open waters of the Bras d'Or — will stay with you long after you descend the mountain. Back at the look-off on the main road, a steep path leads downhill to a beach of crushed marble sand. The turquoise water is ice-cold (several spring-fed brooks flow down the hillside) and crystal-clear.

The Dundee Resort is at the head of West Bay. The resort's 60 hotel rooms and 39 cottages are spread out over 223 hectares. Dundee has all the amenities, including an 18-hole championship golf course. The course was built on

a steep slope overlooking the bay, making for great views and challenging golf. The resort also has a large marina where you can arrange a cruise on the Bras d'Or.

At Roberta, not far from Dundee, Kayak Cape Breton offers guided sea-kayaking trips on the Bras d'Or and along the Atlantic Coast. The sheltered waters of the Bras d'Or are ideal for beginners.

Continuing along the scenic south shore of the lake brings you to St. Peter's. You can picnic beside St. Peters Canal, a National Historic Site, while watching ships and pleasure craft pass through the old locks from the Atlantic to the Bras d'Or Lakes. At MacIsaac Kiltmakers, you can order a custom kilt or see how one is made. Next door is the home (now a museum) of renowned photographer Wallace MacAskill. The *Bluenose* on the Canadian dime is from one of MacAskill's prints.

Dundee Resort

At Chapel Island Reserve, one of the oldest Mi'kmaq settlements in the province, a powwow is held in late July featuring traditional dancing, drumming and feasting.

Big Pond is the home of Cape Breton singer Rita MacNeil. Many of her awards and records are on display at Rita's Tea Room, in a converted one-room schoolhouse. You may well see Rita here or at the Big Pond Festival, a weeklong celebration of folk music held each July.

Continue through the charming village of East Bay and the Eskasoni First Nations Reserve to the Grand Narrows Bridge. Across the bridge is Iona, site of the Nova Scotia Museum's Highland Village.

Bras d'Or also attracted European settlers — mostly Scots, like the MacNeils from the Hebridean Island of Barra, who came to Iona towards the end of the 18th century. In 1956, Iona was chosen by the Association of Scottish Societies as the site for a proposed village that would depict the evolution of Scottish settlement in this part of Nova Scotia. Overlooking the Barra Strait, the Nova Scotia Highland Village tells its story through a series of 10 structures, beginning with a Hebridean Black House and ending with an early 20th-century home. Also included in the tour are a blacksmith forge, carding mill and a 19th-century church, recently relocated to the site after being floated down the lake from the community of Malagawatch.

From Iona you have two choices. You can take a car ferry at Little Narrows back to Highway 105, on which you can return to Baddeck or go to the Canso Causeway. Or, if you want to complete the drive around the northern loop of the Bras d'Or, recross the Grand Narrows bridge and

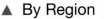

The Margaree
Valley

follow Route 223.

If you have travelled from the Canso Causeway to
Baddeck via the Trans-Canada Highway and driven the
Cabot Trail in a counter-clockwise direction, you might
carry on through the Margaree Valley towards Margaree
Forks and back to the 105. Or, if you are returning to the
Canso Causeway, you might consider taking the alternative
Route 19 (the Ceilidh Trail) at Margaree Forks. The
Ceilidh Trail, as its name suggests, is the musical heartland
of Cape Breton. It passes through villages like Judique and
Mabou that have produced Celtic music luminaries John
Allan Cameron, Natalie MacMaster, the Rankins, Celtic
"bad boy" Ashley MacIsaac and many others. The Western
Shore's strong Scottish identity is preserved in its music,
schools and institutions. Mabou and Port Hood offer Gaelic
in their schools. The series of summer ceilidhs and square
dances held along the shore at Broad Cove, held between
Margaree Valley and Judique, draw great crowds from the
local population as well as visitors.

The Ceilidh Trail rivals the Cabot Trail for beautiful (if
more pastoral) views — especially between Inverness and
Mabou and along the Colindale Road between Mabou and
Port Hood. And there is great saltwater swimming at
Inverness, Mabou and Port Hood beaches, as well as the
shore road between Port Hood and Judique. (The water of
the Northumberland Strait is comfortably warm during
summer.)

Glenora Inn and
Distillery

Inverness is the largest community on the Ceilidh Trail
and provides all services. The Inverness Miners' Museum

presents the coal mining history of
the area. Local arts and crafts are
available here and at the Inverness
County Centre for the Arts. Just 5
kilometres from Inverness is Broad
Cove, site of one of the biggest
Scottish music events of the year.
The Broad Cove Concert has been
held on the last Sunday in July
since 1957. Accommodations in the
area include motels, cottages and
bed and breakfasts. The Mabou
Highlands hiking trail provides

panoramic views of the highlands and seascapes and opportunities for bald eagle sightings.

The Glenora Inn & Distillery Resort offers nine comfortable rooms, as well as six hillside chalets in a unique complex. Glenora is North America's only distiller of single malt whisky. Tours are provided and the single malt, Kenloch, is on sale in the gift shop. Inland from Glenville, amidst the rolling hills of the Mabou Highlands, is Lake Ainslie. The 53-kilometre, fairly level, route around the lake is a popular cycling trail. In West Lake Ainslie, Tulloch Inn, with six bright, airy rooms, licensed dining room and gift shop, caters to environmental sensitivities.

Ashley MacIsaac

The Duncreigan Country Inn, overlooking Mabou Harbour, has eight spacious guest rooms with bay windows. The menu at the inn's excellent dining room includes seafood and local lamb seasoned with garden-fresh herbs. An on-site gift shop features the work of Maritime artists and artisans. The Mull Café and Deli, operated by the Mullendores of The Duncreigan, offers informal, family oriented dining with the same quality you'd find at the inn. The Red Shoe Pub, owned by the musically famed Rankin sisters, is housed in an extensively renovated, 130-year-old Mabou storefront. The Shoe features traditional music every evening and offers a full menu of Nova Scotia home cooking until closing seven days a week. The An Drochaid (The Bridge) Museum in Mabou presents the Gaelic culture of the area.

Port Hood marks the end of the Mabou Highlands, which stretch from Inverness and Lake Ainslie. Port Hood is a full-service community with some fine accommodation and dining. Haus Treuburg Inn & Cottages is a heritage house with European-style cottages. Its licensed gourmet restaurant features a unique "German Sunday morning breakfast" available daily. There are a number of warm-water beaches around Port Hood. The Chestico Museum reflects the history of the Port Hood area and traces rural life over the last 200 years.

Judique is another staunchly Scottish community, whose musical traditions are preserved and promoted at the Celtic Music Interpretive Centre. Find out about performances and ceilidhs by visiting the centre's website at www.celticmusicsite.com.

If the Cabot Trail is your destination, it may be well worth your while to plan on making the journey one way,

Cap Auguet
Eco-Trail Area,
Isle Madame

either up or back, along the richly scenic and cultural
Ceilidh Trail.

Fleur-de-Lis and Marconi Trails

The eastern edge of Cape Breton Island has a French
flavour. Starting at Port Hawkesbury, near the Canso
Causeway, the Fleur-de-Lis Trail follows the rugged
coastline through picturesque Acadian villages. Fishing has
been a way of life along this coast since Basque and
Portuguese fishermen sought shelter here in the early
1500s. In little coves and harbours you will see colourful
houses, lovely wooden churches and wharves stacked with
nets and traps. You will hear French spoken and taste
Acadian cuisine along the way. At the magnificent Fortress
of Louisbourg National Historic Site, the Fleur-de-Lis Trail
meets the Marconi Trail, which carries on to Glace Bay,
linking three sites of Guglielmo Marconi's historic wireless
transmissions.

At Louisdale, cross the Lennox Passage Bridge to the
cluster of islands that make up lovely Isle Madame, where
there are picturesque old fishing villages. Arichat was a
busy seaport in the mid-18th century and throughout the
era of tall ships. Le Noir Forge museum, on the waterfront,
is a restored French stone blacksmith shop. There are
several accommodations in Arichat. L'Auberge Acadienne
has eight rooms in the inn, nine motel units and a dining
room. Vollmer's Island Paradise on nearby Janvrin Island
offers six fully equipped log cottages and a small — but
very good — dining room. You must book a day or two in
advance, as all the meals are made from scratch. Petit-de-
Grat is the oldest fishing settlement in the area. Nearby,
Little Anse is a picturesque spot with a hiking trail leading
to a view of the lighthouse that guards the entrance to the
Strait of Canso. With its many little coves, bays and inlets,
this area is well suited to exploring by sea kayak. Cycling
is also a good way to see Isle Madame. D'Escousse, settled
in the 1700s, is another pretty fishing village. Rejoining
Route 4 on the mainland you will pass through scenic
River Bourgeois to historic St. Peter's. The trail follows
Route 247 to L'Ardoise. The excellent sandy beach at
nearby Point Michaud is a good place to stop for a picnic.
Continuing on, Route 327 leads to Marion Bridge, "down
on the Mira," the river of the famous song, which is also
famous for fishing. Nearby, Two Rivers Wildlife Park

displays many native Nova Scotian animals in a natural setting overlooking the Mira and Salmon rivers.

A trip to Louisbourg, where the reconstructed Fortress of Louisbourg National Historic Site brings history to life, provides one of the province's most rewarding experiences.

Tourism has replaced the fishery as the economic mainstay of the modern town, which is situated at the sheltered northern end of the harbour. The Louisbourg lighthouse is adjacent to the ruins of Canada's first lighthouse, which dates back to 1734. Visitors can enjoy a stroll along the harbourfront boardwalk, and nearby are Louisbourg Market Square, shops, museums, a ship chandlery, accommodations and a post office.

Visitors can take in live theatre and Cape Breton music at the 17th-century-style Louisbourg Playhouse during the summer and fall, and in early August the Louisbourg Crab Festival celebrates the bounty of the sea. The Sydney & Louisbourg Railway Museum houses the visitor information centre, along with exhibits and rolling stock that tell the story of the railway and railway technology.

A few minutes' drive from the town, you will find the entrance to the 18th-century fortress and the gateway to a living museum.

By the Treaty of Utrecht in 1713, the French agreed to leave their fishing station at Placentia, in Newfoundland, and give up Acadia (which included present-day mainland Nova Scotia) to the British. In exchange, France was allowed to hold onto the islands in the Gulf of St. Lawrence. Île-Royale (Cape Breton) would emerge as the most important of these, and within a short time, the French had established the Fortress of Louisbourg on its southeastern shore. There, they were soon landing 13.6 million kilograms of cod a year, worth two to three times the value of the fur trade of Quebec and Montreal. They also had an imposing fortress that lay between the British colonies of Newfoundland and Nova Scotia and, in the fishery, a ready-made training ground for their navy. It is no wonder that the French said of the bargain that they had received an ingot of gold for a bar of silver.

As an entrepôt — a clearinghouse for commodities from France, New France, New England and the West

Indies — Louisbourg flourished. Outbound ships, their holds brimming with cod, would return to Louisbourg laden with West Indian rum and sugar, cloths from Carcassonne and the wines of Provence. Enticed by such rich cargoes, wealthy New England merchants supplied wood products and foodstuffs in exchange for them. To a lesser extent, traders from Nova Scotia and Quebec did the same. Atlantic trade filled Louisbourg's harbour and quickened its waterfront.

The quay was a lively place. Scores of shallops (small boats) manoeuvred between large traders so that fishermen could bring their codfish to shore, where they would soon be drying on flakes. Sailors on leave crowded into the inns and taverns that lined the south side of the quay — and Louisbourg fathers made sure their daughters were accounted for. Commercial necessity overcame the difficulty of haggling with someone who spoke a different language. Goods flowed back and forth between ship and shore.

By 1760 it was over — the town deserted, the fortress destroyed. Louisbourg's commercial promise had been fulfilled, but its military promise had not.

Twice in its short history, Louisbourg fell. When France declared war on Britain in 1744, Louisbourg's commander went on the offensive in the New World, and the British outpost at Canso was captured. A campaign against Annapolis Royal was less successful, but reprisals seemed unlikely. Louisbourg was too well defended and the British seemed unwilling to expend much effort against it.

An attack did come in 1745 — from an unexpected quarter. William Shirley, Governor of Massachusetts, succeeded in raising a force of 4,000 New England militiamen for the purpose. Shirley was strongly supported by wealthy merchants, and the proposed campaign was, in part, a reflection of their desire to take over control of the rich Louisbourg fishery. The militia, under the leadership of General Pepperell, and with the help of a British naval squadron from the West Indies, succeeded in taking the fortress after a 46-day siege.

During the intense negotiations that followed the end of the war in 1748, the British sacrificed Louisbourg in order to hold on to some of their European gains. The following year, Louisbourg was returned to the French. New Englanders were outraged.

In 1756, when war broke out again, the British strategy was to attack France through its colonies and foreign trade. Louisbourg was an obvious target. The town endured several blockades until 1758, when an irresistible combination of British land and sea power overwhelmed the fortress. The French surrendered Louisbourg in July. Two years later, rather than run the risk that Louisbourg would be returned to the French in future negotiations, British engineers were ordered to blow up the fortifications.

The town barely survived. A few people settled in the sheltered northern end of the harbour. Daily, fishermen made the melancholy trip out of the harbour, past the Royal Battery, around Careening Point, to gaze upon the desolation of the fortress on their way to the fishing grounds.

The reconstruction of Fortress Louisbourg began in 1963 as a creative response to severe unemployment in Cape Breton's coal mines. More than 150 out-of-work coal miners were employed in the project as stonemasons, labourers and carpenters. Researchers had found the original drawings for the military buildings in Paris. Archaeological and graphic evidence was used to reconstruct civilian buildings. The entire effort was characterized by a meticulous devotion to Louisbourg's past.

Proof of this devotion abounds. Buildings sit on their original foundations. Dormer windows jut from gabled roofs, as they did in Poitou, Saintonge and Brittany in the 18th century. Plank siding and a clutter of chimneys speak to an ongoing struggle with cold and damp. Everywhere, timber, sod, stone, mortar and mud have been used to resurrect one-quarter of the original town — more than 50 buildings in all.

Louisbourg's authenticity goes beyond architecture. Bread is baked in the Royal Bakery; savoury dishes simmer in the Engineer's House. The Governor's Apartments are appointed according to Governor Jean-Baptiste-Louis Le Prevost Duquesnel's inventory. They are comfortable and luxurious, well suited to sipping fine Bordeaux. This is a marked contrast to the Hotel de la Marine — a sturdy tavern run by a fisherman where rum and sapinette (spruce beer) flowed freely.

Finally, there are the people. Parks Canada has endeavoured to recreate a moment in the summer of 1744, and the players know their roles. And, whether by design or not, they seem to fit them. The woman who plays the 18th-century harpsichord in the Ordonnateur's Property does not look out of place. Neither do the soldiers who bear precise reproductions of 1734 French-made flintlock

View of reconstructed French City, Fortress of Louisbourg

Costumed interpreters at the Fortress of Louisbourg

muskets. The man carting firewood to houses along the quay looks just right. Children roll hoops through the streets.

Plan on taking an entire day to fully appreciate Fortress Louisbourg. Ask questions of those who work there. Their answers do more than just inform — they lend flavour to this 18th-century French garrison town.

Should you choose to stay overnight in the town of Louisbourg, there are many good accommodations available. The Louisbourg Harbour Inn is a century-old sea captain's house with balconies overlooking the fortress and the harbour. Five of the inn's eight rooms have jacuzzis. Louisbourg Heritage House B&B is a handsomely restored Victorian (c.1886) rectory with six guest rooms. Close to the fortress entrance, the Cranberry Cove Inn is another restored turn-of-the-century home. It, too, combines antique furnishings and other traditional touches with modern conveniences like gas fireplaces and jacuzzis. Point of View Suites, at the Louisbourg gates, offers views of the fortress and the ocean from its 16 suites, as well as nightly lobster and crab dinners. There is also an RV park near the fortress.

The former city of Sydney, now the hub of Cape Breton Regional Municipality, has long prided itself on being the "industrial heart of Cape Breton." Founded in 1785 by Col. J. F. W. DesBarres, Sydney was first settled by Loyalists from New York State, who were followed by immigrants from the Scottish Highlands. The construction early in this century of the Dominion Steel and Coal Company steel plant (now Sydney Steel) took full advantage of the large protected harbour and provided the mainstay of the city's economy for nearly 100 years.

Wentworth Park, a narrow green area near the city centre, has duck ponds, walking paths, picnic areas and a bandstand. A 3-kilometre boardwalk along the harbourfront is a focal point of summer activity. Cossit House, built in 1787 on Charlotte Street, is the city's oldest, and now is a provincial museum. Nearby are Jost Heritage House and the Cape Breton Centre for Heritage and Science. Tiny St. Patrick's Church, the oldest Catholic Church in Cape Breton, has been restored as a museum depicting Sydney's past. Centre 200 is the venue for sports and culture events throughout the year.

Canadian aboriginal and local Mi'kmaq arts and crafts are available at Petroglyph Gifts in the Membertou Trade and Convention Centre. The centre houses a steak and seafood restaurant. The Cambridge Suites and Delta hotels offer reliable accommodation in Sydney, as do some very good B&Bs. There is a casino in Sydney.

In other parts of this area there are still places that reveal the pride and prosperity that were such a part of the island's past. The Gowrie House in Sydney Mines was

built in 1830 for Samuel Archibald, agent-general of the General Mining Association, which ran the coal mines. It remained in the Archibald family until 1975, when the present owner purchased it. For an overnight stay in metropolitan Cape Breton, there is no better spot. Guest rooms and common areas have since been furnished with beautiful things — Staffordshire figurines, Chippendale chairs and more. A four-course dinner is served each evening; reservations are a must. Visitors to and from Newfoundland find the Gowrie House especially convenient, as it is only minutes away from the ferry terminal in North Sydney.

In Glace Bay, the Savoy Theatre on Union Street is another reminder of a time when Cape Breton industry boomed and the population of coal-mining towns exploded. Built in 1901, the theatre quickly became the venue for a host of cultural activities that Glace Bay residents demanded and could easily support. When the entire Union Street block burned to the ground in 1927, Glace Bay's prosperity was on the wane, but still sufficient enough to quickly rebuild the Savoy — this time with ornamental touches that included the iron rococo chandeliers that hang from the ceiling today. The 761-seat theatre stages theatrical and musical productions throughout the year and is considered one of the finest performance venues in the Atlantic region.

At the edge of town, a national historic site commemorates Guglielmo Marconi's experiments with wireless communication. After he received the first trans-Atlantic signal at St. John's, Newfoundland, in 1901, several Canadian communities courted Marconi. He chose to conduct his experiments in Glace Bay. In December 1902, Marconi successfully transmitted signals from here to Poldhu, Cornwall. His story is well told at the museum.

Visitors to Glace Bay can also take an underground tour at the Cape Breton Miners' Museum. Retired coal miners tell of the dangerous and gritty life below the surface, and of the men who died in explosions, cave-ins, floods and even in union clashes with company police. The Men of the Deeps, a choir of Cape Breton coal miners, which has gained worldwide recognition, performs several concerts at the museum during the summer.

Along the Eastern Shore:
Marine Drive

Martinique Beach

The Eastern Shore, which extends along the Atlantic coast between Halifax and Canso, is rugged and relatively undeveloped. A vast network of wilderness lakes and rivers makes the area a favourite with canoeists and campers, hikers and bird watchers. Coastal kayaking is also popular, especially in the area around Tangier. Outdoor enthusiasts can explore the beaches, harbours and islands or the inland forests, lakes and rivers. Several good museums interpret the fishing, lumbering and gold-mining history of this coast.

But to those who choose the Eastern Shore's Marine Drive as an alternative to the Trans-Canada Highway for the trip from Halifax to Cape Breton, take heed. You will find some spectacular coastal scenery, but the 400-kilometre drive along winding roads is best spread over two days.

Eastern Shore

Lawrencetown Beach

Lawrencetown Beach is just east of Dartmouth. A provincial park, this steep, sandy beach is supervised from the end of June to early September and has change and canteen facilities. Lawrencetown is relatively exposed, and large waves make it a favourite with Nova Scotia surfers and windsurfers.

Farther along, to the south of Musquodoboit Harbour, is Martinique Beach (the name is tropical, but the crystal-clear water is not). Because of its distance from Halifax, on some summer days you will have this 5-kilometre-long stretch to yourself. The fine white sand hardens at the waterline, making Martinique ideal for long walks. Nearby, the Martinique Beach Game Sanctuary is the northernmost wintering ground of the Canada goose. Auberge Salmon River House Country Inn, at Salmon River Bridge, offers 7 well-appointed guest rooms in an area where accommodations are scarce. On-site outdoor activities include hiking, boating, hunting and fishing. The Fisherman's Life Museum in neighbouring Jeddore Oyster Pond recalls the lives of a turn-of-the-century inshore fisherman, his wife and their 13 daughters. The museum's costumed interpreters are local people who have some wonderful stories to tell.

At Lake Charlotte, Memory Lane Heritage Village recalls the more recent past — rural Nova Scotia in the 40s, with bicycles and a 1949 truck for touring the site. You can get a lumberjack meal at the cookhouse.

Clam Harbour Beach comes next. Its fine, white sand is ideal for sandcastles. In mid-August, thousands come here for the Clam Harbour Beach Sandcastle and Sculpture Contest, with group and individual competitions for young and old. Some of the sculptures are extremely intricate. On Route 224 toward Middle Musquodoboit is the Moose River Gold Mines Museum, which describes gold mining history and the famous mine disaster of 1936.

Highway 7 continues east through Tangier on its way towards Sherbrooke Village. Tangier is home to Willy Krauch's Danish Smokehouse. Open year-round, Krauch's wood-smoked salmon, eel and mackerel have won customers from around the world. Tangier is the centre for sea kayaking. Sea birds, seals and wrecks can be seen from its many inlets and islands. Lessons, rentals and tours can be arranged here.

Sherbrooke Village

Farther along Highway 7, on a peninsula that juts into the Atlantic, is Taylor Head Provincial Park, where there are a number of boardwalks and trails. Both the beach and the views of the ocean are spectacular.

Sherbrooke Village has been restored to appear as it was during the last half of the 19th century. Area residents work at the village dressed in period costumes and take pride in its lumbering and shipbuilding history. The result is a low-key living museum, where the past rubs shoulders comfortably with the present.

This area along the banks of the St. Marys River has attracted many people over the centuries. The Mi'kmaq were drawn by the large runs of salmon in the river, as were New England fishermen. In 1755, the French established a fur trading post here (Fort Sainte Marie), where they traded with the Mi'kmaq, fished and cultivated the soil until they were driven out by an English force in 1769.

Around 1800, about 50 settlers from the Truro and Pictou areas moved cross-country to establish new homes. The new arrivals took advantage of the area's most valuable resource, timber, and sawmills began producing lumber for small shipbuilding operations. Sherbrooke, so named in 1815 after Sir John Coape Sherbrooke, Lieutenant-Governor of Nova Scotia, exported timber to Great Britain in locally built ships. Families like the Cummingers and the MacDonalds were involved in both ends of the operation, and grew quite wealthy. During the 1860s and 1870s, their shipyards turned out several barques in excess of 500 tons for the carrying trade, as well as many smaller boats for the fishery.

The contributions of these families feature prominently in the restored village. The general store was operated by the Cumminger brothers, Samuel and John. You need only look at the store's elaborate counters to gain some appreciation of their wealth and the woodworking skills associated with shipbuilding. Superior craftsmanship is also apparent at Greenwood Cottage, built by John and Sarah Cumminger in 1871.

The reconstruction of the MacDonald Brothers' water-powered, up-and-down sawmill is located a few minutes

Sawmill at
Sherbrooke Village

away from the main village, and it is wonderful. You can feel the power of the water wheel and see it in the rise and fall of the huge saw blade. All the workings — great belts and pulleys — are exposed.

There is much more. Sherbrooke Village has a blacksmith shop, which has operated continuously since it was built in 1870. The Sherbrooke Drug Store was given most of its stock by the Nova Scotia Pharmaceutical Society and has a wonderful display of turn-of-the-century medicines. Among the many other buildings on-site are a Temperance Hall, a boat building shop, a village potter, a Presbyterian church and a courthouse. Tea and more substantial meals are served at the What Cheer Tea Room. One of the largest salmon smokehouses in Canada is situated on the St. Marys River near Sherbrooke.

The provincially run Liscombe Lodge Resort and Conference Centre at nearby Liscomb Mills (about 20 minutes from Sherbrooke Village) offers first-rate accommodation in the lodge or cottages and chalets in peaceful riverside surroundings with beautiful walking trails.

The lighthouse at Port Bickerton, which protected the region's seafaring folk since the 1920s, has been refurbished to its original decor, and has been reopened as the Nova Scotia Lighthouse Interpretive Centre. Inside, interpretive panels show the history behind the 166 lights that dot Nova Scotia's coastline. Visitors can also find detailed information on the Sable Island and Sambro lighthouses, along with local history concerning the 16 lights in Guysborough County. Stepping from old to new, there is a CD-ROM in English and German, detailing all of the Guysborough County lights. A trail leads from the lighthouse to a beautiful sandy beach.

Lighthouse at Port
Bickerton

Country Harbour is crossed by a ferry that makes regular crossings year-round. Along this wild and rugged stretch of coastline from Isaacs Harbour to Canso are several interesting little communities that provide shelter and necessaries. If you want to stop along the way and savour the sea for a while, there are secluded housekeeping bungalows at New Harbour, and an inn with all the amenities and fine dining at Charlos Cove.

Near the end of a peninsula that juts far out into the Atlantic is the fishing village of Canso, one of Nova Scotia's oldest communities. The widow's walk at Whitman House, home of the Canso Museum, offers a splendid view.

It was the rugged and beautiful nature of this area that inspired some of the most memorable songs of Stan Rogers. His music and his place in local folklore are celebrated at the Stan Rogers Folk Festival in early July. Offshore, Grassy Island was the site of a community of New England fishermen and merchants that prospered until 1744, when the fishing station was sacked by a French force from Louisbourg. The Canso Islands National Historic Site visitor centre tells the story through a brief audiovisual presentation and a series of life-size exhibits detailing the interiors of three Grassy Island properties — a tavern, a merchant's house and the home of a military officer. Between June and mid-September, a daily boat service takes visitors to the island, where an interpretive trail links 8 designated sites.

Route 16 along the edge of Chedabucto Bay takes you to the old town of Guysborough. Along the way you will pass the Queensport lighthouse, and at Halfway Cove, another lighthouse museum. Whales can sometimes be spotted from the road. At Guysborough you will find luxury accommodation at the gracious DesBarres Manor Inn, good food and ale at The Rare Bird, a lively waterfront brewpub, a snug harbour with full-service marina and a delightful gallery, Skipping Stone, showcasing Nova Scotia artists and crafts. At Boylston you can either continue on Route 6, a faster inland route to Trans-Canada Highway 104, or complete the Marine Drive on Route 344 that hugs the scenic coast until Aulds Cove and the Canso Causeway to Cape Breton.

The Eastern Shore is a popular place for sea kayaking

Listings: Contents

★ **denotes a location recognized by the publisher for its high quality.**

Getting There

By Land

The Trans-Canada Highway enters Nova Scotia from New Brunswick. Visitors from the United States must pass through Canada Customs checkpoints before entering the country.

- Greyhound from New York (800 231-2222) connects with Acadian Lines (800 567-5151; www.acadianbus.com) in Bangor, Maine, and Orléans Express from Montreal (888 999-3977; www.orleansexpress.com) connects with Acadian in New Brunswick for service to most Nova Scotia destinations.
- VIA Rail Canada (888 842-7245) provides train service to Halifax via Montreal.
- The 12.9-kilometre Confederation Bridge joins Borden-Carleton, Prince Edward Island, and Cape Jourimain, New Brunswick, near the Nova Scotia border.

By Sea

There are several options for car-ferry trips to Nova Scotia.

Bar Harbor, Maine, or Portland, Maine to Yarmouth, Nova Scotia

Daily service from May to October aboard the Cat. Contact: Bay Ferries Ltd., 877 359-3760; www.catferry.com.

Saint John, New Brunswick to Digby, Nova Scotia

Daily ferry service across the Bay of Fundy. Contact Bay Ferries Ltd., 888 249-7245; www.nfl-bay.com for up-to-date information.

Prince Edward Island to Nova Scotia

Daily service between May 1 and December 20 from Wood Islands, PEI, to Caribou, NS. Northumberland Ferries, 800 565-0201 in NS or PEI; elsewhere 902 566-3838. No reservations.

Newfoundland to North Sydney, Nova Scotia

Daily service from Port-aux-Basques to North Sydney; additional service during peak periods. Tuesday, Thursday and Saturday service from Argentia to North Sydney, mid-June through mid-September only. 800 341-7981 in the USA and Canada; www.marine-atlantic.ca

By Air

- Air Canada (888 247-2262; www.aircanada.ca) provides daily flights to Nova Scotia from most Canadian cities. Air Canada Jazz (www.flyjazz.ca), a subsidiary of Air Canada, is a regional carrier providing short-haul and connector flights between many cities in Canada and the US.
- WestJet (800 538-5696, www.westjet.com) is a discount airline offering economy flights to Halifax from many Canadian and US cities.
- Porter (www.flyporter.com) offers service from New York, Toronto, Ottawa and Montreal to Halifax.

Air Canada, in partnership with United Airlines, services destinations in the United States and worldwide through all major US airports.

Several airlines offer regularly scheduled flights between Halifax and a number of European destinations (ask about charters as well). For up-to-date flight information consult www.flyhalifax.com.

Most air traffic to Nova Scotia touches down at the Halifax Stanfield International Airport, with connecting flights to Yarmouth and Sydney. Car rentals may be arranged at all three airports.

Airporter Inc. offers a shuttle service approximately every hour to Halifax's major downtown hotels. One-way fare is $18, children under ten ride free. The Halifax airport is located about 40 kilometres northeast of the city, and the 30- to 40-minute cab or limousine ride to downtown Halifax costs about $53.

Travel Essentials

Money

American currency can be exchanged at any bank in Nova Scotia at the prevailing rate. There are also currency exchange booths at the visitor information centre in Yarmouth and at the Halifax Stanfield International Airport. Units of currency are similar to those of the United States, except for Canadian two-dollar and one-dollar coins.

Traveller's cheques, major US credit cards and debit cards are accepted throughout Nova Scotia, although you may require cash in some rural areas. Traveller's cheques in Canadian funds can be purchased in the US. Cheques issued by Visa, American Express and Thomas Cook are widely recognized.

American visitors may also use bank or credit cards to make cash withdrawals from automated teller machines that are tied into international networks such as Cirrus, Interac and Plus. These can be found in most towns throughout the province.

Passports

As of summer 2009, American visitors, regardless of how they enter Canada, may require a valid passport. At the border, expect to be asked where you live, why you are coming to Canada and for how long. Before travelling it would be wise to check with Canada Border Services Agency (506 636-5064; www.cbsa.gc.ca) for the latest information. Citizens of other countries should check with the nearest Canadian embassy, High Commission or Consulate regarding entry requirements (www.cic.gc.ca). Visitors should also check with their home country regarding document requirements for re-entry.

Customs

Arriving

Visitors to Canada may bring certain duty-free items into the country as part of their personal baggage. These items must be declared to Customs upon arrival and may include up to 200 cigarettes, 50 cigars, 200 grams of manufactured tobacco and 200 tobacco sticks. Visitors are also permitted 1.14 litres (40 oz.) of liquor or 1.5 litres (52 oz.) of wine, or 8.5 litres (24 12-oz. cans or bottles) of beer.

Gift items — excluding tobacco and alcohol products — for Canadian residents that do not exceed $60 are also duty-free. Packages should be marked "Gift" and the value indicated.

Boats, trailers, sporting equipment, cameras and similar big-ticket items may enter Canada free of duty. However, Canada Border Services may require a refundable deposit to ensure that these goods are not sold for profit. It might be better to register such items with customs officials in your own country, so that when you re-enter you have evidence that they were not bought in Canada.

Some items are strictly controlled in Canada. Weapons and firearms are prohibited, with the exception of rifles and shotguns for hunting purposes, which must be declared. Regulations for temporarily importing firearms or for borrowing firearms while in Canada have changed within the past couple of years. For detailed current information contact the Canadian Firearms Centre at 800 731-4000; www.cfc-cafc.gc.ca. Plant material will be examined at the border (www.inspection.gc.ca). Veterinarian's certificates are required for all pets.

For further information on Canadian customs regulations, contact Canada Border Services at 800 461-9999; www.cbsa.gc.ca.

Departing

To find out about US customs regulations and what other restrictions and exemptions apply, contact your local customs office or US Customs and Border Protection, www.cbp.gov/xp/cgov/travel/. Ask for a copy of *Know Before You Go*.

Travellers from other countries should also check on customs regulations before leaving home.

Taxes

Harmonized Sales Tax (HST)

Most goods and services sold in Nova Scotia are subject to the Harmonized Sales Tax, a 13 percent federal/provincial tax that may be either included in or added to prices.

Guides

The *Nova Scotia Doers' and Dreamers' Guide* is an indispensable aid to visitors. To obtain a copy call 800 565-0000 toll-free, or see NovaScotia.com. The guide is also available at visitor information centres throughout Nova Scotia.

Getting Acquainted

Time Zone

Nova Scotia falls within the Atlantic Time Zone, which is one hour later than the Eastern Time Zone. Daylight Saving Time, when the clocks are advanced one hour, is in effect from early March until late October.

Climate

Nova Scotia's climate is influenced by the sea. Summers are cooler and winters milder than in central Canada. Average daily maximum temperatures for Halifax:

Jan. 1°C	33°F
Feb. 1°C	33°F
Mar. 4°C	39°F
Apr. 9°C	48°F
May 14°C	58°F
June 19°C	67°F
July 23°C	73°F
Aug. 24°C	74°F
Sept. 19°C	67°F
Oct. 14°C	58°F
Nov. 9°C	48°F
Dec. 3°C	37°F

Getting Around

Bus Tours

Seasonal bus tours of the province are available through a number of tour operators, including Ambassatours (800 565-7173; www.ambassatours.com), Aberdeen Tours (866 831-2277; www.aberdeentours.ca) and Trius Tours Ltd. (800 903-5664). Several tour operators will arrange customized itineraries for groups.

By Car

Nova Scotia highway maps are available at visitor information centres throughout the province. Highways are generally well maintained. Speed limits vary depending on the type of highway, with the 100-series controlled access highways having the highest limit, 110 km/hr (65 mph). The speed limit is 50 km/hr (30 mph) in cities and towns. In Nova Scotia, seat belt use is compulsory for driver and passengers.

A valid United States driver's license is also valid in Nova Scotia. Evidence of the car's registration is required (a car rental contract will also serve). US motorists may obtain a Non-Resident Inter-Province Motor Vehicle Liability Insurance Card through their own insurance companies as evidence of financial responsibility within Canada.

Car Rentals

All major car rental agencies are represented in Nova Scotia.

Representatives at the Halifax International Airport are listed below:
- Avis: 902 429-0963, 800 437-0358; www.avis.ca
- Budget: 800 268-8900; www.budget.com
- Hertz: 800 263-0600; www.hertz.ca
- Thrifty: 800 847-4389; www.thrifty.com
- National Car and Truck Rental: 800 227-7368; www.nationalcar.com

Consult the Yellow Pages of local telephone directories for local agencies that may offer lower rates.

Lodging

For a complete listing of accommodations in the province, including campgrounds, consult the *Nova Scotia Doers' and Dreamers' Guide* (see *Travel Essentials*). Hostellers should contact Hostelling International Nova Scotia, 1253 Barrington St, Halifax, Nova Scotia, B3J 1Y3; 902 422-3863; www.hihostels.ca. Visitors who are interested in bed-and-breakfast-style accommodation in Nova Scotia can consult *Atlantic Canada Bed & Breakfasts*, a comprehensive listing of B&Bs published by Formac and updated frequently. Other resources available at local bookstores include an illustrated guide to Nova Scotia's most distinctive inns — Elaine Elliot and Virginia Lee's *Maritime Flavours* (6th ed., Formac Publishing, 2002).

Many establishments are members of the Nova Scotia Information and Reservation Service (see *Travel Essentials*). Membership is indicated by a check mark in the *Nova Scotia Doers' and Dreamers' Guide*. In general, the accommodations listed below are the best of their kind in Nova Scotia. Most have distinguishing features that will enhance your stay. Approximate prices are indicated, based on the average cost at time of publication for two persons staying in a double room (excluding taxes): $ = less than $100; $$ = $100 – $150; $$$ = more than $150.

Halifax Metro

- Courtyard by Marriott Halifax Downtown, 5120 Salter St., Halifax; 902 428-1900; www.courtyardhalifax.com. All amenities. Centrally located, near waterfront, harbour views. $$$

- Delta Barrington, 1875 Barrington St., Halifax; 800 268-1133; www.deltabarrington.com. Close to the Historic Properties and most attractions. Adjoins Barrington Place Mall, restaurants and pubs. Open year-round. $$$
- Delta Halifax, 1990 Barrington St., Halifax; 800 268-1133; www.deltahalifax.com. Top-floor restaurant with sweeping view of the city and harbour. All amenities. Adjoins Scotia Square shopping mall. Open year-round. $$$
- Four Points by Sheraton, 1496 Hollis St., Halifax; 866 444-9494. Central to downtown. All amenities. Indoor parking. Open year-round. $$$
- Halifax Marriott Harbourfront, 1919 Upper Water St., Halifax; 800 943-6760; www.halifaxmarriott.com. Luxury accommodation on the Halifax waterfront. Indoor pool, health club, whirlpool. Underground parking. Next to casino. Adjacent to the Historic Properties. Open year-round. $$$
- ★ The Halliburton, 5184 Morris St., Halifax; 888 512-3344; www.thehalliburton.com. An elegant boutique hotel near downtown. Registered Heritage Property incorporating 3 19th-century townhouses in downtown Halifax. Fine dining. Open year-round. $$$
- Inn on the Lake, 3009 Hwy. 2, Fall River; 800 463-6465; innonthelake.com. Two hectares of parkland with private freshwater beach and outdoor pool, courtesy shuttle to airport (10 minutes away). Open year-round. $$$
- Lord Nelson Hotel and Suites, 1515 South Park St., Halifax; 800 565-2020; www.lordnelsonhotel.com. Renovated historic hotel opposite Public Gardens and near shopping. Dining room, fitness centre, business services. Open year-round. $$$
- Pepperberry Bed & Breakfast, 2688 Joseph Howe Dr., Halifax; 877 246-3244; www.pepperberryinn.com. Parklike setting near Armdale Roundabout. Heritage property decorated with artistic panache. Full breakfast. Open year-round. $$$
- ★ Prince George Hotel, 1725 Market St., Halifax; 800 565-1567; www.princegeorgehotel.com. Central downtown location with all amenities. Fine dining. Underground parking. Open year-round. $$$
- Radisson Suite Hotel Halifax, 1649 Hollis St., Halifax; 800 333-3333; www.radissonhalifax.com. Two-room suites, most overlooking harbour. All amenities. Pool, fitness centre, club room. Complimentary continental breakfast. Open year-round. $$$
- Sterns Mansion B&B, 17 Tulip St., Dartmouth; 800 565-3885; www.sternsmansion.com. Four guest rooms with four-poster beds, two with jacuzzis. Full breakfast (in bed if you like). Close to downtown and ferry. Open year-round. $$$
- Westin Nova Scotian Hotel, 1181 Hollis St., Halifax; 877 993-7846; www.westin.ns.ca. Comfortable rooms, historic hotel, a short walk south of downtown at the train station. Indoor pool, sauna, spa, tennis court. Open year-round. $$$

Along the South Shore
Peggys Cove to Hubbards
- Oceanstone Inn & Cottages, 8650 Peggys Cove Rd., Indian Harbour; 866 823-2160; www.oceanstone.ns.ca. Secluded 20-acre oceanfront getaway. Housekeeping cottages with fireplace; rooms or suites in inn. Beach, spa, fine dining. Open year-round. $$
- Rosewood on the Cove Cottages, 187 Shore Club Rd., Hubbards; 888 265-9950; www.rosewoodonthecove.com. Ten well-furnished 1-3 bedroom seaside cottages with full kitchen, fireplace, gas BBQ, deck. Heated outdoor pool. Open year-round. $$$
- Surfside Inn, 9609 Hwy. 3, Queensland; 800 373-2417; www.thesurfsideinn.com. Victorian elegance with modern amenities. Rooms or suite. Ocean views. Full breakfast included. Casual fine dining. Open year-round. $$

Chester and Mahone Bay
- Bayview Pines Country Inn, 678 Oakland Rd., Indian Point, Mahone Bay; 866 624-9970; www.bayviewpines.com. A 14-acre property with hilltop view of Mahone Bay; century-old farmhouse and converted barn with stylish furnishings. Open year-round. $$
- Mahone Bay Bed & Breakfast, 558

Main St., Mahone Bay; 866 239-6252; www.bbcanada.com/4078.html. A much-photographed 1860 stately home; antiques, art, wrap-around porch. $
- Mecklenburgh Inn, 78 Queen St., Chester; 902 275-4638; www.mecklenburghinn. Casual and eclectic heritage B&B with good breakfasts, water views. Open May – Dec. $$
- Oak Island Resort, 36 Treasure Dr., Western Shore; 800 565-5075; www.oakislandresortandspa.com. Oceanfront resort hotel and chalets. Restaurant, pool, tennis, golf, sailing and whalewatching packages. Open year-round. $$$
- Sword and Anchor B&B, 5306 Hwy. 3, Chester Basin; 877 639-3966; www.swordandanchor.com. Eight rooms in 1882 waterfront property; one oceanfront cottage. Full breakfast. Open year-round. $
- Three Thistles B&B and Apartment, 389 Main St., Mahone Bay; 902 624-0517; www.three-thistles.com. Comfortable lodging in historic parsonage. Organic full breakfast. Environmentally friendly products used. Yoga studio. Open year-round. $/$$

Lunenburg and Area
- 1880 Kaulbach House Historic Inn, 75 Pelham St., Lunenburg; 800 568-8818; www.kaulbachhouse.com. Award-winning restoration in old Lunenburg, this is a gracious B&B with six air-conditioned rooms. Offers gourmet breakfast, harbour views. Walk to town attractions. Open May – Dec. $$
- Addington Arms, 27 Cornwallis St., Lunenburg; 877 979-2727; www.addingtonarms.com. Steam room, aroma and sound therapy. Full breakfast. Downtown, waterviews. Open year-round. $$$
- Boscawen Inn & McLachlan House, 150 Cumberland St., Lunenburg; 800 354-5009; www.boscawen.ca. Two heritage properties in the heart of old Lunenburg. One-of-a-kind rooms. Upscale and casual dining rooms. Open May – Oct. $$
- Lunenburg Arms, 94 Pelham St., Lunenburg; 800 679-4950; www.lunenburgarms.com. A 24-room hotel and spa in Old Town

with harbour views and amenities; dining room. Open year-round. $$$
- Lunenburg Inn, 26 Dufferin St., Lunenburg; 800 565-3963; www.lunenburginn.com. An 1893 heritage inn with sun deck and covered verandah. Complimentary full breakfast. Open May – Oct. $$
- MacLeod Cottages, 85 Green Bay Rd., Petite Rivière; 902 688-2866; www.macleodcottages.ca. Twenty-three quintessential summer cottages, some old, some newer; no frills, all the necessities, beach, canteen. Open May – Oct, weekly only Jul. – Aug. $$
- Salty Rose Beach Houses, Rose Bay; 877 766-4923; saltyrose.com. Six secluded oceanfront housekeeping cottages, loft bedrooms, fully equipped, tastefully appointed, wood stoves, screened decks, gas BBQs. Open year-round. $$$

Liverpool and Shelburne
- Cooper's Inn, 36 Dock St., Shelburne; 800 688-2011; www.thecoopersinn.com. Loyalist home built around 1785. Seven guest rooms and one luxury suite in main building and adjoining cooperage, with views of Shelburne Harbour. Full breakfast. Open Apr. – Oct. $$
- Lane's Privateer Inn, 27-33 Bristol Ave. (Rte. 3), Liverpool; 800 794-3332; www.lanesprivateerinn.com. Twenty-seven rooms in restored heritage property overlooking Mersey River. Dining room and pub. Open year-round. $$
- Quarterdeck Beachside Villas & Grill, 6499 Hwy. 3, Summerville Centre; 800 565-1119; www.quarterdeck.ns.ca. Beachside condos and cottages with all amenities including jacuzzis, fireplaces and kitchen facilities. Dining room. Open year-round. $$$
- White Point Beach Resort, White Point Beach; 800 565-5068; www.whitepoint.com. Seventy-four-room resort with extensive recreational facilities, including golf, tennis, boating, swimming pools and kilometre-long white sand beach. Also 44 cottages with fireplaces. Open year-round. $$$
- Whitman Inn, 12389 Hwy. 8, Kempt; 800 830-3855;

www.whitmaninn.com. Close to Kejimkujik National Park. Turn-of-the-century homestead with indoor pool and sauna. Park-related recreational packages for canoeing, bicycling and cross-country skiing. Open year-round. $

Yarmouth
- Charles C. Richards House B&B, 17 Collins St., Yarmouth; 866 798-0929; www. charlesrichardshouse.ns.ca. Three guest rooms in Queen Anne mansion in historic district. Full breakfast, high tea. Open year-round. $$
- Guest-Lovitt House B&B, 12 Parade St., Yarmouth; 866 742-0372; www.guestlovitt.ca. Interesting, well-appointed heritage house with widow's watch. Open year-round. $$$
- Harbour's Edge Bed and Breakfast, 12 Vancouver St., Yarmouth; 902 742-2387; www.harboursedge.ns.ca. Large rooms in heritage house with harbour views. Open year-round. $$
- Manor Inn Lakeside, 1023 Hwy. 1, Hebron; 888 626-6746; www.manorinn.com. Inn, coach house and adjacent motel set on 9 acres of landscaped grounds on Doctors Lake. Breakfast included. Pool, restaurant. Open year-round. $$/$$$
- Rodd Grand Yarmouth, 417 Main St., Yarmouth; 800 565-7633; www.rodd-hotels.ca. Modern full-service hotel with indoor pool. Open year-round. $$$
- Trout Point Lodge, 189 Trout Point Rd., East Kemptville, off Hwy. 203; 902 482-8360; www.troutpoint.com. Granite and log lodge; seafood restaurant. Nature retreat on 200 acres in Tobeatic wilderness area. Fishing, kayaking, canoeing, nature trails. Open May – Oct. $$$

Annapolis Valley
Wolfville to Middleton
- Blomidon Inn, 195 Main St., Wolfville; 800 565-2291; www.theblomidon.net. Sea captain's mansion from the grand shipbuilding era of the 1880s. Fine dining. Victorian gardens, gift shop. Open year-round. $$/$$$
- By the Dock of the Bay Cottages, Haddock Alley, Margaretsville; 800 407-2856; www.cottagesnovascotia.com. Two-

and three-bedroom housekeeping beach houses on the Bay of Fundy, very near water's edge amidst gorgeous gardens. Open Mar. – Dec. $$$
- Century Farm Inn, 10 Main St., Middleton; 800 237-9896; www.centuryfarminn.com. Victorian farmhouse on 110-acre estate. Complimentary full breakfast. Open June – Sept. $
- Falcourt Inn, 8979 Hwy. 201, Nictaux; 800 464-8979; www.falcourtinn.ns.ca. Restored 1920s lodge on Nictaux River. Eight guest rooms (one wheelchair accessible) and 3 2-bedroom guest houses. Complimentary breakfast, evening dining. Open year-round. $$$
- Olde Lantern Inn & Vineyard., 11575 Hwy. 1, Grand Pré; 877 965-3845; www.oldlanterninn.com. Replica of 1700s Cape-style house situated in vineyard next to winery and restaurant. Views of Bay of Fundy. Open year-round. $$
- Tattingstone Inn, 620 Main St., Wolfville; 800 565-7696; www.tattingstone.ns.ca. Tastefully decorated B&B inn and carriage house (c. 1874) with tennis court, outdoor pool. Open year-round. $$
- Victoria's Historic Inn and Carriage House B&B, 600 Main St., Wolfville; 800 556-5744; www.victoriashistoricinn.com. Picturesque 1893 Registered Heritage Property. Luxury suites with jacuzzi whirlpool bath. Full breakfast, afternoon tea. Open year-round. $$/$$$

Annapolis Royal and Digby
- Bread and Roses Inn, 82 Victoria St., Annapolis Royal; 888 899-0551; www.breadandroses.ns.ca. Restored Queen Anne Revival mansion with many unique architectural details, antique furnishings. Full breakfast included. Open Apr. – Nov. $$
- Brier Island Lodge & Restaurant, 557 Water St., Westport, Brier Island; 800 662-8355; www.brierisland.com. Forty modern motel rooms with ocean view. Dining room. Excellent opportunities for whale- and bird-watching. Open May – Oct. $/$$
- ★ The Digby Pines Golf Resort & Spa, 103 Shore Rd., Digby; 800

667-4637; www.signatureresorts.com. Full-scale luxury resort with championship golf course and all other amenities. Hotel rooms and suites plus 31 cottages with stone fireplaces. Open May – mid-Oct. $$$

- Dockside Suites, 34 Water St., Digby; 866 445-4950; www.fundyrestaurant.com. Six air-conditioned housekeeping suites overlooking the Digby scallop fleet. Restaurant. Open year-round. $$
- Garrison House Inn, 350 St. George St., Annapolis Royal; 866 532-5750; www.garrisonhouse.ca. Small inn overlooking Fort Anne, built in 1854. Fine dining. Open May – Dec. $$/$$$
- Harbourview Inn, 25 Harbourview Rd., Smiths Cove; 877 449-0705; www.theharbourviewinn.com. Nine comfortable rooms in century inn; water views and lovely gardens. Open mid-May – mid-Oct. $$
- Milford House, 5296 Hwy. 8, South Milford; 877 532-5751; www.milfordhouse.ca. Secluded historic lodge amidst large wooded acreage between Annapolis Royal and Kejimkujik National Park. Twenty-seven rustic lakeshore cabins with fireplaces. Country breakfasts and dinners in the main lodge (MAP). Open July – mid-Oct. Two winterized cabins available year-round. $$
- Queen Anne Inn, 494 Upper St. George St., Annapolis Royal; 877 536-0403; www.queenanneinn.ns.ca. A grand Victorian mansion. Breakfast in elegant dining room. Dinners served. Open Apr. 15 – Oct. 31. $$$
- Thistle Down Country Inn, 98 Montague Row, Digby; 800 565-8081; www.thistledown.ns.ca/theinn. Edwardian inn on the water's edge. Twelve comfortable rooms (6 modern harbourside units). Dinner for guests. $$

Along the Fundy Shore

Amherst

- Regent Bed & Breakfast, 175 East Victoria St., Amherst; 866 661-2861; www.theregent.ca. One of Amherst's fine old homes, now a fine B&B. Open year-round (March by reservation). $$

Truro and Maitland

- Irwin Lake Chalets, Old Barns (near Truro), Rte. 236, off Hwy. 102, exit 14; 866 554-7946; www.irwinlakechalets.com. Six comfy lakeside log chalets in 500-acre unspoiled wilderness setting; 1- and 2-bedroom, heated, wood stoves, covered decks, BBQs. Fishing, hiking, canoeing. Open year-round. $$
- The John Stanfield Inn, 437 Prince St., Truro; 800 561-7666; www.johnstanfieldinn.com. Impressive Queen Anne-style mansion, beautiful woodwork, period furnishings, modern amenities. Fine dining. Open year-round. $$$

Economy to Parrsboro

- Four Seasons Retreat, 320 Cove Rd., Economy; 888 373-0339; www.fourseasonsretreat.ns.ca. Eleven beautiful housekeeping cottages with fireplaces, on the cliffs overlooking Minas Basin. Swimming, skiing, hiking trails. Open year-round. $$/$$$
- Gillespie House Inn, 358 Main St., Parrsboro; 877 901-3196; www.gillespiehouseinn.com. Victorian farmhouse with antiques, fireplaces, down duvets. Lovely gardens and lawns. Near Fundy hiking, rockhounding. Open year-round. $/$$
- Lightkeeper's Kitchen & Guest House, Cape d'Or, Advocate; 902 670-0534; www.capedor.ca. Right next to the lighthouse. Spectacular views. Restaurant. Open May – mid-Oct. $$
- Parrsboro Mansion Inn, 3916 Eastern Ave., Parrsboro; 866 354-2585; www.parrsboromansion.com. Three large, attractive guest rooms and one suite. Walk to Fundy shore. Open July – Oct. $$

Along the Northumberland Shore

Lorneville to Tatamagouche

- ★ Amherst Shore Country Inn, 5091 Rte. 366, Lorneville; 800 661-2724; www.ascinn.ns.ca. Small inn with lovely ocean view, private beach. Renowned dining room. Open May – Oct., weekends Dec. – Apr. $$
- The Cottages at Cambra Sands, 643

North Shore Rd., Malagash; 866 559-0705; www.cambrasands.com. Well-appointed housekeeping cottages (1-, 2- and 3-bedroom) with all amenities; private beach. Open year-round. Weekly. $$$
- StoneGarden Chalets, 1120 Sand Point Rd., Tatamagouche; 866 657-0024; www.stonegardenchalets.com. Seaside log chalets on Barrachois Bay. Full kitchen, living room and 1 or 2 bedrooms. Open May – Oct. $$$
- Train Station Inn, 21 Station Rd., Tatamagouche; 888 724-5233; www.trainstation.ca. Three guest rooms in restored century-old train station plus 7 guest cabooses reflect its railway past. All modern amenities. Dining car. Open Apr. – Oct. $$

Pictou and Antigonish
- Antigonish Victorian Inn, 149 Main St., Antigonish; 800 906-5558; antigonishvictorianinn.ca. Magnificent turreted Victorian mansion-cum-B&B; sumptuously decorated rooms with mod cons. Open year-round. $$
- Braeside Inn, 126 Front St., Pictou; 800 613-7701; www.braesideinn.com. Eighteen air-conditioned rooms. Dining with harbour view. Open year-round. $$
- Consulate Inn, 157 Water St., Pictou; 800 424-8283; www.consulateinn.com. Bed-and-breakfast accommodation in a restored c. 1810 property overlooking Pictou harbour. Open year-round. $$
- Customs House Inn, 38 Depot St., Pictou; 902 485-4546; www.customshouseinn.ca. On Pictou waterfront; walk to all attractions. Open year-round. $$
- Pictou Lodge Resort, 172 Lodge Rd., Braeshore; 800 495-6343; www.pictoulodge.com. Rustic 1920s resort with modern amenities. Hotel rooms, suites or log cottages with huge stone fireplaces and some screened-in sunporches. Open mid-May – mid-Oct. $$$
- Stonehame Lodge & Chalets, 310 Fitzpatrick Mountain Rd., Scotsburn; 877 646-3468; www.stonehamechalets.com. Modern rustic retreat with all amenities and great views. Some units barrier-free; chalets pet friendly. Open year-round. $$

Along the Eastern Shore
- DesBarres Manor Inn, 90 Church St., Guysborough; 902 533-2099; www.desbarresmanor.com. Ten large, well-appointed rooms in elegant mansion. Fine dining. Open year-round. $$$
- ★ Liscombe Lodge Resort, 2884 Hwy. 7, Liscomb Mills; 800 665-6343; www.liscombelodge.ca. Full-service resort featuring sport fishing packages (guides available), boat rentals and cottage-style accommodations, some overlooking the beautiful Liscomb River. Enclosed pool and fitness centre. Fine dining. Open mid-May – Oct. $$$
- Lonely Rock Seaside Bungalows, 150 New Harbour Rd., New Harbour; 866 248-1877; www.lonelyrock.com. Fully equipped family housekeeping cottages with ocean views and sand beach. Open year-round. $$$
- Salmon River House Country Inn, 9931 Hwy. 7, Salmon River Bridge; 800 565-3353; www.salmonriverhouse.com. Seven well-appointed guest rooms. On-site hiking, boating, hunting and fishing. Licensed dining. Open May – Oct. $$
- Seawind Landing Country Inn, 1 Wharf Rd., Charlos Cove; 800 563-4667; www.seawindlanding.com. Oceanfront inn with dramatic seascapes. Fine dining. Open mid-May – mid-Oct. $$

Cape Breton Island
Cabot Trail
- Auberge Giselle's Inn, 387 Shore Rd., Baddeck; 800 304-0466; www.giseles.com. Seventy-five rooms overlooking gardens and Bras d'Or Lakes. All amenities. Dining room. Open May – Oct. $$$
- Broadwater Inn and Cottages, Bay Rd., Baddeck; 877 818-3474; www.broadwater.baddeck.com. Historic property with charming B&B and 7 housekeeping log cottages overlooking Bras d'Or. Cottages open year-round; B&B Apr. – Oct. $$
- Cabot Shores Adventure and Retreat Centre, 30 Buchanan Dr., Indian Brook; 866 929-2585;

Lodging

www.cabotshores.com. Rustic comfort in environmentally responsible lodge and cabins. Outdoor activities for the whole family. Open year-round. $$$

- Cabot Trail Sea and Golf Chalets, 71 Fraser Doucet Lane, Cheticamp; 877 224-1777; www.SeaGolfChalets.com. Modern, tasteful, fully equipped cottages adjacent to Le Portage golf course. Open mid-May – mid-Oct. $$

- Castle Moffett, 11980 Hwy. 105, Bucklaw, Baddeck; 888 756-9070; www.castlemoffett.com. Luxury suites with king or queen canopy or four-poster beds, fireplaces, sauna, views of Bras d'Or Lakes. Fine dining. Open May – Oct. $$$

- Castle Rock Inn, 39339 Cabot Trail, Ingonish Ferry; 888 884-7625; www.ingonish.com/castlerock. Overlooks Middle Head Peninsula, the Atlantic Ocean and the Highlands. Avalon fine-dining restaurant. Open year-round. $$

- Chanterelle Country Inn and Cottages, 48678 Cabot Trail, North River; 866 277-0577; www.chanterelleinn.com. Environmentally friendly property in tranquil setting overlooking St Ann's Bay. "Slow food" dining. Open May – Oct. $$

- Cheticamp Island Resort, Cheticamp Island; 902 849-6444; www.cheticampislandresort.com. Two-bedroom housekeeping cottages. Ocean swimming. Daily and weekly rates. Open mid-June – mid-Oct. $$

- Crown Jewel Resort Ranch, 992 Westside Baddeck Rd., 8 km north of Baddeck; 902 295-1096; www.crownjewelresort.com. Fly-in adventure vacation on 800-acre ranch with working animals, eco-adventures. Fine dining. Open year-round. $$$

- Dundee Resort & Golf Club, 2750 West Bay Hwy., Dundee; 800 565-5660; www.capebretonresorts.com/dundee.asp. Golf with outstanding views of the Bras d'Or; marina and boat rentals, indoor and outdoor pools; lighted tennis. Sixty hotel rooms, 38 1- and 2-bedroom cottages. Open mid-May – Oct. $$

- Inverary Resort, 368 Shore Rd., Baddeck; 800 565-5660; www.InveraryResort.com. Seven cottages, 125 rooms and 6 suites. Sauna, indoor pool, tennis, beach, marina. Licensed restaurant and pub. Open May – Dec. $$

★ Keltic Lodge Resort & Spa, Middle Head Peninsula, Ingonish Beach; 800 565-0444; www.kelticlodge.ca. Full-scale luxury resort with championship golf course (many say the best in Nova Scotia). Original main lodge, inn or cottages. Outdoor heated pool, hiking trails. Open mid-May – mid-Oct. $$$

- Laurie's Motor Inn, 15456 Laurie Rd., Cheticamp; 800 959-4253; www.lauries.com. Forty-six motel units, 6 suites. Dining room. Whale cruises arranged. Open Apr. – Oct. $$

- Lynwood Inn, 441 Shore Rd., Baddeck; 877 666-1995; www.lynwoodinn.com. Lovely guest rooms in century inn and modern suites. Open year-round. $$

- MacNeil House, 257 Shore Rd., Baddeck; 888 662-7484; www.silverdart.com. Luxury suites with fireplaces, kitchens. Swimming pool or saltwater swimming in the Bras d'Or. Dining room. Open mid-May – mid-Oct. $$$

★ Markland Coastal Resort, 802 Dingwall Rd., Dingwall; 800 872-6084; www.marklandresort.com. Secluded coastal resort with log cabins, heated outdoor pool, ocean beach, concert hall, outdoor adventure tours. Fine dining. Open mid-June – mid-Oct. $$$

- Normaway Inn, 691 Egypt Rd., Margaree Valley; 800 565-9463; normaway.com. Relaxing old-style resort, 9 rooms in lodge, 17 cabins with woodstoves and screened porches (7 have jacuzzis). Fine dining and entertainment. Excellent salmon and trout fishing nearby. Open mid-June – mid-Oct. $$$

- Pilot Whale Chalets, 15775 Cabot Trail, Cheticamp; 902 224-1040; www.pilotwhalechalets.com. Well-equipped 2- and 3-bedroom pine log chalets with views of Highlands. Open year-round. $$$

- Sea Parrot Oceanview Manor, 45227 Cabot Trail, North Shore; 902 929-2530; www.seaparrotoceanview manor.com. Open May – Oct. $$

- Water's Edge Inn, 18-22 Water St., Baddeck; 295-3600; www.thewatersedgeinn.com.

Tastefully decorated rooms, art gallery. Café. Open June – mid-Oct. $$

Ceilidh Trail

• Duncreigan Country Inn, 11409 Hwy. 19, Mabou; 800 840-2207; www.duncreigan.ca. Four spacious guest rooms with antique furnishings in main inn and 4 large rooms in adjacent Spring House, 1 suite. Fine dining. Open year-round. $$

• Glenora Inn and Distillery Resort, 13727 Hwy. 19, Glenville; 800 839-0491; www.glenoradistillery.com. 9 rooms and 6 housekeeping chalets. Dining room and pub. Tours of Canada's only single-malt distillery. Open mid-May – mid-Oct. $$

• Haus Treuburg, 175 Main St., Port Hood; 902 787-2116; www.haustreuburg.com. Guest house and cottages close to warm saltwater swimming. German-style breakfast available daily. Licensed restaurant. Open May – Dec. $$

• Tulloch Inn, 2795 Tulloch Lane, West Lake Ainslie; 866 707-4300; www.tulloch-inn.ca. One wheelchair-accessible room and one environmentally friendly room in family-friendly inn. Breakfast, licensed dining room. Open year-round. $$

Fleur-de-lis and Marconi Trails and Metro Cape Breton

• Cambridge Suites Hotel, 380 Esplanade, Sydney; 800 565-9466; www.cambridgesuitessydney.com. On Sydney waterfront. Suite accommodation with housekeeping facilities. Rooftop spa pool and exercise facilities. Complimentary breakfast. Open year-round. $$$

• Cranberry Cove Inn, 12 Wolfe St., Louisbourg; 800 929-0222; www.cranberrycoveinn.com. Seven guest rooms (6 with jacuzzis) in a century-old home near fortress. Full breakfast. Open May – Oct. $$

• Delta Sydney, 300 Esplanade, Sydney; 800 268-1133; www.deltasydney.com. Harbour view with 152 rooms, all amenities, pool, waterslide. Open year-round. $$/$$$

★ Gowrie House Country Inn, 840 Shore Rd., Sydney Mines; 800 372-1115; www.gowriehouse.com.

Beautifully furnished 1830 home with elegant antique-filled guest rooms. Renovated caretaker's cottage with fireplace. Exceptional dining. Open May – Oct. $$$

• L'Auberge Acadienne, 2375 Hwy. 206, Arichat; 877 787-2200; www.acadienne.com. 19th century Acadian-style country inn on Isle Madame. Dining room. Open year-round. $$

• Louisbourg Harbour Inn, 9 Lower Warren St., Louisbourg; 888 888-8466; www.louisbourgharbourinn.com. Eight well-appointed guest rooms in a century-old captain's house overlooking Louisbourg Harbour. Full breakfast. Open mid-June – mid-Oct. $$

• Louisbourg Heritage House B&B, 7544 Main St., Louisbourg; 888 888-8466; www.louisbourgheritagehouse.com. Victorian rectory, well-decorated rooms in period style. Open June – mid-Oct. $$

• Point of View Suites, 15 Commercial St. Ext., Louisbourg; 888 374-8439; www.louisbourgpointofview.com. Sixteen oceanfront suites near the gates of fortress Louisbourg; balconies and decks overlooking Fortress and ocean. Open mid-May – mid-Oct. $$/$$$

• Vollmer's Island Paradise, 1489 Main Street, Janvrin's Harbour; 902 226-1507; www.vipilodge.com. Environmentally friendly log cottages in secluded setting. Gourmet dining. Scuba diving. Open May – Oct. $$

Dining

Nova Scotia cuisine is a delight. Tastefully and imaginatively prepared seafood, fresh Annapolis Valley produce and Pictou County lamb are among the many specialties of Nova Scotia restaurants. Local wines are inexpensive and surprisingly good.

Where to Eat in Canada (Oberon Press) is updated annually and includes many of the province's finer restaurants. *Maritime Flavours* (7th ed., Formac Publishing, 2008) is an illustrated guide to the best and most distinctive dining establishments in the Maritime provinces, accompanied by a selection of their favourite recipes. See *Dining* p. 32.

Dining

Approximate prices are indicated, based on the average cost, at time of publication, of dinner for two including wine (where available), taxes and gratuity: $ = less than $70; $$ = $70–100; $$$ = over $100.

Halifax

- Baan Thai, 1569 Dresden Row, Halifax; 902 446-4301; www.baanthai.ca. Very good, reasonably priced Thai food. Open daily, 5–10 pm; closed Mon. $$
- Bear Restaurant, 1241 Barrington St, Halifax; 902 425-2327. Global, fusion, contemporary cuisine using fresh local ingredients. Call for hours. $$$
- ★ Bish World Cuisine, Bishop's Landing, 1475 Lower Water St., Halifax; 902 425-7993; www.bish.ca. Wonderful waterfront location with outdoor patio in summer; imaginative appetizers; local seafood and rack of lamb; good wine list. Open Mon–Sat 5:30–10 pm. $$$
- Cheelin, Brewery Market, 1496 Lower Water St., Halifax; 902 422-2252; www.cheelinrestaurant.com The best Chinese food in Halifax. Open for dinner Tues–Sun 5:30–10 pm, lunch Mon–Sat 11:30 am–2:30 pm. $$
- The Chickenburger, 1531 Bedford Highway, Bedford; www.chickenburger.com. A landmark since the 1940s. Still has a juke box (although it now plays compact discs). Chicken burgers and real, old-fashioned milkshakes are the staples. Open 9 am–1 am daily. $
- Chives Canadian Bistro, 1537 Barrington St., Halifax; 902 420-9626; www.chives.ca. Changing menu of traditional Nova Scotian fare with local seasonal ingredients. Open daily, 5–9:30 pm. $$$
- Cut Steakhouse and Urban Grill, 5120 Salter St., 902 429-5120; www.cutsteakhouse.ca. Dry-aged beef for the steak connoisseur. Open daily, Grill: lunch, noon–3 pm, 5–11 pm; Steakhouse: from 5:30 pm. $$$
- da Maurizio, 1496 Lower Water St., Halifax; 902 423-0859; www.damaurizio.ca. Elegant Italian dining in the restored Brewery Market complex. One of Nova Scotia's best restaurants. Open Mon–Sat 5:30–10 pm; closed Sun. $$$

- Economy Shoe Shop, 1661–63 Argyle St., Halifax. 902 423-7463; www.economyshoeshop.ca. Open daily, 11 am–late. $$
- Fid, 1569 Dresden Row, Halifax; 902 422-9162; www.fidcuisine.ca. Small, creative, fusion menu featuring seasonal and local ingredients. Open daily for dinner 5–10 pm, lunch Wed–Fri 11:30 am–2 pm, closed Mon. $$
- Gio, 1725 Market St., Halifax; 902 425-1987; www.giohalifax.com. In the Prince George Hotel. Two award-winning chefs provide some of the finest dining in Nova Scotia. Open for dinner daily except Sunday; lunch, Mon–Fri. $$$
- Hamachi House, 5190 Morris St., Halifax; 902 425-7711; www.hamachihouse.com. Japanese menu and floating sushi bar. Open Mon–Sat 11:30 am–11 pm, Sun 4–10 pm. $$
- Hamachi Steakhouse, Bishop's Landing, 1477 Lower Water St., Halifax; 902 422-1600. Japanese-style steakhouse with interesting seafood dishes as well. Open Mon–Sat 11:30 am–2:30 pm, dinner 5–10 pm, Fri and Sat till 11 pm, Sun 4–10 pm. $$$
- Inn-on-the-Lake, Fall River; 902 861-3480; www.innonthelake.com. Located on beautiful Lake Thomas, meals are served in the dining room, on the terrace or in Oliver's pub. Open daily, 7 am–10 pm. $$$
- ★ Jane's on the Commons, 2394 Robie St., Halifax; 902 431-5683; www.janesonthecommon.com. Imaginative, inexpensive dining in a diner format. Short wine list. Open for lunch and dinner Tues–Sun, brunch Sat and Sun. $$
- La Perla, 73 Alderney Dr., Dartmouth; 902 469-3241; www.laperla.ca. Distinctive northern Italian cuisine, a minute's walk from the ferry terminal. Open for lunch Mon–Fri, dinner Mon–Sat; closed Sun. $$$
- The Lower Deck, Historic Properties, Lower Water St., Halifax; 902 425-1501; www.lowerdeck.ca. Pub with lively entertainment; patio. Open daily, 11:30 am–10 pm. $
- The Old Triangle, 5136 Prince St., Halifax; 902 492-4900; www.oldtraingle.com. Good pub fare and live entertainment. Open daily,

11 am– midnight, Tues–Sat later. $
- Onyx, 5680 Spring Garden Rd., Halifax; 902 428-5680; www.onyxdining.com. Fine dining, superlative service, sophisticated décor. Open Mon–Sat from 4:30 pm. $$$
- Opa! 1565 Argyle St., Halifax; 902 492-7999: www.opataverna.com Atmospheric taverna featuring grilled seafood and traditional Greek favourites. Open Mon–Sat, 11 am–11 pm; Sun 4:30–11 $$
- Press Gang, 5218 Prince St., Halifax; 902 423-8816; www.thepressgang.ca. Fine dining in an intimate and historic setting. Popular both with locals and visiting celebrities. Open daily for dinner. Reservations recommended. $$$
- Saege, 5883 Spring Garden Rd., Halifax; 902 429-1882; www.saege.ca. Stylish, creative and delicious dishes in a cozy bistro atmosphere. Excellent wines. Open Tues–Fri, 11:30 am–10 pm; Sat and Sun, 8–10; closed Mon. $$$
- Satisfaction Feast Vegetarian Restaurant, 3559 Robie St., Halifax; 902 422-3540; satisfaction-feast.com. Delicious and inexpensive vegetarian fare, especially the soups and breads. Open Tues, Thurs and Sun 10 am–8 pm; Wed 10 am–3:30 pm; Fri and Sat 10 am–9 pm; closed Mon. No liquor. $
- Stories at The Halliburton, 5184 Morris St., Halifax; 902 444-4400; www.thehalliburton.com. Specialties include fresh Atlantic seafood and wild game entrees. Light fare and cocktails in the outdoor garden café. Open daily, 5–9 pm; closed Mon. $$$

Along the South Shore

Peggys Cove and Hubbards
- The Finer Diner, 9976 Peggys Cove Rd., Hackett's Cove; 902 821-3434. Classic diner food. Patio overlooking Boutilier's Cove. Open Wed–Sun 8 am–8 pm. $
- Rhubarb Grill & Café at Oceanstone Inn & Cottages, 8650 Peggys Cove Rd., Indian Harbour; 866 823-2160; www.oceanstone.ns.ca. Casual fine dining in a unique seaside setting. Open daily in summer, 2–9:30 pm. $$$

- Shore Club Lobster Supper, Hubbards; 902 857-9555; www.lobstersupper.com. Boiled lobster, mussels and salad bar; children's menu. Open Wed–Sun, 4–8 pm, June–early Oct. $$
- Sou'wester, Peggys Cove; 902 823-2561. Chowders, lobster and traditional Nova Scotia desserts like gingerbread and apple crisp. Open daily, 8 am–8:30 pm. $$

Chester and Mahone Bay
- The Biscuit Eater, 16 Orchard St., Mahone Bay; 902 624-2665; www.biscuiteater.ca. A delightful café with excellent teas and coffees, unusual sandwiches and sweets, amidst stacks of books in a warm, eclectic atmosphere. Open daily, 8:30 am–5:30 pm, Sun from 11 am; closed Mon, Tues in winter. $
- Cheesecake Gallery, 533 Main St., Mahone Bay; 902 624-0579. Fine casual dining. Open daily in summer. $$
- Innlet Café, Kedy's Landing, 249 Edgewater St., Mahone Bay; 902 624-6363. Pasta, seafood, salads. Try the front terrace on a warm evening, with a view of the water and Mahone Bay's three churches. Open daily, 11:30 am–9 pm. $$
- Julien's Pâtisserie, Bakery & Café, 43 Queen St., Chester; 902 275-2324; www.juliens.ca. Croissants, French pastries, European breads, light lunches (famous lobster sandwiches) and deli. Open daily, 8 am–6 pm. Shorter hours and closed Monday during off-season. $
- Kiwi Café, 19 Pleasant St., Chester; 902 275-1492; www.kiwicafechester.com. Home cooking from scratch with fresh ingredients. Open daily, 8:30 am–4 pm, year-round. $
- Nicki's Inn, 28 Pleasant St., Chester; 902 275-4342; www.aco.ca/nickis.html. Open Wed–Sat 5–9 pm; Sun 4–8 pm (carvery). Fine dining. Good wine list. $$$
- Seaside Shanty, Hwy. 3, Chester Basin; 902 275-2246. Big helpings of fresh seafood. Great chowder. Open daily, 11:30 am–10 pm; shorter hours off-season. $$

Lunenburg
- Black Forest. Hwy. 3, Martin's Brook; 902 634-3600. German and

Canadian fare. Specialities are schnitzel and spaetzle. Open mid-Apr.–mid-Dec., 11.30 am–9 pm. $$

- Boscawen Inn, 150 Cumberland St., Lunenburg; 902 634-3325. A restored Victorian mansion specializing in fresh local seafood. Afternoon tea in the drawing rooms. Open daily for breakfast and dinner, Easter–Dec. $$$

★ Fleur de Sel, 53 Montague St., Lunenburg; 902 640-2121; www.fleurdesel.net. Highly lauded fine dining with European flair; changing menu features local seafood and organic vegetables. Open daily in summer for dinner from 5 pm; Sunday brunch 10 am–2 pm; shorter hours off-season. $$$

- LaHave Bakery, LaHave; 902 688-2908. Home baking using clear spring water and locally grown, fresh-milled grains. Sandwiches made to order. Open Mon– Fri, 9 am–5:30 pm, weekends 9 am–7 pm; longer hours during season. No liquor. $

- Magnolia's Grill, 128 Montague St., Lunenburg; 902 634-3287. Bustling atmosphere, tasty and innovative dishes and lots to look at on the walls while you wait. Key lime pie for dessert. Open Mon–Sat for lunch and dinner, Apr.–late Oct. $$

- The Old Fish Factory Restaurant, at the Fisheries Museum, Lunenburg; 902 634-3333; www.oldfishfactory.com. Good selection of seafood. Watch the sunset over the harbour as you dine. $$

- Salt Shaker Deli, 124 Montague St., Lunenburg; 902 640-3434; www.saltshakerdeli.com. Open daily, 11 am–9 pm. $$

- Sweet Indulgence, Lincoln St., Lunenburg next to the post office. Superb baked goods. Open daily.

- Trattoria della Nonna, 9 King St., Lunenburg; 902 640-3112; www.trattoriadellanonna.ca. Very good authentic Italian food. Open for lunch Tues–Fri from 11:30 am; dinner Tues–Sat from 5 pm; Sunday brunch 10:30. $$$

Liverpool and Shelburne

- Charlotte Lane Café, 13 Charlotte Lane, Shelburne; 902 875-3314; www.charlottelane.ca. Relaxed dining, meals prepared by award-winning chef in a heritage property. Open May–Dec., Tues–Sat, lunch 11:30 am–2 pm, dinner 5–8 pm (evening reservation recommended). $$

- Lane's Privateer Inn, 27 Bristol Ave., Liverpool; 902 354-3456; www.lanesprivateerinn.com. Dining room and pub. Good pasta and seafood. Open daily, 7 am–10 pm (9 pm in winter). $$

- Quarterdeck Beachside Villas and Grill, Summerville Centre; 902 683-2998; www.quarterdeck.ns.ca. Bright restaurant with view of white-sand beaches, serving good food. Open daily, 11:30 am–10 pm, early May–mid-Oct. $$

- Seawatch Restaurant, White Point Beach Resort, White Point; 902 354-2711; www.whitepoint.com. Informal dining room, suitable for children, serves steak and seafood. Open daily for breakfast, lunch and dinner. $$

Yarmouth

- Chez Bruno Café, 278 Main St., Yarmouth; 902 742-0031. Organic vegetables, fresh fish and free-range chicken, all impeccably prepared. Open daily, 10 am–8 pm. $$

- Rudder's, 96 Water St., Yarmouth; 902 742-7311. A seafood restaurant and microbrewery in a historic building overlooking the water. Open year-round, 11 am until late. $$

Annapolis Valley

Windsor to Kentville

- Acton's Grill and Café, 406 Main St., Wolfville; 902 542-7525. Elegant summer lunches, chilled soups, and an interesting buffet; open-air patio. One of Nova Scotia's very best restaurants. Open daily for lunch and dinner. $$$

- Between the Bushes, 1225 Middle Dyke Rd., Sheffield Mills; 902 582-3648; www.novaagri.com/between_ the_bushes. Fine dining in the middle of a big blueberry field; notable fresh scallops and haddock and, of course, blueberry desserts. Open Tues–Sun for lunch, Fri–Sun for dinner. $$$

- Blomidon Inn, 195 Main St., Wolfville; 902 542-2291; www.blomidon.ns.ca. Dine in an elegant restored sea captain's mansion, built in 1877. Open daily, year-round for lunch and dinner, 11:30 am–2 pm and 5–9:30 pm. $$$

- Cocoa Pesto Bistro, Woodshire Inn,

494 King St., Windsor; 902 472-3300; www.cocoapesto.com. Licensed bistro serving fresh and interesting food. Open daily, 5 pm–9 pm; lunch, Mon–Fri 11:30 am–2 pm; Sunday brunch 11:30–2, year-round. $$

- Evangeline Café, Evangeline Motel, 11668 Hwy.# 1, Grand-Pré; 902 542-2703; www.evangeline.ns.ca. Fabulous Valley fruit pies. Open daily to 7 pm, early May–late Oct. No liquor. $

- Falcourt Inn, 8979 Hwy. 201, Nictaux; 902 825-3399; www.falcourtinn.ns.ca. A restored fishing lodge with an exceptional view, specializing in seafood and creative beef and chicken dishes. Open daily, 5–8:30 pm, year-round. $$

- Le Caveau at Grand Pré Winery, 11611 Hwy. 1, Grand Pré; 902 542-7177; www.grandprewines.ns.ca. Northern European cuisine served in an attractive vineyard setting. Open daily, Apr.–Dec. for lunch and dinner. Reservations recommended. $$$

- Lobster Pound, Halls Harbour; 902 679-5299, www.hallsharbourlobster.ns.ca. Some of the best lobster to be had anywhere. Take it away to cook yourself, or take it to the boiling shack. Open noon–7 pm, May–Oct; 11:30 am–8:30 pm, Jul. and Aug. $

- Tempest, 117 Front St., Wolfville; 902 542-0588. Fine dining, world cuisine, ethnic lunches, fusion dinners and French accents. Open daily, 11:30 am–2:30 pm, 5:30–9 pm; no Monday lunch, May–Oct. $$$

Annapolis Royal to Digby

- Brier Island Lodge, Westport, Brier Island; 902 839-2300; www.brierisland.com. Acadian dishes and lots of seafood, from fish cakes to Solomon Gundy. Open daily, 7 am–9:30 pm, June–mid-Oct. $$

- Cape View Restaurant, Mavillette Beach; 902 645-2519. Seafood and Acadian specialties. Great view of Mavillette Beach. $$

- Chez Christophe, Hwy. 1, Grosses Coques; 902 837-5817; www.chezchristophe.ca. Acadian cooking: chicken fricot, rappie pie

and seafood as well, served in a homey atmosphere. Open Tues–Sun, 6 am–9 pm. $

★ Digby Pines Resort, Annapolis Room, Shore Rd., Digby; 902 245-2511; www.digbypines.ca. Specializing in local fish and seafood, in the luxurious surroundings of the Pines Resort Hotel. One of Nova Scotia's best restaurants. Open daily, May–mid-Oct., breakfast 7–10 am, lunch at 19th Hole noon–2 pm, dinner 6–9 pm; Sunday brunch mid-June–Sept. $$$

- Fundy Restaurant, 34 Water St., Digby; 866 445-4950; www.fundyrestaurant.com. Open daily, year-round, 7 am–10 pm in summer, 11 am–9 pm in winter. $$

- Garrison House Inn Restaurant, 350 St. George St., Annapolis Royal; 532-5750; www.come.to/garrison. Understated entrees with fresh and simple vegetable accompaniments. Save room for dessert — the strawberry rhubarb pie is wonderful! Open for dinner 5:30 pm–9 pm, early May–mid-Dec. $$

- Leo's Café, St. George St., Annapolis Royal; 902 532-7424. Tasty soups and sandwiches. Don't expect a quick lunch in mid-summer, it's apt to be crowded. Open mid-Mar.–late Dec. daily 11:30 am–6 pm,. Licensed for beer and wine only. $

- Queen Anne Inn, 494 Upper St. George St., Annapolis Royal; 902 532-7850; www.queenanneinn.ns.ca. Fine dining in elegant surroundings. Open Tues–Sat for dinner. Call for reservations. $$

- Restaurant Chez Christophe, 2655 Rte. 2, Grosses Coques; 902 837-5817. Acadian favourites and more. Open 11:30 a –2 pm and 4:30 pm–8 pm, year-round. Reservations recommended. $

Along the Fundy Shore

- Diane's Restaurant, 81 Wharf Rd., Five Islands; 902 254-3190. A good feed of fried clams right at the source. $`

- Lightkeeper's Kitchen, Cape d'Or, Advocate Harbour; 902 670-0534. Great seafood and organic vegetables served up in a charming old lightkeeper's house. Open 11 am–4 pm; 5:30–9 pm, mid-May–Oct. $$

- Murphy's Fish & Chips, 88 Esplanade, Truro; 902 895-1275. One of the best of its kind in Canada. Fried Digby clams and the seafood platter are favourites. Open Mon–Thurs 11 am–7 pm, Fri and Sat until 8 pm, Sun noon–7 pm. $

Along the Northumberland Shore

- Amherst Shore Country Inn, Hwy. 366, Lorneville; 902 661-2724; www.ascinn.ns.ca. A different four-course gourmet meal each night. Dinner daily at 7:30 pm, May–Oct.; Fri and Sat in winter. By appointment only. $$$
- The Bistro, 216 Archimedes St., New Glasgow; 902 752-4988; www.thebistro.ca. Open Tues–Sat from 5 pm, year-round. Reservations required. $$$
- ★ Gabrieau's Bistro, 350 Main St., Antigonish; 902 863-1925; gabrieaus.com. Innovative appetizers, light pasta and exceptional desserts. Open Mon–Thurs 8 am–9:30 pm, Fri and Sat to 10 pm, year-round. $$
- Hebels Restaurant, 71 Stellarton Rd., New Glasgow; 902 695-5955; www.hebelsrestaurant.ca. Open Tues–Sat from 5 pm. Call for reservation. $$$
- Mill Room, Balmoral Hotel, Hwy. 6, Tatamagouche; 902 657-2000. German specialities including sausages, sauerkraut and schnitzel, as well as Canadian dishes featuring local seafood. Open daily, noon–8 pm. $
- Pictou Lodge Resort, 172 Lodge Rd., Braeshore; Pictou; 902 485-4322; www.pictoulodge.com. Fireside and ocean-view dining in this resort since the 1920s. Open mid-May–mid-Oct, hours vary seasonally. $$$
- Sugar Moon Farm, Alex MacDonald Rd., Earltown; 902 657-3348; www.sugarmoon.ca. Rustic Pancake House on sugar maple farm. See how maple syrup is made and eat your fill. Open year-round. $

Along the Eastern Shore

- Des Barres Manor Inn, 90 Church St., Guysborough; 902 533-2099; www.desbarresmanor.com. Fresh local produce, seafood and lamb. Open daily at 7 pm, year-round, by reservation only. $$$
- Liscombe Lodge, Hwy. 7, Liscomb Mills; 800 665-6343; www.liscombelodge.ca. A relaxed resort setting and casual dining room with an accomplished kitchen. Planked salmon is a speciality; watch it being cooked on the outdoor open fire. Open daily for breakfast, lunch and dinner, mid-May–Oct. $$$
- Rare Bird Pub, Guysborough; 902 533-2128. A fine brewpub on the waterfront with good pub food. Open daily, 11 am–10 pm; weekends until 1 am, June–mid-Oct. $
- Salmon River House, 9931 Hwy. 7, Head of Jeddore; 902 889-3353; www.salmonriverhouse.com. Fresh boiled lobster and steaks on the verandah overlooking the Salmon River. Open daily for lunch and dinner, May–Oct. $$
- SeaWind Landing Country Inn, 1 Wharf Rd., Charlos Cove; 800 563-4667; www.seawindlanding.com. Picnic lunches available to guests. Open to the public for dinner by reservation only, mid-May–mid-Oct. $$

Cape Breton Island

- Castle Rock Inn, Cabot Trail, Ingonish Ferry; 888 884-7625; www.ingonish.com/castlerock. Seasonal cookery featuring local ingredients in a spectacular location overlooking Ingonish Bay. Open daily for breakfast and dinner. $$
- Chanterelle Country Inn, Cabot Trail, North River, St. Anns Bay; 866 277-0577; www.chanterelleinn.com. Cuisine based on organically grown ingredients in an attractively appointed setting overlooking St. Anns Bay. Open for dinner 6–8:30 pm by reservation; closed Mon; May–Oct. $$$
- Chowder House, Cabot Trail, Neil's Harbour; 902 336-2463. $
- Duncreigan Country Inn, 11409 Hwy. 19, Mabou; 800 840-2207 for reservations only; www.duncreigan.ca. High-quality country dining in a tranquil setting. Open 5:30–8:30 pm, year-round, by reservation. $$$
- Haus Treuburg, 175 Main St. (Hwy. 19), Port Hood; 902 787-2166. Try the homemade soup, Atlantic salmon and apple strudel for dinner. Open daily, 7–10 pm, June–Oct., by reservation only. $$$

- Herring Choker Deli, on the Trans-Canada Highway between Baddeck and Whycocomagh; 902 295-2275. Coffee shop and family restaurant. Specialty and natural food items. Bakery treats. Open daily, 8 am–8 pm, year-round. $
- Inverary Inn and Resort, 368 Shore Rd., Baddeck; 295-3500; www.capebretonresorts.com/inverary. Flora's dining room offers a full-scale menu, with Scottish touches like smoked salmon and bannock. Lakeside Café on the waterfront is more casual, and features seafood appetizers and entrees. Open daily, May–Dec. for breakfast, lunch and dinner; café, lunch and dinner only. $$$
- ★ Keltic Lodge, Middle Head Peninsula, Ingonish Beach; 800 565-0444; www.kelticlodge.ca. Fine formal dining in the Purple Thistle dining room. Five-course evening meal, menu changes daily. Open daily for breakfast, and dinner to 9 pm, mid-May–mid-Oct. $$$
- Markland Coastal Resort, Dingwall; 902 383-2246; www.marklandresort.com. Fresh lamb and local seafood, with a beautiful view of Aspy Bay from the oceanside deck. Enjoy a walk on the beach before dinner. Open 7:30–10:30 am, 6–9 pm, mid-June–mid-Oct. $$$
- The Mull Café, 11630 Cabot Trail, Mabou; 902 945-2244. Casual and quick, hearty deli sandwiches with takeout available. Open daily, 11 am–8 pm; shorter hours off-season. $
- Normaway Inn, Egypt Rd., Margaree Valley; 800 565-9463; www.normaway.com. Beautifully situated in the Margaree Valley. Four-course country gourmet meals with attentive but unobtrusive service. Open for breakfast and dinner mid-June–mid-Oct. $$$
- Red Shoe Pub, 11533 Hwy. 19, Mabou; 902 945-2996; www.redshoepub.com. Owned by the Rankin family. Entertainment every evening. Open June–mid-Oct., full menu served 11:30 am 9:30 pm. Late night menu served 10 pm–1:30 am.
- Restaurant Acadien, in the Co-operative Artisanale, 15067 Main St., Cheticamp; 902 224-3207. Authentic Acadian specialities including tourtière, chowders and fish cakes. Open daily, early May – late Oct., 7 am–9 pm. Hours vary seasonally. $$
- Rita's Tea Room, Big Pond; 902 828-2667, www.ritamacneil.com/tearoom.htm. Baked goods and Rita's Tea Room Blend Tea. Rita MacNeil's awards and photographs are on display. Open daily, 10 am–6 pm, late June–mid-Oct. $
- The Water's Edge, 22 Water St., Baddeck; 902 295-3600, www.thewatersedgeinn.com. An interesting menu of dishes that are a little out of the ordinary, and excellent desserts. A nice setting in the middle of town. Open noon–9 pm, June–Oct. $

Fleur-de-lis and Marconi Trails
- Gowrie House, 840 Shore Rd., Sydney Mines; 800 372-1115; www.gowriehouse.com. Antique-filled country inn, beautiful grounds and gardens. Fine meals are prepared from the freshest Nova Scotia ingredients. One of the province's best dining experiences. Open daily, one sitting at 7:30 pm, May–Oct. Reservations essential. Dinner for residents only rest of the year. Bring your own wine. $$$
- Vollmer's Island Paradise, 1489 Main Street, Janvrin's Harbour; 902 226-1507; www.vipilodge.com. Make reservations a day ahead for fish or meat. No smoking. Open daily, 7 pm May–Oct., by appointment only. $$

Attractions

The *Nova Scotia Doers' and Dreamers' Guide* (see *Travel Essentials*) provides exhaustive listings of the province's attractions. Guided walking tours or brochures for self-guided tours are available for many Nova Scotia communities (make inquiries at the closest tourist information centre). Here we provide a selective listing of many of the points of interest. See Museums p. 14 and Regions p. 74.

Metro Halifax
- Alexander Keith's Nova Scotia Brewery, 1496 Lower Water St., Halifax; 877 612-1820;

Attractions

- www.keiths.ca. Costumed guides lead historic tours of the oldest working brewery in North America.
- Anna Leonowens Gallery, 1891 Granville St., Halifax; 902 494-8223; www.nscad.ns.ca (Nova Scotia College of Art and Design University).
- ★ Art Gallery of Nova Scotia, 1723 Hollis St., Halifax; 902 424-7542; www.agns.gov.ns.ca
- Bedford Institute of Oceanography, located near the Dartmouth end of MacKay Bridge; 902 426-4306/2373; www.bio.gc.ca
- Black Cultural Centre for Nova Scotia, 1149 Main St., Rte. 7 at Cherrybrook Rd., Dartmouth; 800 465-0767; www.bccns.com
- *Bluenose II*, at the wharf by the Maritime Museum of the Atlantic when in Halifax; 866 579-4909; www.schoonerbluenose2.ca
- Cathedral Church of All Saints, 1320 Tower Rd., Halifax; 902 423-6002; www.cathedralchurchofallsaints.com
- Cole Harbour Heritage Farm Museum, 471 Poplar Dr., Cole Harbour (outside Dartmouth); 902 434-0222
- Dartmouth Heritage Museum, 26 Newcastle St., Dartmouth; 902 464-2300; www.dartmouthheritagemuseum.ns.ca
- Discovery Centre, 1593 Barrington St., Halifax; 902 492-4422; www.discoverycentre.ns.ca
- Grand Parade, between Barrington St. and Argyle St., Halifax.
- Halifax Citadel National Historic Site of Canada, overlooking downtown Halifax (you can't miss it); 902 426-5080; www.pc.gc.ca/lhn-nhs/ns/halifax/
- ★ Halifax Public Gardens, Spring Garden Rd. at South Park St., Halifax
- Halifax Regional Library, 5381 Spring Garden Rd., Halifax; 902 490-5700; www.halifaxpubliclibraries.ca/
- Hemlock Ravine Park, Kent Ave., off Bedford Highway.
- Historic Properties, 1869 Upper Water St., on the Halifax waterfront; 902 429-0530; www.historicproperties.ca
- HMCS *Sackville*: Canada's Naval Memorial, at the wharf of the Maritime Museum, Halifax; 902 429-2132; www.hmcssackville-cnmt.ns.ca
- Little Dutch (Deutsch) Church, Brunswick St. at Gerrish, Halifax; 902 423-1059.
- Maritime Command Museum, Admiralty House, 2725 Gottingen St., Halifax; 902 427-0550 ext 8250; users.pspmembers.com/marcommuseum
- ★ Maritime Museum of the Atlantic, 1675 Lower Water St., Halifax; 902 424-7890; museum.gov.ns.ca/mma
- Museum of Natural History, 1747 Summer St., Halifax; 902 424-7353; museum.gov.ns.ca/mnh
- Nova Scotia Centre for Craft and Design, 1061 Marginal Rd., Halifax; 902 492-2522; www.craft-design.ns.ca
- Old Burying Grounds and Welsford-Parker Monument, Barrington St. (across from Government House), Halifax; 902 429-2240.
- Old Town Clock, at the base of the Citadel. Halifax's most famous landmark.
- Pier 21 National Historic Site of Canada, 1055 Marginal Rd., Halifax; 902 425-7770; www.pier21.ca
- Prince of Wales Tower National Historic Site of Canada, Point Pleasant Park (Tower Rd. entrance), Halifax; 902 426-5080; www.pc.gc.ca/lhn-nhs/ns/prince
- ★ Province House, 1726 Hollis St., Halifax; 902 424-4661; www.gov.ns.ca/legislature
- Quaker House, 57–59 Ochterloney St., Dartmouth; 902 464-2253; www.dartmouthheritagemuseum.ns.ca/quaker.html
- ★ St. George's Round Church, 2222 Brunswick St., Halifax; 902 423-1059; www.roundchurch.ca
- St. Paul's Anglican Church, at the Grand Parade, Halifax; 902 429-2240; www.stpaulshalifax.org
- Shearwater Aviation Museum, at CFB Shearwater; 902 720-1083; www.shearwateraviationmuseum.ns.ca
- Sir Sanford Fleming Park (the Dingle), Dingle Rd., off Purcell's Cove Rd. on Northwest Arm, Halifax.
- York Redoubt National Historic Site of Canada, Purcell's Cove Rd., Halifax; 902 426-5080; www.pc.gc.ca/lhn-nhs/ns/york

Along the South Shore

Peggys Cove and Hubbards
- deGarthe Gallery, Peggys Cove; 902 823-2256.
- The Shore Club, Hubbards; 902 857-9555; www.shoreclub.ca
- SwissAir Memorial, Hwy. 333.
- Village of Peggys Cove and lighthouse; Hwy. 333.
- William E. deGarthe Memorial Monument, Peggys Cove.

Chester to Mahone Bay
- Amos Pewter, interpretive workshop, 589 Main St., Mahone Bay; 800 565-3369; www.amospewter.com
- Lordly House Museum and Park, 133 Central St., Chester; 902 275-3842
- Mahone Bay Centre, 45 School St., Mahone Bay; 902 624-0890; www.mahonebaycentre.com
- Mahone Bay Settlers' Museum, 578 Main St., Mahone Bay; 902 624-6263; www.settlersmuseum.ns.ca
- Ross Farm Living Museum of Agriculture, New Ross (on Rte. 12, exit 9 from Hwy. 103 at Chester Basin); 902 689-2210; museum.gov.ns.ca/rfm/
- The Three Churches, Edgewater Rd., Hwy. 3, Mahone Bay.

Bridgewater and Lunenburg
- ★ *Bluenose II*, at the Fisheries Museum wharf, Lunenburg; 866 579-4909; www.schoonerbluenose2.ca
- Captain Angus J. Walters House Museum, 37 Tannery Rd., Lunenburg; 902 634-2010
- DesBrisay Museum, 130 Jubilee Rd., Bridgewater; 902 543-4033; www.town.bridgewater.ns.ca/museum.htm
- ★ Fisheries Museum of the Atlantic, Montague St. (on the waterfront), Lunenburg; 866 579-4909; fisheries.museum.gov.ns.ca
- Fort Point Museum, Fort Point Rd., off Rte. 331, LaHave; 902 688-1632; www.fortpointmuseum.com. Site of Fort Ste. Marie de Grace, the first capital of New France (1632–1636).
- Lunenburg Academy, Kaulbach St., Lunenburg; it can be seen from any road into Lunenburg.
- Knaut-Rhuland House Museum, 125 Pelham St., Lunenburg; 902 634-3498; www.lunenburgheritagesociety.ca

- St. John's Church, Cumberland St., Lunenburg; 902 634-4994; www.stjohnslunenburg.org
- Wile Carding Mill, 242 Victoria Rd., Bridgewater; 902 543-8233; cardingmill.museum.gov.ns.ca

Liverpool and Shelburne
- Archelaus Smith Museum, Rte. 330, Centreville, Cape Sable Island (across the causeway); 902 745-3361; www.archelaus.org
- Argyle Township Courthouse & Gaol, 8168 Hwy. 3, Tusket; 902 648-2493; www.argylecourthouse.com
- Dory Shop Museum, Dock St., Shelburne; 902 875-3219; doryshop.museum.gov.ns.ca
- Fort Point Lighthouse Park, 21 Fort Lane, end of Main St., Liverpool; 902 354-5260
- Hank Snow Country Music Centre, 148 Bristol Ave., Liverpool; 888 450-5525; www.hanksnow.com
- Perkins House Museum, 105 Main St., Liverpool; 902 354-4058; wperkins.museum.gov.ns.ca
- Queens County Museum, 109 Main St., Liverpool; 902 354-4058; www.queenscountymuseum.com
- Rossignol Cultural Centre, 205 Church St., Liverpool; 902 354-3067; www.rossignolculturalcentre.com
- Ross-Thompson House and Store Museum, 9 Charlotte Lane, Shelburne; 902 875-3141; museum.gov.ns.ca/rth
- Shelburne County Museum, 20 Dock St., Shelburne; 902 875-3219; www.historicshelburne.com
- Sherman Hines Museum of Photography & Galleries, 219 Main St., Liverpool; 902 354-2667; www.shermanhinesphotographymuseum.com

Barrington
- Barrington Woolen Mill Museum, 2368 Hwy. 3, Barrington; 902 637-2185; woolenmill.museum.gov.ns.ca
- The Old Meeting House, 2048 Hwy. 3, Barrington; 902 637-2185; meetinghouse.museum.gov.ns.ca
- Seal Island Light Museum, Hwy. 3, Barrington; 902 637-2185; maxwelbm@gov.ns.ca

Pubnico and Yarmouth
- Cape Forchu Light, Rte. 304, Cape Fourchu Scenic Drive; 902 742-4522; www.district.yarmouth.ns.ca/go.aspx?ID=10

Attractions

- Firefighters' Museum of Nova Scotia, 451 Main St., Yarmouth; 902 742-5525; firefighters.museum.gov.ns.ca
- Killam Brothers Shipping Office, 90 Water St., at the foot of Central St. on the waterfront; 902 742-5539; yarmouthcountymuseum.ednet.ns.ca
- Musée Acadien, Hwy. 103, exit 31, West Pubnico; 902 762-3380; www.museeacadien.ca
- Le Village Historique Acadien (Historical Acadian Village), Hwy. 103, exit 31, Old Church Rd., West Pubnico; 902 762-2530; acadianvillage.museum.gov.ns.ca
- Yarmouth County Museum and Archives, 22 Collins St., Yarmouth; 902 742-5539; yarmouthcountymuseum.ednet.ns.ca

Annapolis Valley and Acadian Shore

Mount Uniacke, Windsor and Wolfville

- Fort Edward National Historic Site, near exit 6 on Hwy. 101, Windsor; 902 798-4706; www.pc.gc.ca/lhn-nhs/ns/edward
- Grand-Pré National Historic Site, 866 542-3631; www.grand-pre.com
- ★ Haliburton House Museum, 414 Clifton Ave., Windsor; 902 798-2915; haliburton.museum.gov.ns.ca
- Harriet Irving Botanical Gardens, Wolfville; 902 585-5242; botanicalgardens.acadiau.ca
- Howard Dill Enterprises, 400 College Rd., Windsor; 902 798-2728; www.howarddill.com
- Prescott House, 1633 Starr's Pt. Rd. (off Hwy. 358), Starr's Point (near Wolfville); 902 542-3984; prescott.museum.gov.ns.ca
- Randall House Historical Museum, 259 Main St., Wolfville; 902 542-9775; wolfvillehs.ednet.ns.ca
- Robie Tufts Nature Centre, Front St., Wolfville.
- Shand House Museum, 389 Avon St., Windsor; 902 798-8213; shand.museum.gov.ns.ca
- Uniacke Estate Museum Park, 758 Main Rd. (Hwy. 1), Mount Uniacke; 902 866-2560; uniacke.museum.gov.ns.ca
- Windsor Hockey Heritage Centre, 128 Gerrish St., Windsor; 902 798-1800; www.birthplaceeofhockey.com

Kentville to Middleton

- Annapolis Valley Macdonald Museum, 21 School St., Middleton; 902 825-6116; www.macdonaldmuseum.ca
- Kentville Agricultural Centre and Blair House Museum, Rte. 1, Kentville; 902 679-5333
- Kings County Museum, in the Old Kings Courthouse, 37 Cornwallis St., Kentville; 902 678-6237; www.okcm.ca
- Oaklawn Farm Zoo, Hwy. 101, exit 16, Aylesford; 902 847-9790; www.oaklawnfarmzoo.ca

Digby and Annapolis Royal

- Admiral Digby Museum, 95 Montague Row, Digby; 902 245-6322; www.admuseum.ns.ca
- ★ Annapolis Royal Historic Gardens, 441 Saint George St., Annapolis Royal; 902 532-7018; www.historicgardens.com
- Annapolis Tidal Generating Station, at the Annapolis River Causeway; 902 532-5454.
- deGannes-Cosby House, 477 St. George St., Annapolis Royal.
- First Nations Heritage and Cultural Centre, Bear River; 902 467-0301; www.bearriverculturalcenter.com
- Fort Anne National Historic Site, St. George St., Annapolis Royal; 902 532-2321; www.pc.gc.ca/fortanne
- North Hills Museum, 5065 Granville Rd., Granville Ferry; 902 532-2168; northhills.museum.gov.ns.ca
- O'Dell House Museum, 136 Lower St. George St., Annapolis Royal; 902 532-7754; www.annapolisheritagesociety.com
- ★ Port Royal National Historic Site of Canada (the Habitation), Rte. 1 to Granville Ferry, 12 kilometres southwest at Port Royal; 902 532-2898; www.pc.gc.ca/portroyal
- Sinclair Inn Museum, 232 St. George St., Annapolis Royal; 902 532-7754; www.annapolisheritagesociety.com
- Upper Clements Park, 2931 Hwy. 1, 6 kilometres west of Annapolis Royal; 888 248-4567; www.upperclementsparks.com
- Upper Clements Wildlife Park, Hwy. 1, 6 kilometres west of Annapolis Royal; 532-5924; www.upperclementsparks.com

Acadian Shore
- L'Église Saint-Bernard (St. Bernard Church), Hwy. 1, St. Bernard; 902 837-5687; www.baiesaintemarie.com
- L'Église Sainte-Marie (St. Mary's Church), and St. Mary's Museum, Church Point; 769-2832; www.baiesaintemarie.com/ste-marie
- Université Sainte-Anne, Church Point; 769-2114; www.usainteanne.ca

Along the Fundy Shore
Amherst and Springhill
- Anne Murray Centre, 36 Main St., Springhill; 902 597-8614; www.annemurray.com
- Cumberland County Museum, 150 Church St., Amherst; 902 667-2561; www.cumberlandcountymuseum.com
- Springhill Miners' Museum, 145 Black River Rd., Springhill; 902 597-3449.

Joggins to Parrsboro
- Age of Sail Centre, 8334 Hwy. 209, Port Greville; 902 348-2030; www.ageofsailmuseum.ca
- Fundy Geological Museum, 162 Two Islands Rd., Parrsboro; 866 856-3466; www.fundygeo.museum.gov.ns.ca
- Joggins Fossil Centre, Main St., Joggins; 902 251-2727; jogginsfossilcliffs.net/
- Parrsboro Rock and Mineral Shop and Museum, 349 Whitehall Rd., Parrsboro; 902 254-2981; www.parrsbororockandmineralmuseum.com

Truro, Maitland and Shubenacadie
- Burntcoat Head Park, Noel. Site of world's highest recorded tides. Lighthouse and walking trail.
- Glooscap Heritage Centre, 65 Treaty Trail, (exit 13A off Hwy. 102) just outside Truro; 902 843-3496; www.glooscapheritagecentre.com
- Lawrence House Museum, 8660 Hwy. 215, Maitland; 902 261-2628; lawrence.museum.gov.ns.ca
- Shubenacadie Provincial Wildlife Park, near exit 11 on Hwy. 102, Shubenacadie; 902 758-2040; wildlifepark.gov.ns.ca
- Victoria Park, Park Rd. and Brunswick St., Truro; 893-6078; www.colchester.ca/Services/Trails/victoria.htm

Along the Northumberland Shore
Pictou to Antigonish
- Cape George Lighthouse, Cape George Point overlooking Cape George Bay. Hwy. 337 from Antigonish.
- Hector Exhibit & Research Centre, 86 Haliburton Rd., Pictou; 902 485-4563; www.rootsweb.com/~nspcghs
- Hector Heritage Quay, 33 Caladh Ave., Pictou; 877 574-2868; www.townofpictou.com
- McCulloch House Museum, 100 Haliburton Rd., Pictou; 902 485-4563; museum.gov.ns.ca/mch
- Northumberland Fisheries Museum, 71 Front St., Pictou; 902 485-4972; www.northumberlandfisheriesmuseum.com
- Nova Scotia Museum of Industry, 147 North Foord Street, Hwy. 104 at exit 24, Stellarton; 902 755-5425; museum.gov.ns.ca/moi
- St. Ninian's Cathedral, 121 St. Ninian St. Antigonish; 902 863-2338.

Tatamagouche to Amherst
- Balmoral Grist Mill Museum, 660 Matheson Brook Rd., off Rte. 311, Balmoral Mills; 902 657-3016; gristmill.museum.gov.ns.ca
- Creamery Square Museum and Archives, 257 Main St., Tatamagouche; 902 657-3500; www.creamerysquare.ca
- Jost Vineyards, off Rte. 6, between Tatamagouche and Pugwash at Malagash; 800 565-4567; www.jostwine.com
- Northumberland Arts Council Fraser Cultural Centre, Main St., Tatamagouche; 902 657-3285, 902 657-3667 (off-season).
- Sugar Moon Farm, Alex MacDonald Rd., Earltown. Atlantic Canada's Maple Syrup Economuseum. 866 816-2753; www.sugarmoon.ca
- Sutherland Steam Mill Museum, off Rte. 326, Denmark; 902 657-3016; steammill.museum.gov.ns.ca

Along the Eastern Shore
- Canso Islands National Historic Site, Union St., 1 km off the coast of Canso; 902 295-2069; www.pc.gc.ca/lhn-nhs/ns/canso
- Canso Museum, Whitman House, 1297 Union St., Canso;

Attractions

902 366-2170 or 902 366-2525.
- Fisherman's Life Museum, 58 Navy Pool Loop, Jeddore Oyster Pond, off Rte. 7; 902 889-2053; fishermanslife.museum.gov.ns.ca
- Memory Lane Heritage Village, Rte. 7, Lake Charlotte; 877 287-0697; www.heritagevillage.ca
- Moose River Gold Mines Museum, Moose River Rd., Rte. 224; Moose River Gold Mines; 902 384-2484; www.mvta.net
- Musquodoboit Railway Museum, Main St., Rte. 7, Musquodoboit Harbour; 902 889-2689; www.trainweb.org/canadianrailways /Museums/NovaScotia.html
- Nova Scotia Lighthouse Interpretive Centre, Rte. 211, Port Bickerton; 902 364-2000
- Sherbrooke Village, off Rte. 7, near the modern village of Sherbrooke; 888 743-7845; sherbrookevillage.museum.gov.ns.ca

Cape Breton Island
Cabot Trail
- Acadian Museum, 15067 Main St. (at Co-operative Artisinale de Cheticamp Ltée), Cheticamp; 902 224-2170; www.co-opartisanale.com
- ★ Alexander Graham Bell National Historic Site, Chebucto St. (Hwy. 205), Baddeck; 902 295-2069; www.pc.gc.ca/lhn-nhs/ns/grahambell
- Cape Breton Highlands National Park, 902 224-2306; www.pc.gc.ca/pn-np/ns/cbreton
- Centre de la Mi-Carême, 12615 Cabot Trail, St. Joseph du Moine; 902 224-1016 or 902 224-2665.
- Giant MacAskill Museum, Rte. 312, Englishtown; 902 929-2925
- The Great Hall of the Clans at the Gaelic College of Celtic Arts and Crafts, South Gut St. Anns; 902 295-3441; www.gaeliccollege.edu
- Highland Village Museum, 4119 Hwy. 223, Iona; 866 442-3542; highlandvillage.museum.gov.ns.ca
- Joe's Scarecrow Theatre, Cap Le Moine, Cabot Trail.
- L'Église Saint-Pierre (Church of St. Peter), Cheticamp; 902 224-2062
- Les Trois Pignons Museum of the Hooked Rug and Home Life, Dr. Elizabeth LeFort Gallery, 15584 Main St., Cheticamp; 902 224-2642 or 902 224-2612; www.lestroispignons.com
- Lone Shieling, at the base of North Mountain, Cape Breton Highlands National Park.
- MacAskill House Museum, St. Peter's. Works of great marine photographer Wallace MacAskill.
- Margaree Salmon Museum, 60 East Big Intervale Rd., North East Margaree; 902 248-2848; www.invernessco.com/margaree_ museum.html
- Orangedale Station Museum, 1428 Main St., Orangedale. Rolling stock and rail history of the area; 902 756-3384; fortress.uccb.ns.ca/historic/oranstat.html
- St. Peters Canal National Historic Site, St. Peter's. Links the Atlantic Ocean with the Bras d'Or Lakes.
- Wagmatcook Culture and Heritage Centre, Wagmatcook; 866 295-2999; www.wagmatcook.com
- Whale Interpretive Centre, Pleasant Bay; 902 224-1411.

Ceilidh Trail
- An Drochaid (The Bridge) Museum, 11513 Rte. 19, Mabou; 902 945-2790
- Cape Breton's Celtic Music Interpretive Centre, Judique; 902 787-2708; www.celticmusicsite.com
- Chestico Museum, 8095 Rte. 19, Harbourview, just south of Port Hood; 902 787-2244 or 902 787-3104; www.porthood.ca/attractions/view/ chestico-museum
- Glenora Distillery, Single Malt Whisky Economuseum; 800 839-0491; www.glenoradistillery.com
- Inverness Miners' Museum, 62 Lower Railway St., in the old CNR station, Inverness; 902 258-3822.

Fleur-de-lis and Marconi Trails and Metro Cape Breton
- Cape Breton Centre for Heritage and Science, 225 George St., Sydney; 902 539-1572.
- Cape Breton Miners' Museum, 42 Birkley St., Quarry Point, Glace Bay; 902 849-4522; www.minersmuseum.com
- Cossit House Museum, 75 Charlotte St., Sydney; 902 539-7973 or 902 539-1572; cossit.museum.gov.ns.ca
- ★ Fortress of Louisbourg National Historic Site of Canada, Louisbourg; 902 733-2280 or 902 733-3546; www.pc.gc.ca/louisbourg

- Jost Heritage House, 54 Charlotte St., Sydney; 902 539-0366.
- LeNoir Forge Museum, Lower St., Arichat; 902 226-9364.
- Marconi National Historic Site of Canada, Timmerman St., Glace Bay; 902 295-2069; www.pc.gc.ca/lhn-nhs/marconi
- St. Patrick's Church Museum, 87 Esplanade, Sydney; 902 562-8237
- Sydney and Louisburg Railway Museum, Louisbourg; 902 733-2720; fortress.uccb.ns.ca/historic/s_l.html
- Two Rivers Wildlife Park, Grand Mira North Rd., Marion Bridge (off Rte. 327); 902 727-2483; www.tworiverspark.ca

Festivals & Events

What follows is a listing by area of some of the best and most popular festivals and events in the province. For a complete listing, consult the *Nova Scotia Festivals and Events Guide*, available at visitor information centres or at NovaScotia.com. The scheduling of many of these events is subject to change; the Nova Scotia Information and Reservation Service (800 565-0000) will provide updated information. See Festivals and Events p. 39

Province-wide

May/June
- Musique Royale. Early and traditional music in historic venues all summer. www.musiqueroyale.com

Sept/Oct
- Discover the Wines of Nova Scotia Fall Festival. Wine tastings, grape stomps, wine pairings. www.winesofnovascotia.ca

Halifax

Year-round
- St. Cecilia Concert Series. Classical music at Lilian Piercey Concert Hall in the Maritime Conservatory of Performing Arts and other venues; www.stcecilia.ca
- Symphony Nova Scotia. Concerts at Rebecca Cohn Auditorium in the Dalhousie Arts Centre and other venues, Sept – May; www.symphonynovascotia.ca

May/June
- Scotia Festival of Music. Internationally renowned festival of chamber music. www.scotiafestival.ns.ca

June
- Greek Festival. Three-day feast put on by the Halifax Greek community. www.greekfest.org
- Halifax Celtic Feis. Celebration of Scottish and Irish heritage. www.halifaxcelticfeis.com
- Halifax Highland Games and Scottish Festival. The Garrison Grounds, Halifax. www.halifaxhighlandgames.com
- Multifest (Nova Scotia Multicultural Festival), Dartmouth. Food, music and dancing offered by Nova Scotia's different ethnic communities. www.multifest.ca

July
- Africville Reunion. The spirit of the Black community of Africville is revived at Seaview Park; picnic, church service and dance.
- Atlantic Jazz Festival. Outdoor concerts and late-night sessions in city bars. www.jazzeast.com
- Halifax Highland Games and Scottish Festival, Dartmouth. www.halifaxhighlandgames.com
- Maritime Fiddle Festival, Dartmouth. Top-notch competitors from Canada and the United States. www3.ns.sympatico.ca/marfiddlefest
- Nova Scotia Designer Crafts Council Summer Festival. A juried market draws many of the province's best craftspeople. www.nsdcc.ns.ca
- Royal Nova Scotia International Tattoo. A musical extravaganza with a military flavour. www.nstattoo.ca

August
- Halifax International Busker Festival. Street performers, including jugglers and clowns, provide 10 days of fun along the waterfront. www.buskers.ca

September
- Atlantic Film Festival. Independent films and parties celebrating the industry. www.atlanticfilm.com
- Atlantic Fringe Festival. Alternative plays performed around the city. www.atlanticfringe.com
- DRUM! A musical production of

drums and dance of four cultures on the waterfront, Sept.–mid-Oct. www.drumshow.ca
- Maritime Fall Fair. Brings the country to the city; animals, food, entertainment. www.maritimefallfair.com
- Nova Scotia International Airshow. Atlantic Canada's largest demonstration of aerial acrobatics. www.nsairshow.ca
- Word on the Street. Book sales, displays, author readings and entertainment. www.thewordonthestreet.ca

October
- Halifax Pop Explosion, Halifax. halifaxpopexplosion.co

Along the South Shore

May
- Birding and Nature Festival. Shelburne County. www.discovershelburnecounty.com/birdfestival.html
- Liverpool International Theatre Festival (every second year). www.astortheatre.ns.ca
- Mahone Bay Mussel Festival. Mahone Bay and Indian Point. www.mahone bay.com

June/July
- Festival Acadien International de Par-en-Bas, Wedgeport, Argyle. Celebrates Acadian heritage through music, food and dance. festivalacadien.net
- Music at the Three Churches, Mahone Bay. Classical music every second Friday all summer. www.threechurches.com
- Privateer Days. Liverpool. Includes historical re-enactments, guided tours. www.privateerdays.com
- Tern Festival. West Pubnico. www.museeacadien.ca/english/events/tern.htm

July
- Boxwood Festival. Lunenburg. Celebrates traditions of the flute. www.boxwood.org
- Lunenburg Festival of Crafts. Quality crafts from the province's top artisans.
- Music at the Three Churches. Classical music in Mahone Bay (July and August). www.threechurches.com

- Shelburne Founders' Days. Commemorates the arrival of thousands of United Empire Loyalists in the 1780s. www.shelburnenovascotia.com/foundersdays
- South Shore Exhibition, Bridgewater. Century-old agricultural exhibition featuring ox-pulls, among the many events. www.thebigex.com
- Yarmouth Seafest. A celebration of life by the sea with a parade, chowder cook-off and fish feast, and other events. www.seafest.ca

August
- Chester Race Week. Atlantic Canada's largest regatta. The Front and Back harbours are crowded with sleek yachts. www.chesterraceweek.com
- Hank Snow Tribute. Bridgewater Exhibition Grounds.
- Lunenburg Fishermen's Picnic and Reunion. A festival for the fisheries that features unusual and entertaining competitions like net mending, scallop shucking and dory racing.
- Lunenburg Folk Harbour Festival. The Lunenburg waterfront provides an idyllic setting for a series of performances by folk musicians. www.folkharbour.com
- Mahone Bay Classic Boat Festival. Boatbuilding competitions and demonstrations, and events recalling the town's shipbuilding tradition. www.woodenboatfestival.org
- Nova Scotia Folk Art Festival. Celebrates the work of Nova Scotia's best folk artists. www.nsfolkartfestival.com

September
- Lights Along the Shore Lighthouse Festival, at various sites along the South Shore. www.ssta.com
- Whirligig & Weathervane Festival, Shelburne Harbour. Prizes for contestants. Observers help judge and may buy the wonderful, whimsical creations. www.whirligigfestival.com

October
- Great Scarecrow Festival and Antique Fair, Mahone Bay. Dozens of vendors in three venues; music, food, activities for kids, and scarecrows everywhere. www.mahonebay.com

November/December
- Father Christmas Festival, Mahone Bay. Larger than life Father Christmas figures, candle-lit streets, horse-drawn taxi, Victorian carolers. www.mahonebay.com

Annapolis Valley and Acadian Shore

May
- Annapolis Valley Apple Blossom Festival, Windsor to Digby. Community-based celebrations herald the arrival of another growing season. www.appleblossom.com
- Musique de la Baie, Venues throughout the District of Clare. Acadian kitchen parties all summer. www.baiesaintmarie.com

June
- Fox Mountain Bluegrass Festival, Berwick. www.foxmountaincampingpark.com
- Musique Saint-Bernard, Saint Bernard. Fine music in St. Bernard Church, Sunday afternoons in summer. www3.ns.sympatico.ca/musiquestb
- Rhododendron Sunday, Kentville Agricultural Centre.

July
- Bear River Cherry Carnival. Bear River.
- Festival Acadien de Clare. Colourful Acadian celebration that runs the length of the Acadian Shore. www.festivalacadiendeclare.ca
- Heart of the Valley Days, Middleton. Parade, concert and fireworks. www.town.middleton.ns.ca
- Journée Acadienne de Grand-Pré, Grand-Pré. Acadian music, heritage, culture. www.grand-pre.com
- Music and Martinis. Domaine de Grand Pré Winery, Grand Pré. Thursday evenings during July and August.

August
- Annapolis Valley Exhibition, Lawrencetown. Showcase of Valley agriculture, with top-name entertainment.
- Digby Scallop Days. A feast of Digby scallops and a scallop-shucking competition. www.townofdigby.ns.ca
- Natal Days Craft and Antique Show, Annapolis Royal. Fast-growing community of craftspeople displays its wares.

September/October
- Deep Roots Music Festival. Wolfville. A celebration of the music of the peoples who have settled Nova Scotia. www.deeprootsmusic.ca
- Hants County Exhibition, Windsor. North America's oldest agricultural fair. www.hantscounty.com
- Pumpkin Festival, Hants County Exhibition Grounds, Windsor. Growers of giant pumpkins vie for the World's Biggest Pumpkin title. www.worldsbiggestpumpkins.com
- Pumpkin Regatta, Windsor. Giant gourds take to the water for riotous races. www.worldsbiggestpumpkins.com

Along the Fundy Shore

May
- Truro International Tulip Festival. www.downtowntruro.ca

August
- Dutch Mason Blues Festival, Truro. Blues, bike show and BBQ. www.dutchmason.com/festival
- Nova Scotia's Gem and Mineral Show, Parrsboro. Guided walks, lectures, demonstrations. museum.gov.ns.ca/fgm/mineralgem/show.html
- Nova Scotia Provincial Exhibition, Truro. Parade, equestrian events, animals, food, entertainment. www.nspe.ca
- Wild Blueberry Harvest Festival, throughout central Nova Scotia. Teas, suppers, pancake breakfasts. www.wildblueberryfest.com

September
- Maitland Launch Day, Maitland. Costumed villagers, parade and re-enactment of launch of the *W.D. Lawrence*.

Along the Northumberland Shore

July/September
- New Scotland Days, Pictou. Events throughout the summer.

July
- Antigonish Ceilidhs, Antigonish. At Piper's Pub.

Festivals & Events

- Antigonish Highland Games. Highland competitions from dancing to caber tossing make this Nova Scotia's best Scottish festival. www.antigonishhighlandgames.com
- Evolve Festival. Antigonish. Summer celebration of music, culture and social awareness. www.evolvefestival.com
- Gathering of the Clans and Fishermen's Regatta, Pugwash. A Scottish festival capped off by a lobster dinner. www.pugwashvillage.com/gathering.html
- Kites and Kayaks Festival, Pictou Lodge, Pictou. Family fun on the water and in the sky.
- New Glasgow Riverfront Music Jubilee, New Glasgow. Some of the best of East Coast music. Late July–early August. www.jubilee.ns.ca
- Pictou Lobster Carnival. Fishermen's competitions and Northumberland Strait lobsters are the highlights at this community festival. www.townofpictou.com
- Pictou Summer Musical Showcase, Pictou. On the waterfront Sundays and Mondays in July and August.

August

- Festival of the Tartans, New Glasgow. Massed bands, Highland dance competitions and all things Scottish. www.festivalofthetartans.ca
- Hector Festival, Pictou. Celebrates the coming of the Scots to Nova Scotia aboard the *Hector*. www.townofpictou.ca
- Race on the River, the Pictou County Dragon Boat Festival, New Glasgow.

September

- Oktoberfest, Tatamagouche. Post-war immigration to the North Shore gave rise to this traditional German celebration. www.nsoktoberfest.ca

Along the Eastern Shore

July

- St. Mary's Chowderfest & Sherbrooke Shindig, Sherbrooke. Good eating, music and dancing. museum.gov.ns.ca/sv/chowderfest.php
- Sherbrooke Village Courthouse Concert Series. Sherbrooke. Jul.–Oct. Folk, pop and traditional music. museum.gov.ns.ca/sv/concert-series.php
- Stan Rogers Folk Festival, Canso. A celebration of the music of one of Canada's most celebrated folk musicians. www.stanfest.com

August

- Clam Harbour Beach Sand Castle and Sculpture Contest. The fine, white sand along one of Nova Scotia's best beaches is an ideal building material.

November

- Old Fashioned Christmas, Sherbrooke. Crafts, concerts, dining and family activities. museum.gov.ns.ca/sv/christmas.php

Cape Breton Island

April

- Cape Breton International Drum Festival, Sydney, at the Membertou Centre. Some of the world's best drummers. www.cbdrumfest.ca

June to September

- Ceilidhs at the Creamery, Port Hawkesbury. Tuesdays, all summer. www.ceilidh.ca
- Mabou Ceilidhs. See for yourself why this village of 400 is home to several of Nova Scotia's best musicians. Tuesdays. There are also Wednesday-night ceilidhs throughout July and August in Judique. www.invernessco.com/ceilidhs.html

July

- Big Pond Festival. Cape Breton music, highlighting Big Pond's most famous resident, Rita MacNeil.
- Broad Cove Scottish Concert, near Inverness. A highlight of the summer ceilidh season. www.broadcoveconcert.ca
- Judique-on-the-Floor Days. More of Cape Breton's best music. www.invernesscounty.com
- Pow Wow, Chapel Island First Nation. potlotek.ca/cifn/powwow.html. A tribal gathering with drumming, dancing and feasting.

July/August

- Festival de l'Escaouette, Cheticamp. An Acadian celebration, featuring a special mass in Cheticamp's exquisite church. www.festivallescaouette.com
- Granville Green Concerts, Port Hawkesbury. Free concerts every

Sunday. www.granvillegreen.com
- Inverness Gathering, Inverness. Ceilidhs, dinners, song and dance.
- Louisbourg Crab Festival, Louisbourg. Early August.

August
- Baddeck Regatta. The highlight of Baddeck's summer sailing season since 1904.
- Feast of St. Louis. An 18th-century feast at the Fortress of Louisbourg.
- Gaelic Mod, South Gut St. Anns. Music and other Gaelic arts at the home of the Gaelic College. www.gaeliccollege.edu

September/October
- Celtic Colours. An island-wide celebration of Celtic music featuring Cape Breton and international performers. www.celtic-colours.com
- Hike the Highlands Festival, on the Cabot Trail. Ten days of guided hikes; entertainment, BBQs and more. www.hikethehighlandsfestival.com

Theatre

Halifax is home to Neptune Theatre, Nova Scotia's only professional live repertory theatre group. Also, a surprising number of communities throughout the province, including Halifax, are summertime venues for live theatre. Many productions are distinctly Nova Scotian, revealing much about the province and its people. See *Theatre* p. 24.
- 2b Theatre Company, 5670 Macara St., Halifax; 902 453-6267; www.2btheatre.com
- Alderney Landing Theatre, 2 Ochterloney St., Dartmouth; 902 461-4698; 888 311-9090; www.alderneylanding.com/theatre/theatre.html
- Atlantic Fringe Festival; 902 471-7081; 800 565-0000; www.atlanticfringe.ca. Five stages in downtown Halifax.
- Bicentennial Theatre, 12390 Hwy. 224, Middle Musquodoboit; 902 384-2819; www3.ns.sympatico.ca/bicentennial.theatre
- Bus Stop Theatre, Arts Space, 2203 Gottingen St., Halifax.
- Centrestage Theatre, 363-R Main St., Kentville; 902 678-8040; www.centrestagetheatre.ca

- The Chester Playhouse, Pleasant St., Chester; 902 275-3933, 800 363-7529; www.chesterplayhouse.ns.ca. Site of the Chester Theatre Festival, Jul.–Aug.
- DalTheatre, 6135 University Ave., Halifax; 800 874-1669; www.theatre.dal.ca
- Dartmouth Players Theatre, 5 Crichton Ave., Dartmouth; 465-7529; www.dartmouthplayers.ns.ca
- deCoste Entertainment Centre, Water St., Pictou; 800 353-5338; www.decostecentre.ca
- Eastern Front Theatre, Alderney Landing, Dartmouth; 902 463-7529; www.easternfront.ns.ca
- Festival Antigonish Summer Theatre, Bauer Theatre, St. Francis Xavier University, Antigonish. Jul.–Aug. 902 867-3333; 800 563-7529; www.festivalantigonish.com
- Grafton Street Dinner Theatre, 1741 Grafton St., Halifax; 902 425-1961; www.graftonstdinnertheatre.com
- Halifax Feast Dinner Theatre, Maritime Centre, Barrington St., Halifax; 902 420-1840; www.feastdinnertheatre.com
- Irondale Ensemble, 2182 Gottingen St., Halifax; 902 429-1370; www.irondale.ca. Critical and thoughtful alternative theatre.
- King's Theatre, Lower St. George St., Annapolis Royal; 800 818-8587; www.kingstheatre.ca. Site of the Annapolis Royal Summer Theatre Festival in July and August.
- Liverpool International Theatre Festival (bi-annually in May), Astor Theatre, Gorham St., Liverpool; 902 354-5250; www.litf.ca
- Louisbourg Playhouse, 11 Aberdeen St., Louisbourg; 902 733-2996; 888 733-2787, June-Oct.; www.louisbourgplayhouse.com
- Mermaid Theatre, Mermaid Imperial Performing Arts Centre, Windsor; 902 798-5841; www.mermaidtheatre.ns.ca. Unique puppetry adaptations of children's literature.
- Mulgrave Road Theatre, 68 Main St., Guysborough; 902 533-2092; www.mulgraveroad.ca. Creates, develops and produces original plays.
- Neptune Theatre, 1593 Argyle St., Halifax; 902 429-7070; 800 565-7345; www.neptunetheatre.com. Professional repertory theatre.

Theatre

- Octagon Performing Arts Centre, Dingwall; 902 383-2246; www.octagonarts.com. Chamber and Ceilidh concerts.
- The Rebecca Cohn, Dalhousie Arts Centre, University Ave., Halifax; 902 494-3820; www.dal.ca/artscentre. A variety of live performances, including the Symphony Nova Scotia concert series.
- Savoy Theatre, 19 Union St., Glace Bay; 902 842-1577; 902 564-6668; www.savoytheatre.com. A lively blend of Celtic music and humour all summer long.
- Shakespeare by the Sea, Halifax. Open air theatre in Point Pleasant Park; 902 422-0295; www.shakespearebythesea.ca
- Ship's Company Theatre, 18 Lower Main St., Parrsboro; 902 254-5000; 800 565-7469; www.shipscompany.com. New theatre incorporating MV *Kipawo*, a restored car ferry Jul.– Sept.
- The Space, 2353 Agricola St., Halifax; 902 429-8742.
- Theatre Arts Guild, The Pond Playhouse, from Armdale Roundabout, off Purcell's Cove Rd., 6 Parkhill Rd., Halifax; 902 477-2663; www.tagtheatre.com
- Th'YARC Playhouse and Arts Centre, 76 Parade St., Yarmouth; 902 742-8150; 800 561-1103; www.thyarc.ca. Theatre and concerts.
- Two Planks and a Passion Theatre Company, www.twoplanks.ca. Touring company.
- Zuppa Circus, www.zuppacircus.com. Original performances by innovative theatre company.

Shopping

Art and Craft shops and studios

See *Arts & Crafts* p. 19.

- Amicus Gallery, 20 Pleasant St., Chester; 902 275-2496. Fine art and fine craft.
- Argyle Fine Art, 1869 Upper Water St., Halifax; 902 425-9456; www.argylefa.com. Wide variety of contemporary art by established and emerging Canadian artists. Open Mon–Sat, year-round.
- Arts North, just west of Cape North on the Cabot Trail. Specializing in Cape Breton pottery and jewellery, the gallery also features silk, weaving, prints, quilts and basketry by resident artisans. Open daily from mid-June–mid-Oct.
- ArtWare, Diligent River; 902 254-2972; www.artware.ns.ca. Krista Wells makes masks, prints, collage jewellery from found materials, painted clay and handmade paper. Open by chance or appointment.
- Barry Colpitts, 15359 Hwy. 7, East Ship Harbour; 902 772-2090. Weird and wonderful folk art. Almost always home.
- Black Duck, 8 Pelham St., Lunenburg. A long-standing craft co-operative with adjoining art gallery and a fine selection of books on Nova Scotia and the Maritimes. Open year-round.
- Bob Hainstock, The Printmaker Studio & Gallery, 1688 Brow of Mountain Rd., North Mountain, off Hwy. 359 north towards Halls Harbour. Open most afternoons.
- Co-operative Artisanale de Cheticamp Ltée, 15067 Cabot Trail, Cheticamp. This is the place for hooked rugs in all shapes and sizes (as well as mats, coasters and wall-hangings). Watch how the hooking is done during one of the frequent daily demonstrations here or at any one of the numerous craft shops in Cheticamp. Open daily, 8 am–9 pm, June 15–Sept. 15; variable hours in off-season.
- David Lacey Gallery, 4092 Rte. 359, Halls Harbour; 902 679-7073; www.davidlaceygallery.com.
- Dawn MacNutt, Weaver, Sculptor, 5226 Little Harbour Rd., New Glasgow. 902 752-3378; www.dawnmacnutt.com. Sculptures of woven metal or fibre.
- Deanne Fitzpatrick, 7 Eclectic St., Amherst; 800 328-7756; www.hookingrugs.com. Original hooked rugs. Open Wed–Sat 10 am–3 pm, year-round.
- deWeever's Wovens, 3486 Hwy.1, Aylesford. Contemporary styling in quality handwoven clothing.
- Flight of Fancy, Main St., Bear River. Selling the works of more than 200 craftspeople, this is a beautifully appointed shop in the picturesque village of Bear River —

Shopping

worth a trip just for the drive. Open Mon–Sat 9–7, May–Oct.

- Flora's, Point Cross (near Cheticamp) on the Cabot Trail. Large craft shop with a wide selection of hooked rugs. Open daily during tourist season.
- Folk Art by Reed Timmons, Pleasant Bay on the Cabot Trail. Specializing in hand-carved whales, gulls, roosters and fishermen. Open daily, June–Oct.
- Gallery Shop, Art Gallery of Nova Scotia, 1741 Hollis St. at Cheapside, Halifax. Good selection of works by a wide variety of Nova Scotia artists and craftspeople. Open daily, except Monday. Evening hours on Thursday.
- Glooscap Trading Post, Hwy. 102, exit 13, Truro. Traditional Mi'kmaq crafts, featuring woven baskets and twig furniture. The wonderful smell of sweet grass will make you want to browse just a little longer. Open 9 am–5:30 pm, year-round.
- Grey Seal Weaving, 3886 Michaud Pt., Lower L'Ardoise; 902 587-2777. Damask silk scarves, shawls and framed pieces woven by E. Del Zoppo on a draw loom. Open by chance or appointment.
- Houston North Gallery, 110 Montague St., Lunenburg; 902 634-8869. Large selection of Inuit carvings and prints, Nova Scotia folk art, silk screens and intaglio. Open year-round.
- Inverness County Centre for the Arts, Hwy. 19, Inverness; www.invernessarts.ca. Gallery and gallery shop. Open Mon–Fri 10 am–5 pm, year-round; summer weekends 1–5 pm.
- Iron Art and Photographs, 48084 Cabot Trail, Tarbot; 902 929-2821; www.ironart.ca. Fine art photography by Carol Kennedy and metal sculptures and iron work by Gordon Kennedy. Open 10 am–6 pm, June–Oct.
- Jennifer's of Nova Scotia, 5635 Spring Garden Rd., Halifax. Easy to find on Halifax's main downtown shopping street, Jennifer's features Nova Scotian crafts, especially pottery, pewter and knitted items. Open 9 am–6 pm Mon, Tues, Sat; Wed, Thurs and Fri to 9 pm; Sun 11 am–5 pm.
- John Little Ironwork, 11 Scott's Point Rd., East Dover; 902 852-2541; johnlittleironwork.tripod.com. Blacksmith, working studio.
- Joy Laking Studio Gallery, 6730 Rte. 2, Portapique; 800 565-5899; www.joylakinggallery.com. Original watercolours and serigraphs. Open year-round by chance or appointment.
- Kath and Rob Rutherford, 544 West Petpeswick Rd., Musquodoboit Harbour; 902 889-3344; www.originalprintsns.com. Silkscreen and mezzotints. Open Sun, noon–5 and by chance or appointment.
- Kenny Boone Studio and Gallery, 230 Neville Street, Dominion; 902 849-5820; www.kennyboone.ca. Watercolour landscapes and seascapes of Cape Breton.
- Krista Wells, Artware Studio, 9874 Hwy. 209, Diligent River (12 km west of Parrsboro); 902 254-2972; www.artware.ns.ca. Mixed media. Open by chance or appt.
- Leather Works by John Roberts, 45808 Cabot Trail, Indian Brook; 902 929-2414; www.leather-works.ca. Historic reproductions and a variety of contemporary leather goods. Open daily, May–Oct.
- Le Motif, 15423 Cabot Trail, Cheticamp. Specializing in rag rugs, carvings, twig baskets and the folk art of proprietor Diane Bourgeois. Open daily, June–mid-Oct.
- Leslie Hauck, The Spinner's Loft, 1626 West Jeddore Rd., Head of Jeddore; 902 889-2829; www.thespinnersloft.ca. Hand spinning of unusual fibres, even dog hair. Knitted products and spinning workshops.
- Lyghtesome Gallery, 166 Main St., Antigonish; 902 863-5804; www.lyghtesome.ns.ca. Local and Maritime artists. Open Mon–Sat, 9 am–5 pm.
- Maritime Painted Saltbox, 265 Petite Rivière Rd., Petite Rivière; 902 624-1544; www.paintedsaltbox.com. Fine and folk art by Tom Always and Peter Blais. Open daily, May–Oct.
- Out of Hand, 135 Montague St., Lunenburg. Arts and crafts gallery, unusual gifts. Open 9 am–6 pm, May–Dec.; 9 am–9 pm, Jul.–Aug.
- Page and Strange Gallery, 1869 Granville St., Halifax; 902 422-8995; www.pageandstrange.com.

Shopping

Established artists with a special connection to Nova Scotia. Open Mon–Wed 10 am–5pm, Thur–Fri 10 am–6 pm, Sat 11–5 pm.

- Roger Savage, 611 Shore Rd., Liverpool. Gallery features the artist's latest water-colours and original prints. Open 10 am–7 pm, Jul.–Sept.
- Secord Gallery, 6301 Quinpool Rd., Halifax; 902 423-6644; www.secordgallery.com. Nova Scotian artists. Open Mon–Thurs 9:30 am–5:30 pm; Fri 9:30 am–8 pm, Sat 10 am–5 pm.
- Sheep's Clothing, North East Margaree, 902 248-2921; www.sheepsclothing.ca. Hand-knitted traditional and custom clothing and accessories, and historic reproductions.
- Skipping Stone Craft and Art Gallery, Guysborough; 902 533-2078. Works by Nova Scotian artists and artisans. Open mid-May–Oct.
- Sous le Soleil, Little Brook, between Yarmouth and Digby. Original stained glass and other media.
- Steady Brook Saddlery, James Brown, 303 Etter Rd., Mount Uniacke; 902 866-4055; www.steadybrooksaddlery.ca
- Steven Kennard Studio, 9545 Borden St., Canning; 902 582-3795; www.stevenkennard.com. Woodturner and furniture maker.
- Studio 21, 1223 Lower Water St., Halifax. 902 420-1852; www.studio21.ca. Original contemporary art by top Canadian artists. Open Tues–Fri 11 am–6 pm; Sat 10 am–5 pm; Sun noon–5 pm.
- Sun Room Glass, Upper Clements. Emery and Sheila Salsman offer their beautiful stained glass in the gallery.
- Sunset Art Gallery, Cheticamp. Bright, whimsical wood carvings (lots of people and birds) by William Roach. Open daily, May 24–Oct. 15 or by appointment.
- Tin Pot Textiles, 429 Lakeside Rd., Yarmouth; 902 742-1978. Knitting and rug-hooking studio. Open by chance or appointment.
- Trees Gallery, 3 Edgewater St., Mahone Bay; 902 531-8733. Fine art and craft inspired by the forest. Open daily in summer.
- Tudor Tile, 1003 Little Harbour Rd., Sable River; 902 656-3298.

Handmade custom-designed ceramic tile. Open by chance or appointment.
- Water's Edge Gallery, Water St., Baddeck; 902 295-1209. A collection of artworks with a primarily maritime theme and featuring new and established artists of Atlantic Canada.
- Zwicker's Gallery, 5415 Doyle St., Halifax; 902 423-7662; www.zwickersgallery.ca. Eastern Canada's oldest gallery. Works of over 80 Maritime and Canadian artists. Open Mon–Fri 9 am–5 pm; Sat from 10 am.

Fine Jewellery and Crystal

- Fire Works Gallery, 1569 Barrington St., Halifax. An eclectic mix of silver and gold jewellery, some made by the shop's resident jewellers, art glass, and pottery by well-known local artists. Open daily, except Sunday.
- Nova Scotian Crystal, 5080 George St., at Lower Water St., Halifax. Canada's only mouth-blown and hand-cut crystal in the centuries-old tradition of Waterford. Stemware, vases, bowls, giftware. Open daily.

Pewter

- Amos Pewter, 589 Main St., Mahone Bay. Interpretive workshop and studio. Contemporary designs, including picture frames, goblets and jewellery. Open Mon–Sat 9 am–5:30 pm, Sun. afternoons.
- Seagull Pewter, Rte. 6, 9926 Durham St., Pugwash. Full line of pewter products. Canada's largest giftware manufacturer, now international in scope. Open daily. Also at 5475 Spring Garden Rd., Halifax.

Pottery

- Birdsall-Worthington Pottery Ltd., 590 Main St., Mahone Bay. Slip-decorated earthenware pottery, including commemorative plates and handmade earrings. Open Mon–Sat 10 am–5 pm; Sun 1 pm–5 pm; Jul.–Sept.; limited hours in off-season.
- Cape Breton Clay, East Big Intervale Rd., Margaree Valley; 902 235-2467; www.capebretonclay.com. Pottery features maritime motifs of trout, lobster and mussels. Open

daily, June–Oct.
- Lucky Rabbit Pottery, 15 Church St., Annapolis Royal; 902 532-0928; www.luckyrabbitpottery.ca. Studio and shop of Deb Kuzyk, ceramic artist and Ray Mackie, master potter.
- Nova Scotia Folk Pottery, Front Harbour, Chester; 902 275-3272. Colourful platters, bowls, vases and serving dishes by Jim Smith. Open daily, 10 am–6 pm, Sun noon–6 pm, June–Sept.; off-season by appointment.
- Nova Terra Cotta Pottery, 10 Dufferin St., Lunenburg. 902 634-8902; www.joanbruneau.com. Open daily, 9:30 am–5:30 pm in summer; shorter hours in fall.
- Shape Shift Pottery, at St. Anns on the Cabot Trail. Deanie Cox makes raku and functional dinnerware. Open daily, 9 am–5 pm, June–Sept.

Gift Shops
- Blomidon Inn's House of Gifts, Wolfville. Kitchen wares, glass, pottery, knitted garments. Open May–Christmas.
- Blue Heron Gift Shop, Chebucto St., Baddeck. Large selection of Nova Scotian books and CDs. Open daily, year-round; 9 am–9 pm in summer.
- Frieze and Roy General Store, 8787 Hwy. 215, Maitland. Oldest continuously operating general store in Canada (since 1839). Gifts and Canadian crafts.
- Kidston Landing, Chebucto St., Baddeck. Extensive selection of Nova Scotia crafts, Scottish woolens, men's and women's clothing, including wool and cotton sweaters. Open daily, 9 am–9 pm.
- Sea Shanty Antiques and Crafts, Beach Point at the Englishtown Ferry. Interesting collectibles, including vintage china and glassware, and a good selection of new and antique quilts. Open daily, mid-May–mid-Oct.
- Seawinds Chandlery, on the Government Wharf, Baddeck. Fine handmade sweaters, gift items and marine supplies. Open daily during tourist season, 9 am–9 pm.
- Sou'wester Gift Shop, Peggys Cove. Large selection of Nova Scotia crafts, souvenirs and gifts. Open year-round.
- Sunrise Mercantile, Tatamagouche; 902 657-1094; www.sunmerc.com.

An eclectic yarn and fibre arts studio, gift shop and gourmet food store. Open daily, 8 am-8 pm, Sun 1-8 pm May-Oct.; shorter winter hours.
- Suttles and Seawinds, 466 Main St., Mahone Bay. Vibrant quilts, jewellery and fashion accessories. Open year-round.
- The Teazer, Edgewater Rd. (Rte. 3), Mahone Bay. Upscale local crafts and imported gift items, kitchen ware. Open year-round.
- Warp and Woof, Water St., Chester. Local art and crafts, fine gift items. Open daily, May–Oct.

Specialty Shops
- Beach Lane Lavender Farm, 147 Carlson Lane, Marshville, near River John. Lavender shop, plants and products; U-pick lavender. Open Aug., Mon–Sat, 10 am–4 pm; Sept., Tues–Sat 10 am–3 pm.
- Box of Delights, Main St., Wolfville. Good general bookstore with the valley's best selection of local titles. Open year-round.
- For The Birds, 647 Main St., Mahone Bay. Feeders, books, binoculars and all bird-related things. Open Mon–Sat, May–Dec.; Tues–Sat, Feb.–Apr.
- Grohmann Knives, 116 Water St., Pictou. Fine knives for every use, made on-site. Plant tours Mon–Fri 9 am–3 pm. Open Mon–Fri 9 am–5 pm, weekends seasonal.
- Halifax Folklore Centre, 1528 Brunswick St., Halifax. Large selection of traditional musical instruments and Nova Scotian recordings. Open Mon–Wed noon–5:30 pm, Thurs–Fri noon–9 pm, Sat 10 am–5 pm.
- Lismore Sheep Farm Wool Shop, 1389 Louisville Rd., River John. Wool, sheepskin and knitted products. Working sheep farm. Open daily, May–Christmas.
- MacIsaac Kiltmakers, 4 MacAskill Dr., St Peter's; 866 343-4000; www.mackilts.com. Handmade kilts and kilt accessories.
- Magasin Campus (Campus Bookstore), Université Sainte-Anne, Pointe de l'Église. Books dealing with the history and culture of the Acadians. Open Mon–Sat 9 am–5 pm.
- Negemow Basket Shop, Whycocomagh. Quality Mi'kmaq

baskets sold by the Googoo family for more than 30 years.

- The Outdoorstore, Chebucto St., Baddeck. Quality outdoor clothing, equipment and gifts. Open daily, 9 am–8 pm, Sun 11 am–7pm, Apr.–Christmas.
- Petroglyph Gifts, Membertou Trade and Convention Centre, 50 Maillard Street, Membertou; 902 562-0444; www.membertoutcc.com. Open Mon–Fri 10 am–6 pm.
- P'lovers, 3 Edgewater Rd., Mahone Bay and 5657 Spring Garden Rd., Halifax; 902 624-1421; 902 422-6060. Environmentally sensitive products. Open year-round; Mahone Bay, shorter hours in winter.
- Port of Wines, 5431 Doyle St., Halifax. Wide selection and knowledgeable staff. Open Mon–Sat.
- Sew Inclined, Wreck Cove on the Cabot Trail. Specializing in designer vests, hats and pants. Custom orders and sewing services available. Open daily, June–Oct.

Treats

- Chase's Lobster Pound, 7935 Hwy. 6, Port Howe; 902 243-2408. Live and freshly cooked lobster.
- Clearwater Lobster Shops, 757 Bedford Hwy., Bedford; Halifax International Airport. Live lobster packed for travel. Open daily.
- Italian Gourmet, 5431 Doyle St., Halifax. A few tables for lunch and lots of Italian goodies to take away. Open Mon–Wed, 9 am–7 pm, Thurs–Sat 9 am–8 pm, Sun 10 am-6 pm.
- Jo-Ann's Deli Market and Bake Shop, 9 Edgewater St., Mahone Bay. Open daily, 9 am–7 pm, June–Oct.
- J. Willie Krauch and Sons Ltd., Tangier. Danish-smoked Atlantic salmon, mackerel and eel; orders filled worldwide. Open daily from 8 am.
- LaHave Bakery, Rte. 331, LaHave. Whole grain and herb breads, and sweets. From Lunenburg, a short drive and cable ferry ride across the LaHave River; also at 3 Edgewater Rd. in Mahone Bay.
- Pete's Frootique, Dresden Row, Halifax and Sunnyside Mall, Bedford; 902 425-5700 or 902 835-4997. The best of victuals from all over. Open daily.
- St. Mary's River Smokehouse, Sherbrooke. thebestsmokedsalmon.com.
- Rumrunners Rum Cake Factory, Bishop's Landing, Halifax. 866 440-7867; www.rumrunners.ca. Rum-soaked cake in a distinctive tin. Open daily, 9 am–9 pm in summer.
- Sugar Moon Farm, Earltown, off Rte. 331; 902 657-3348. Maple syrup, maple sugar and other maple treats. Open weekends year-round; daily in summer.
- The Tangled Garden, Rte. 1, Grand-Pré. Herb jellies and vinegars; also finely crafted dried-flower wreaths and other arrangements. Open daily, 10 am–6 pm.

Wineries

- Blomidon Estate Winery, 10318 Hwy. 221, Canning; 877 582-7565; www.blomidonwine.com. Open daily in summer, 11 am–6 pm; call for off-season hours.
- Domaine de Grand Pré, Grand Pré; 866 479-4637; www.grandprewines.com. Open daily in summer; mid-Mar.–Dec., Wed–Sun. Stroll the grounds, taste the wine, enjoy Swiss cuisine at on-site restaurant.
- Gaspereau Vineyards, 2239 White Rock Rd., Gaspereau 902 542-1455; www.gaspereauwine.com. Boutique winery; tours in summer.
- Jost Vineyards, Rte. 6, Malagash; 800 565-4567; www.jostwines.com. Family run winery on 10 hectares. Retail store, daily tours at 3 pm in summer. Open daily to 6 pm; shorter hours and closed Sundays in off-season.
- Lunenburg County Winery, Newburne; 902 644-2415; www.canada-wine.com. U-pick blueberries and raspberries. Wine tastings and sales. Open year-round 9 am–6 pm, 9 am–9 pm in summer.
- Sainte Famille Wines, corner of Dyke Rd. and Dudley Park Lane, Falmouth; 800 565-0993; www.st-famille.com. Vineyard at site of an early Acadian settlement. Daily tours 11 am and 2 pm. Wine and gift shop. Open daily to 6 pm (Sun noon–5 pm).

Outdoor Recreation

Parks and Natural Attractions

Included among the province's outstanding natural attractions are two national parks, Kejimkujik and Cape Breton Highlands. Nova Scotia also has 125 provincial parks. These range from sites of natural or historical significance to pleasant spots for a picnic or swim. Some have campgrounds. For more information on provincial parks, consult the detailed listings in the *Nova Scotia Doers' and Dreamers' Guide* (see *Travel Essentials*) or write to the Nova Scotia Department of Natural Resources, RR1 Belmont, NS, B0M 1C0.

Halifax

★ Point Pleasant Park, in the south end of Halifax. Although thousands of trees were destroyed by Hurricane Juan in 2003, the park continues to afford peaceful walks and views of Halifax Harbour and the Northwest Arm.
• Seaview Park, near Halifax ramp to the A. Murray McKay Bridge. Site of former community of Africville.
• Shubie Park, off Waverley Rd., Dartmouth. Two locks of the Shubenacadie Canal can be viewed from here.
• Sir Sandford Fleming Park (The Dingle), off Purcells Cove Rd., overlooking the Northwest Arm in Halifax. Beautiful view of the Arm along walking trails. Dedicated in 1912, the Dingle Tower was built to commemorate 150 years of representative government for Nova Scotia.

Peggys Cove

• See the waves, the rocks and the lighthouse at Nova Scotia's most famous fishing village.

Lunenburg

• Blue Rocks, east of Lunenburg on Lunenburg Harbour. This tiny, rockbound fishing village is a favourite haunt of local and visiting artists.
• Ovens Natural Park, Rte. 332 southeast of Lunenburg, near Riverport. Coastal caves and cliffside hiking trails highlight this privately owned park.

Liverpool and Shelburne

• Kejimkujik National Park Seaside Adjunct, off Rte. 3 between Port Joli and Port Mouton. This beautiful stretch of isolated coastline is accessible by hiking trails. This is a nesting area for the endangered piping plover and sections of the beach are closed mid-Apr.–mid-Aug.

Annapolis Valley

• Blomidon Provincial Park, Blomidon. Good hiking, scenic views of Minas Basin and rockhounding.
• Blomidon Look Off, Rte. 358 north of Wolfville, on Cape Blomidon. Panoramic view of the Minas Basin and six river valleys.

Maitland Bridge

★ Kejimkujik National Park, off Rte. 8 between Annapolis Royal and Liverpool. Situated in the interior of southwestern Nova Scotia, this 381-square-kilometre wilderness area is a favourite of campers and canoeists. For more information contact Kejimkujik National Park, Box 236, Maitland Bridge, NS, B0T 1B0; 902 682-2772; www.pc.gc.ca/kejimkujik

Northumberland Shore

• Jitney Trail, Pictou. Scenic 3-km walking trail along Pictou Harbour.
• Melmerby Beach Provincial Park, 6380 Little Harbour Rd., Little Harbour, near New Glasgow. Hwy. 104, exit 27A. Supervised beach.

Fundy Shore

• Amherst Point Migratory Bird Sanctuary, 5 km southwest of Amherst at head of the Bay of Fundy. Good hiking and walking trails.
• Cape Chignecto Provincial Park, near Advocate Harbour. Fifty-one kilometres of coastal wilderness trails; Nova Scotia's premier hiking destination.
• Cape d'Or Lighthouse look-off, off Rte. 209, Advocate Harbour. Breathtaking view of the Bay of Fundy and Minas Channel.
• Cape Split, trailhead at Scott's Bay; 5-hour round-trip hike; spectacular view.
• Economy Falls, off River Philip Rd., Bass River. Fifteen min. hike to falls

and more challenging trails.
- Five Islands Provincial Park, Rte. 2 east of Parrsboro, at Lower Five Islands. Camp, hike or picnic in this beautiful park overlooking five islands in the Minas Basin.
- Joggins Fossil Cliffs, Joggins. Sandstone cliffs with 300-million-year-old fossil material. The cliffs were awarded UNESCO World Heritage Site status in 2008. Tours available (see listing under *Attractions*).
- South Maitland Village Park, South Maitland. Good place to watch the Tidal Bore.
- Victoria Park, Brunswick St. and Park Rd., Truro. Recreational facilities, hiking trails and two waterfalls make this 1000-acre park ideal for family outings.

Eastern Shore
- Taylor Head Provincial Park, Rte. 7 east of Spry Bay. Hiking trails, wildlife habitat and coastal views along Taylor Head Peninsula.
- Tor Bay Provincial Park, Tor Bay (south of Larry's River). Contemplate the vastness of the Atlantic while picnicking on this rocky point.

Cape Breton
- Beulach Bahn Falls, North Mountain, Cabot Trail.
- Black Brook Beach, Cabot Trail between Neil's Harbour and Ingonish.
- Cabot's Landing Provincial Park, Cape North. Reputed to be the site where John Cabot landed in 1497. Picnic and enjoy the pleasant views of Aspy Bay.
- ★ Cape Breton Highlands National Park, northern Cape Breton. Nova Scotia's most spectacular scenery. The 950-square-km park affords abundant opportunities for camping and hiking. For more information contact Cape Breton Highlands National Park, Ingonish Beach, NS, B0C 1L0; 285-2691; www.pc.gc.ca/pn-np/ns/cbreton
- Marble Mountain, on the shores of the Bras d'Or, overlooking the village of the same name. After a steep hike, there are beautiful views of Cape Breton's inland sea. Swimming at the crushed marble beach.
- Uisge Bahn Falls Provincial Park, near Baddeck Bridge. A network of hiking trails leads through hardwood forest to a dramatic gorge and waterfalls.

Golf
There are more than 60 golf courses in Nova Scotia that welcome green-fee players. Golf Nova Scotia members are committed to making tee time available to visitors. For a complete list of member courses contact www.golfnovascotia.com, or for reservations call 800 565-0001. For more information on golf courses in Nova Scotia, visit the Nova Scotia Golf Association website at www.nsga.ns.ca. See Golf p. 44.
- Abercrombie Golf & Country Club (18-hole), New Glasgow; 902 755-4653; www.abercrombiegolf.com
- Amherst Golf & Country Club (18-hole), Amherst; 902 667-8730; www.amherstgolfclub.com
- Antigonish Golf Club (18-hole), Antigonish; 902 863-2228; www.antigonishgolfclub.ns.ca
- Avon Valley Golf and Country Club (18 hole), Falmouth; 902 798-2673; www.avonvalleygolf.com
- Bell Bay Golf Club (18-hole), Baddeck; 800 565-3077; www.bellbaygolfclub.com
- Bluenose Golf Club (9-hole), Lunenburg; 902 634-4260; www.bluenosegolfclub.com
- Chester Golf Club (18-hole), Chester; 902 275-4543; www.chestergolfclub.ca
- Digby Pines Resort Golf Course (18-hole), Digby; 800 667-4637; www.signatureresorts.com
- Dundee Resort and Golf Club (18-hole), Dundee (on the south shore of the Bras d'Or); 902 345-0420; www.dundeeresort.com
- Fox Harb'r Golf Resort & Spa (18-hole), 1337 Fox Harbour Rd.,Wallace; 866 257-1801; www.foxharbr.com
- Fox Hollow Golf Club (18-hole), Stewiacke; 902 639-2535
- Glen Arbour Golf Course (18-hole), Hammonds Plains (near Halifax); 877 835-4653; www.glenarbour.com
- Glen Lovat Golf Club (18-hole), New Glasgow; 877 774-4536; www.glenlovatgolf.ca
- Granite Springs Golf Club (18-hole), Prospect Road (near Halifax); 902 852-4653; www.granitespringsgolf.com
- Highlands Links (18-hole), Ingonish Beach (at Keltic Lodge); 800 441-1118; www.highlandslinksgolf.com
- Ken-Wo Golf & Country Club (18-hole), New Minas; 902 681-5388; www.ken-wo.com

- LePortage Golf Club (18-hole), Cheticamp; 902 224-3338; www.leportagegolfclub.com
- Linacy Greens Golf Club (18-hole), New Glasgow; 866-990-5200; www.linacygreens.com
- Liverpool Golf & Country Club (9-hole), White Point Beach; 800 565-5068; www.whitepoint.com
- Northumberland Links (18-hole), 1776 Gulf Shore Rd., Pugwash; 902 243-2808; www.northumberlandlinks.com
- Ocean Links at Brule Point (9-hole), 738 Brule Point Rd., Tatamagouche; 877 657-2611 www.oceanlinks.ca.
- Osprey Ridge (18-hole), Bridgewater; 902 543-6666; www.ospreyridge.ns.ca
- Paragon Golf & Country Club (18-hole), Kingston; 877 414-2554
- Pictou Golf Club (9-hole), 320 Beeches Rd., Pictou; 902 485-4435; www.nsga.ns.ca/pictou/pi.htm
- River Oaks Golf Club (27-hole), Meaghers Grant (Rte. 357 through the Musquodoboit River Valley); 902 384-2033; www.riveroaksgolfclub.ca
- Truro Golf Club (18-hole), Truro; 902 893-4650; www.trurogolfclub.com

Boat Tours

(Sightseeing, Whale- and Bird-Watching, Fishing)

- Amoeba Sailing Tours, Baddeck; 902 295-7780; 902 295-2481; www.amoebasailingtours.com. Daily 1 ½-hr sailings on schooner *Amoeba*. June–Oct.
- Bird Island Tours Ltd., Big Bras d'Or; 800 661-6680; www.birdisland.net. Narrated tour to Bird Islands; see puffins, seabirds, eagles and seals from covered boat. Mid-May–mid-Sept.
- *Bluenose II*, at the Fisheries Museum, Lunenburg; 902 464-4794, 866 579 4909; www.schoonerbluenose2.ca. Cruises when in port.
- Brier Island Whale and Seabird Cruises, Westport; 902 839-2995; 800 656-3660; www.brierislandwhalewatch.com. Cruises 2 to 5 times daily, 3 to 5-hour cruises on the Bay of Fundy. Greatest variety of whales in Nova Scotia waters. Rainchecks are given on the rare occasions when no sightings are made.
- *Caledonia*, Canadian Sailing Expeditions, Halifax; 902 429-1474; 877 429-9463; www.canadiansailingexpeditions.com. Week-long cruises in Nova Scotia waters.
- Capt. Cox's Whale and Bird Watch, Capstick; 888 346-5556. Seabirds and whales in the waters off Cape Breton's northernmost tip; marine biologist guide. Daily tours. July–mid-Sept.
- Capt. Mark's Whale and Seal Cruise, Pleasant Bay; 888 754-5112; www.whaleandsealcruise.com. Five trips daily (3 off-season). Hear and see whales, cruise past sea caves, waterfalls and pioneer settlements. May–mid-Oct.
- Discovery Sailing Charters, at Oak Island Resort & Spa, Western Shore. 902 275-8377; 877 275-8377; www.discoverysailing.com. CYA certified sailing course.
- Eastern Passage Privateers Schooner Company (*Liana's Ransom*), Historic Properties, Halifax; 406-8687; www.passageprivateers.com
- Four Winds Charters, Halifax Cable Wharf and St. Margarets Bay; 877 274-8421; www.fourwindscharters.com. Whalewatching, history tours, ferry to Georges and McNabs Islands. June–Sept.
- Murphy's on the Water: *Mar II* Tall Ship Sailing Tours, also *Harbour Queen I*, *Haligonian III* and *Theodore Tugboat*. Cable Wharf, Halifax; 902 420-1015; www.murphysonthewater.com
- *Peer's Fancy* Sailing Charters, Hubbards; 902 476 4437; www.peersfancy.com. Cruise or crew between Halifax and Lunenburg.
- Sail Lunenburg Star Charters Ltd., Lunenburg; 902 634-3535; 902 688-2740.
- Sail Mahone Bay, Oakland, Mahone Bay; 902 624-8864. Learn to sail or cruise around Mahone Bay and islands.
- Seaside Whale & Nature Cruises, Cheticamp; 800 959-4253; www.loveboatwhalecruises.com. Three tours daily. Accommodation and cruise packages available through Laurie's Motor Inn (see *Lodging*). Mid-June–mid-Oct.

Outdoor Recreation

- Sou'Wester Adventures, Western Shore; 877 665-4004; www.souwesteradventures.com. Learn to sail programs for adults.
- Tall Ship *Silva*, Halifax; 902 429-9463, 877 429-9463; www.tallshipsilva.com. Canadian Sailing Expeditions. Daily tours around Halifax Harbour. June–Oct.
- Whale Cruisers (Cheticamp), Cheticamp; 800 813-3376; www.whalecruises.com. Frequent sightings of pilot, minke and finback whales. Landward view of the coastline of Cape Breton Highlands National Park. Three cruises daily, mid-May–mid Oct.

Hiking

Hikers will find plenty to choose from in Nova Scotia — spectacular ocean views, desolate highland plateaus, thick boreal forest and more. There are trails suitable for family outings and trails to challenge the most serious hikers. See *Hiking* p. 50.

Useful information for hikers is available from a number of sources. The *Nova Scotia Atlas* (6th ed, co-published by the Province of Nova Scotia and Formac Publishing) includes 90 pages of topographic maps that cover the whole of Nova Scotia at a scale of 1:150,000. It is available from bookstores and online at www.gov.ns.ca/snsmr/maps. *Hiking Trails of Nova Scotia* and *Hiking Trails of Cape Breton*, both by Michael Haynes, are also available in bookstores. These publications can also be purchased at outfitters throughout the province.

For specifications on the 25 marked and serviced trails in the Cape Breton Highlands National Park go to www.pc.gc.ca/pn-np/ns/cbreton/activ/activ1_E.asp For information on the 15 hiking trails in Kejimkujik National Park, check www.pc.gc.ca/pn-np/ns/kejimkujik/activ/activ5_E.asp

Tidal Bore Rafting

The tidal bore on the Shubenacadie River provides a unique rafting experience. Check ahead to find out when the bore is at its peak.

- Shubenacadie River Adventure Tours, South Maitland; 888 878-8687; shubie.com. Open June–Sept. Reservations recommended.
- Shubenacadie River Runners, 8681 Hwy. 215, Maitland; 800 856-5061; www.tidalborerafting.com. Open June–Sept. Reservations recommended.
- Tidal Bore Rafting Park, 12215 Hwy. 215, Urbania; 800 565-7238; www.tidalboreraftingpark.com. Open May–Oct.

Birding

Nova Scotia is an important stopover on the Atlantic flyway for many species of migratory birds. Late summer sees thousands congregate on Fundy shores. Whalewatching tours (see listings above) also provide an excellent opportunity to observe seabirds, guillemots, kittiwakes, gannets, cormorants and more. Atlantic puffins and bald eagles are special attractions. Serious birders can purchase Robie Tufts' beautiful guidebook, *Birds of Nova Scotia*, from local bookstores. See *Birding* p. 67.

Canoeing and Sea Kayaking

Opportunities for freshwater paddling and sea kayaking in Nova Scotia are practically unlimited. Much of the interior of the province is a wilderness area studded with lakes and creased by rivers and streams. There are also long stretches of sheltered coastline on both the Atlantic and the Fundy shores. The *Nova Scotia Doers' and Dreamers' Guide* (see *Travel Essentials*) lists a number of outfitters, as well as suppliers of equipment, maps and useful information. See *Sea Kayaking* p. 61.

Bicycling

An extensive series of secondary roads has helped to make cycling one of the fastest growing sports in Nova Scotia. Serious cyclists can challenge the world-famous Cabot Trail, while others may choose a gentler route like the Sunrise Trail along the shores of the Northumberland Strait. *Nova Scotia by Bicycle* describes the province's most popular cycling routes and can be purchased from Bicycle Nova Scotia, 5516 Spring Garden Rd., 4th Floor, Halifax, NS, B3J 1G6. The *Nova Scotia Bicycle Book*, with extensive route information, is available from Atlantic Canada Cycling, Box 1555, Station CRO,

Halifax, NS, B3J 2Y3; 902 423-2453; www.atlanticcanadacycling.com. See *Cycling* p. 47.

Camping

Nova Scotia's two national parks, Kejimkujik and Cape Breton Highlands, and many of the province's 120 provincial parks have campground facilities (see *Parks and Natural Attractions* for addresses and information). There are also close to 130 privately owned campgrounds in Nova Scotia. Extensive listings and information on camping facilities are provided in the *Nova Scotia Doers' and Dreamers' Guide* (see *Travel Essentials*).

Fishing

Deep-Sea Fishing

Options for saltwater fishing range from relaxing outings — often in combination with some cultural or historical commentary, where sedentary cod, haddock, mackeral and Boston bluefish are the catch — to shark or bluefin tuna angling expeditions. Murphy's on the Water (www.murphysonthewater.com) is one of several charter companies that operate out of Halifax Harbour. For complete listings consult the *Nova Scotia Doers' and Dreamers' Guide* (see *Travel Essentials*).

Freshwater Fishing

Many species are caught in Nova Scotia lakes and rivers, but the province owes its lofty reputation among anglers to the speckled trout and the Atlantic salmon. The Margaree River in western Cape Breton and St. Marys River on the Eastern Shore have attracted anglers from around the world. These rivers and several others in the province are posted for fly-fishing only. Information on scheduled rivers, licenses, seasons and bag limits is available from outfitters and tackle shops or from all district offices of the Department of Natural Resouces. For more information consult the Nova Scotia Fisheries and Aquaculture website: www.gov.ns.ca/fish/sportfishing. For information on the salmon fishery, contact Fisheries and Oceans Canada in Halifax at 902 426-9010 (weekdays 8 am–4:30 pm), 800 565-1633 (24-hour line) or visit www.dfo-mpo.gc.ca

Sailing

Nova Scotia is a popular destination for sailors. The island-studded bays and sheltered harbours of the South Shore and the unique sailing experience afforded by Cape Breton's inland sea, the Bras d'Or, have created yachting havens like Chester and Baddeck. Yacht clubs at these communities and several others, including Halifax, host colourful regattas during the summer months. See Sailing p. 57.

Operators of foreign pleasure craft are required to report to the Canadian Border Services Agency by calling 888 226-7277 on arrival in the first Canadian port of call. For a list of the designated telephone reporting marine sites, call 888-226-7277 before you arrive in Canada. For customs information concerning pleasure craft, go to the CBSA website: www.cbsa.gc.ca.

Useful Addresses

It is possible to make detailed plans for your Nova Scotia vacation before leaving home by contacting the Nova Scotia Information and Reservation Service. Travel counsellors will provide invaluable advice, reservation services and a wealth of written material to make travel planning easier. In North America, call 800 565-0000 or email info@checkinnovascotia.com.

Once in Nova Scotia, the same services are available at provincial and community visitor information centres. These are indicated by a "?" on the Nova Scotia Tourism Regions Map, and can be found at key locations throughout the province, including the New Brunswick-Nova Scotia border, Yarmouth and the Halifax International Airport.

Visitors from the United States who need to contact home in case of an emergency may do so through the Consulate General of the United States of America, Suite 904, Purdy's Wharf Tower II, 1969 Upper Water Street Halifax; 902 429-2480.

Special Travel Services

Visitors with Special Needs

The *Nova Scotia Doers' and Dreamers' Guide* indicates, using international symbols, which lodgings and attractions are wheelchair-accessible, non-smoking and are members of ACCESS Canada. To find out what additional services may be available, visitors are urged to make specific inquiries. Where possible, it is advisable to book in advance. For assistance, contact the Nova Scotia Information and Reservation Service at 800 565-0000 (in North America), www.checkinnovascotia.com or Nova Scotia League for Equal Opportunities at 902 455-6942; nsleo@eastlink.ca. The Abilities Foundation website (www.enablelink.org) and its magazine, *Abilities* (available online), offer some travel information.

Students

Student discounts are available for a variety of travel services. In order to qualify, students are advised to buy an International Student Identity Card. In Canada, cards may be purchased at Travel Cuts, a travel agency for students found on many Canadian university campuses. Halifax branches are located at Dalhousie University, 902 494-2054 and at 1589 Barrington St.; 902 482-8000. Students from the US can call 800 592-2887 for information or the location of the nearest Travel Cuts branch.

To find out about hostelling in the province, contact Hostelling International Nova Scotia, 1253 Barrington St., Halifax, NS, B3J 1Y3; 902 422-3863; www.hihostels.ca

Seniors

Seniors can obtain discounts on many travel services, including transportation and accommodation. Inquire before making reservations and have your senior citizen identification card at the ready.

Many of the private tour operators in the province offer coach tours at reduced rates for seniors (several companies are listed in the *Getting Around* section).

Genealogical Sources

- Acadia University, Vaughan Library, 50 Acadia St., Box 4, Wolfville, NS, B4P 2R6; www.library.acadiau.ca
- Admiral Digby Museum, Box 1644, Digby, NS, B0V 1A0.
- Annapolis Valley Macdonald Museum, 21 School St., Middleton, NS, B0S 1P0; www.macdonaldmuseum.ca
- Argyle Township Courthouse and Archives, Box 101, Tusket, NS, B0W 3M0; www.argylecourthouse.com
- Cape Breton Genealogy and Historical Association, 120 Braemar Dr., Sydney, NS, B1R 1V9; www.rootsweb.com/~nscbgha
- Centre d'Etudes Acadiennes, Université de Moncton, Moncton, NB, E1A 3E9; www.umoncton.ca/etudeacadiennes/centre/cea
- Colchester Historical Society, 29 Young Street, Truro, NS, B2N 5C5; www.genealogynet.com/resident/colchester/index/php
- Cumberland County Genealogical Society, 16 Church St., Amherst, NS, B4H 4E2; www.ccgs.ednet.ns.ca
- Deputy Registrar-General, Box 157, Halifax, NS, B3J 2M9; www.gov.ns.ca/snsmr/vstat
- Genealogical Association of Nova Scotia, Box 641, Station Central, Halifax, NS, B3J 2T3; 902 454-0322; www.chebucto.ns.ca/recreation/GANS
- Kings County Museum, 37 Cornwallis Street, Kentville, NS, B4N 2E2; www.okcm.ca
- Memory Lane Heritage Village, Box 1937, Lake Charlotte, NS, B0J 1Y0; www.heritagevillage.ca
- Nova Scotia Archives and Records Management, 6016 University Ave., Halifax, NS, B3H 1W4; 902 424-6060; www.gov.ns.ca/nsarm. Hours are 8:30 am–4:30 pm, Mon, Tues, Thurs and Fri; 8:30 am–9 pm, Wed; 9 am–5 pm, Sat; closed Sun, holidays and Sat on holiday weekends.
- Pictou County Genealogy and Heritage Society, Box 1210, Pictou, NS, B0K 1H0; www.rootsweb.com/~nspcghs
- Shelburne County Genealogical Society, 168 Water St., Shelburne, NS, B0T 1W0; www.ednet.ns.ca/shelburne/index.php
- South Shore Genealogical Society,

68 Bluenose Dr., Lunenburg, NS,
B0J 2C0;
www.rootsweb.com/~nslssgs
- West Hants Historical Society, 281
King St., Windsor, NS, B0N 2T0;
www.glinx.com/~whhs/links
- Yarmouth County Historical Society,
22 Collins Street, Yarmouth, NS,
B5A 3C8;
yarmouthcountymuseum.ednet.ns.ca

Contributors

COLLEEN ABDULLAH is a writer,
visual communication designer and
marketing consultant. She lives in
Mahone Bay on Nova Scotia's
beautiful South Shore.

LINETTE CHIASSON returned to
her native Halifax after studying
theatre and English in Ottawa.

LESLEY CHOYCE is a prolific
author, journalist, poet, musician,
teacher, activist and outdoorsman. He
is also a passionate surfer in the waters
of the North Atlantic all year round.

SCOTT CUNNINGHAM, a
biologist, is author of *Sea Kayaking in
Nova Scotia*. An Instructor Trainer, he
has developed a national sea kayaking
program for Paddle Canada. He lives
in Tangier, where he operates Coastal
Adventures.

ROB CRAWFORD is a landscape
designer and food service professional
who enjoys gardening and entertaining
at his home in Halifax.

JODI DELONG is a freelance garden
writer and photographer from Scotts
Bay, Nova Scotia.

DALE DUNLOP is a native Nova
Scotian who has explored every
highway and byway in the province
and is co-author, with his wife Alison
Scott, of *Exploring Nova Scotia*. Dale
is a litigation lawyer by profession.

MICHAEL ERNST started Sail
Mahone Bay in 1994. He has enjoyed
sailing for 40 years, and for 20 years
was a sailing instructor in Britain
under the Royal Yachting Association.

SUSAN MACALPINE FOSHAY has
been an art consultant and
administrator, gallery owner and
independent curator and is currently
Director of the Nova Scotia Centre for
Craft and Design and the Mary E.
Black Gallery.

AL KINGSBURY is a journalist and
author who lives in the Annapolis Valley.

ROBERT J. McCALLA is a
geographer and author of *The
Maritime Provinces Atlas*.

JODIE NOILES is an independent
tourism and events consultant based in
the Annapolis Valley, and the
Chairperson of Nova Scotia Festivals
and Events Advisory Council.

TERRY PUNCH is Past President of
the Royal Nova Scotia Historical
Society and has written numerous
books and pamphlets on genealogical
research in Nova Scotia.

JOAN WALDRON is an avid birder,
and since her retirement from the
Nova Scotia Museum she has been
spotting birds around the world.

PEGGY WALT is a publicist with her
ear to the vibes of the music world in
Nova Scotia.

Index

Index

Index

Index

211

Index

Index

Index

Index

Index

PHOTO CREDITS

Legend: Top=T; Centre=C; Bottom=B

Photographs by Keith Vaughan, except as noted below:
Abdallah: 88B, 89B; Alanna Jankov: 32, 38T; Alexander Graham Bell National Historic Site/photography Carol Kennedy: 142B; Andre Charland: 93B; Angela Chartier: 21B; Art Gallery of Nova Scotia: 23C&B, 80; Babs Flamingo: 29B; Bay Ferries Ltd: 112B; Brookes Diamond: 30T; Cape Breton Highlands Project: 50B, 61B, 68; Chris Barber: 29T; Chris Campbell: 84T; Chris Gallow/Highlands Links Golf Course: 44T, 46T; Christen Thomas: 98B, 159; Ctd2005: 112T, 130T; DesBarres Manor Inn: 37C&B; Freewheeling Adventures: 47B, 48, 49; Garry Woodcock: 41B; Golf Nova Scotia: 46C; Greg Hickman: 125B; istockphoto: 1, 5T&B, 6B, 7T, 8T&B, 9T&B, 10, 11B, 15T, 16, 17T&B, 33B, 50T, 53 T&B, 54, 57, 62T, 64, 65, 66, 68T, 69B, 70, 71 T&B, 73C, 74, 75T, 87T, 89T, 94B, 95B, 104B, 106, 118, 137T, 141T, 148T, 149, 150T&B, 151T&B, 152, 153T, 156T, 158, 161, 163, 165, 168; Jason Thibodeau/Nancy Roberts: 25T; Jennifer's of Nova Scotia: 82; Jhoc: 81B, 96B; Joelf: 102-103T; John Beale: 26B; Julian Beveridge: 86T; Kadodee: 122; Kathy Brown: 21T; Kennymatic: 83T; La Société Saint-Pierre: 147; Linda Bucci: 153B; Linda Roach: 20B, 148B; Loimere: 78C&B, 81T, 92B; Lunenburg Folk Harbour Festival: 30B; Luvmycrows: 145; Matthew Ingram: 84B; Meghan Collins: 18, 34B, 52 T&B, 55T, 56B, 72B, 73T, 92T, 108B, 114B, 115B, 119C&B; Murdock Smith: 39; Nova Scotia Department of Tourism, Culture & Heritage: 127B, 136B, 139, 140,154B, 61T; Nova Scotia's Rhapsody Quintet: 31B; Ojbyrne: 87B; Owjklos: 47T; Paul Jerry: 85B; Ray Mackie: 20T; Rena Kossatz: 27T; Robber Esq: 72T, 73B, 76B, 97T, 100T,C&B, 101T, 103B, 104T&C; Royal Nova Scotia International Tattoo/Francois Deschact: 40T, 43B; Ryan MacDonald: 19T; Scott Munn: 24, 27B; Sherbrooke Village/Walley Hayes an Roger Lloyd: 141; Sir Christopher Reynolds: 132, 133T&C; Smudge9000: 85T; Steven Isleifson: 104B; Stewart Applegath: 23T; StickmanUK: 126; Teresa Bergen: 22; The National Geographic Society/Bell Family: 134; Thom C: 28; Tylerc083: 6T; Walknboston: 124T; Wally Hayes: 42, 51.

Maps: Nova Scotia region locator map property of and provided by Nova Scotia Department of Tourism, Culture & Heritage: pp.4, 95, 114-115, 129, 134, 141, 164.
Maps by Peggy McCalla: 76-77.

Formac Publishing Company
5502 Atlantic Street
Halifax, Nova Scotia
B3H 1G4
www.formac.ca

Printed and bound in China

Distributed in the United States by:
Casemate
2114 Darby Road, 2nd Floor
Havertown, PA 19083

Distributed in the United Kingdom by:
Portfolio Books Ltd
Suite 3/4, Great West House,
Great West Road, Brentford,
Middlesex TW8 9DF